Who's Afraid of Bernard Shaw?

THE FLORIDA BERNARD SHAW SERIES

UNIVERSITY PRESS OF FLORIDA

Florida A&M University, Tallahassee
Florida Atlantic University, Boca Raton
Florida Gulf Coast University, Ft. Myers
Florida International University, Miami
Florida State University, Tallahassee
New College of Florida, Sarasota
University of Central Florida, Orlando
University of Florida, Gainesville
University of North Florida, Jacksonville
University of South Florida, Tampa
University of West Florida, Pensacola

Who's Afraid of Bernard Shaw?

Some Personalities in Shaw's Plays

Stanley Weintraub

· FOREWORD BY R. F. DIETRICH ·

University Press of Florida
Gainesville · Tallahassee · Tampa · Boca Raton
Pensacola · Orlando · Miami · Jacksonville · Ft. Myers · Sarasota

Copyright 2011 by Stanley Weintraub
All rights reserved
Printed in the United States of America on acid-free paper

First cloth printing, 2011
First paperback printing, 2013

Library of Congress Cataloging-in-Publication Data
Weintraub, Stanley, 1929–
Who's afraid of Bernard Shaw? : some personalities in Shaw's plays / Stanley
Weintraub ; foreword by R. F. Dietrich.
p. cm.—(The Florida Bernard Shaw series)
Includes index.
ISBN 978-0-8130-3726-4 (cloth: acid-free paper)
ISBN 978-0-8130-4471-2 (pbk.)
1. Shaw, Bernard, 1856–1950—Criticism and interpretation. I. Title.
PR5367.W45 2011
822.'912—dc22   2011011177

The University Press of Florida is the scholarly publishing agency for the State
University System of Florida, comprising Florida A&M University, Florida
Atlantic University, Florida Gulf Coast University, Florida International
University, Florida State University, New College of Florida, University of
Central Florida, University of Florida, University of North Florida, University
of South Florida, and University of West Florida.

University Press of Florida
15 Northwest 15th Street
Gainesville, FL 32611-2079
http://www.upf.com

For Michel Pharand, Shavian & Disraelian

Funding to assist in publication of this book was generously provided by the David and Rachel Howie Foundation.

Contents

Foreword xi

Borrowing People: A Preface xiii

1. Shaw's Jesus and Judas: Passion without "Passion" 1
2. A Shavian Caesar 17
3. Schiller's *Die Räuber* and Shaw's *Don Juan in Hell* 29
4. Shaw's "Secretary for America" and General John Burgoyne 39
5. Cetewayo: Shaw's Hero from Africa 51
6. Disraeli in Shaw 65
7. Shaw's Musician: Edward Elgar 79
8. Shaw's Goddess: Lady Colin Campbell 99
9. Shaw's Sculptress: Kathleen Scott 118
10. Eugene O'Neill: The Shavian Dimension 139
11. Noël Coward and the Avuncular Shaw 161
12. King Magnus and King Minus: A Play and a Playlet 175
13. Who's Afraid of Bernard Shaw? Virginia Woolf and GBS 194

Index 219

Foreword

Stanley Weintraub, as much a historian/biographer as a literary critic, but one who often combines both approaches when dealing with Shaw, is well known for his long career of continuously useful, always expert, and sometimes monumental contributions to Shaw studies, not to mention other fields, and in this collection he doesn't disappoint with the usefulness and expertise which, as usual, add up to "a good read" as well. Here we learn many interesting, and sometimes fascinating, facts about Shaw and his relationships with certain others, contemporary and historical, especially as reflected in his and their works, often revealing of a hidden intertextuality.

But why "Who's Afraid of Bernard Shaw?" The title was borrowed from the article on Virginia Woolf and GBS that closes this collection, but how does it extend to all the other relationships included here? Well, it fits some better than others, but Weintraub explains in his preface that this collection is to illustrate and explain Shaw's use of people who either had reason to fear ending up as a character or being used in some other way in one of Shaw's satiric works, or who *would have had* something to fear if they hadn't already been dead by the time Shaw came along. That is, the question "Who's Afraid of Bernard Shaw?" *could* be answered with "Not the Dead," which of course would be a humorous affirmation of the need of *the living* to be afraid. And of course among the living are disciples with fixed, reverent ideas about the dead who might have something to fear from Shaw's revisionist inclinations. In some cases, however, it would seem that Shaw had more to fear from his subject than his subject had to fear from him, as in the cases of Virginia Woolf and Eugene O'Neill, and in other cases, such as Edward Elgar, Lady Scott, and Lady Colin Campbell, the subjects might have had more to fear from over-praise from Shaw. But never mind the title.

This collection is vintage Weintraub when writing on Shaw, as he draws out, in some articles, the many ways that the dross of historical and contemporary incident has been transmuted by the writer into the gold of art, and in others finds literary or personal influence where it had not previously been known or, if known, not as well developed, with some extra value added in some articles by concerning themselves with unpublished material, all of which is illuminating and adds up to an extraordinary humanizing of the celebrity figure Shaw had become. From Jesus to Virginia Woolf, this work efficiently and quietly shows how more than a dozen historically significant people, and, in some cases, their art, have been assimilated into the playwright's art in minor and major ways, and sometimes vice versa in the case of living contemporaries as Shaw was assimilated into theirs. There are so many wonderful little bits of unique and informative scholarship in this manuscript that the accumulation makes for a very significant scholarly repast, mainly dessert though it may be.

R. F. Dietrich
Series editor

Borrowing People

A PREFACE

People known to Bernard Shaw had every reason to fear becoming recognizable characters in his plays. He turned Beatrice Webb into a witchlike virago in *The Millionairess*, former prime minister H. H. Asquith into an aloof, incompetent fuddy-duddy in *Back to Methuselah*, Winston Churchill into an aspiring, blowhard politician in *John Bull's Other Island*, Lawrence of Arabia into the eccentric army private Napoleon Alexander Trotsky Meek in *Too True to Be Good*. Dozens of further examples populate the plays.

Figures from history had nothing to worry about: they were already dead and beyond condoning or complaining; but Shaw remained timid about portraying one person out of the past. The unique exception was the founding prophet of Islam, whom he aspired to write about, but did not. Although it was not yet the age of the aggressive fatwa, Shaw wanted at least the possibility of performance even when, as with *Don Juan in Hell* and *Back to Methuselah*, he denied that the stage was an essential goal. "I am struggling with the temptation to begin another sketch," he wrote to Charlotte in 1913, then away on holiday in France, "which I planned long ago for [Johnston] Forbes Robertson—Mahomet in the slave market. I could do that . . . in a fortnight. These thumbnail historical sketches amuse me." He had written his Julius Caesar role with Forbes Robertson in mind. "Mahomet," he reminded himself in 1924, "like Joan, needs to be rescued from Voltaire, whose play about him is really an outrage. I thought of him as a play subject at one time." Yet a playlet about the icon of Islam had, realistically, as much chance of production, given Muslim antipathy to images of the prophet of any kind, as Voltaire's *Mahomet* of 1741 had of theatrical revival.

Few other subjects frightened Shaw away. He was fascinated as a small boy—so he told Virginia Woolf—by his father's jocular claim that "after Christ was crucified he got down off the Cross & ran away on the other side of the hill." Shaw would indulge his curiosity as he reached reading age. His play about Jesus and Judas, a first attempt for the theater, would have run into stage censorship barriers in England had he figured out how to complete it. As Shaw was only twenty-one, his audacity suggests not only his ambition but his naïveté about production matters and public outrage. He was writing against type and against expectation, both factors that very likely energized him.

While Shaw appreciated Friedrich Schiller's attempts to develop a new drama, he deplored the "raging romance" of Schiller's St. Joan, who dies on the battlefield. Shaw determined to do better by history, and did, earning in the process a Nobel Prize. He also borrowed a band of brigands from Schiller's own first play, for *Man and Superman*, thus becoming indebted to Schiller in widely contrasting ways. Shaw's heroes from history, whether thumbnail in execution or full length, had at least several characteristics in common. From the iconic Caesar and the youngish general Napoleon and the brash veteran general Burgoyne to the captive Zulu king Cetewayo and the militant Maid of Orleans, they were cocky, determined, and outspoken, and pushed the envelope of decorum.

Shaw's eight contemporaries portrayed here, five men and three women, were also individuals who challenged social and political norms. He promoted Edward Elgar, with whom he had no affinities whatever in politics and religion, as not only the greatest English composer since Henry Purcell but as someone trying to break free into modernism. Elgar was baffled at Shaw's militant missionary zeal in his behalf, and afraid that his conservative friends would see the radical GBS as a bad influence. Eugene O'Neill and Shaw shared Irish backgrounds, but little else other than the compulsion to change modern theater. O'Neill saw Shaw as a role model and his plays as breakthroughs in bringing the stage out of the fusty nineteenth century to confront the realities of the twentieth, and Shaw admired the American's very different results, which somehow remained redolent of Shaw. He championed Noël Coward, although Coward, as a young man, had plagiarized one of Shaw's plays and had been reluctant to show it to GBS's former producer, John Vedrenne, afraid that he would show it to Shaw. Vedrenne did. Rather than sue, Shaw proved an avuncular presence in Coward's career.

Despite his cable code name of "Socialist, London," Shaw viewed parliamentary democracy as a failure because people, however armed with the right to vote, failed to have much impact on their own governance. As he aged, and lost faith in the ballot, he saw values in the continuity of constitutional monarchy and, as his creative interest in heroes from history evidences, preferred government for the people rather than by the people. It is only a surprise, then, that his contemporary British king, who in a little-known playlet mockingly outwits his prime minister (as had the futuristic King Magnus in his *The Apple Cart*), is the little-regarded Edward VIII, wryly awarded more brains by Shaw than by historians. (One of Noël Coward's most successful acting roles would be as Magnus, revived for the coronation of Elizabeth II, Edward VIII's niece.)

Shaw's three women portrayed here also lived and worked against type. Lady Colin Campbell was a statuesque beauty whose social notoriety and separation from her unloved husband (the feeling was mutual) required her to make her own living. Although she should have feared Shaw's reformist pen, he abetted her career as a journalist, even giving "Vera"—her press pseudonym—his own newspaper post as art critic. Kathleen Scott, a sculptress and a bohemian in her formative years, also flouted the social norms, eventually marrying the Antarctic explorer Robert Falcon Scott, bearing his son late in life and becoming his widow, then marrying again, this time a one-armed war hero. In the supportive background of Lady Scott's life was, always, Bernard Shaw, a benign, informal uncle. Virginia Woolf, at the start of their curious relationship, saw GBS as inimical to everything she cared about, from feminism to modernism. By the end of her life they were warm friends, and Virginia became a recognizable Shavian character—Lady Utterword—in *Heartbreak House*.

Whether from history, literature, or his own life, Shaw's relationships to real or imagined personalities reveal a complexity beyond easy formulation. He put himself into a Caesar, a Cetewayo, and even into an Edward VIII; he rehabilitated Lady Colin Campbell (beyond her own real abilities), bolstered Kathleen Scott, and reinvented Virginia Woolf. What he was not, or could not be, himself, he became indirectly and imaginatively as parts of other personalities, past and present. These lives in *Who's Afraid of Bernard Shaw?* are a sampling, extraordinary only in all being dimensions of Bernard Shaw.

· 1 ·

Shaw's Jesus and Judas

PASSION WITHOUT "PASSION"

Rediscovering his first attempt for the stage, Shaw called the failed start "A Passion Play." Yet by definition the "Passion" of Jesus referred to his sufferings between the Last Supper and his Crucifixion. The life of Jesus as Shaw imagined it remained unfinished long before the culminating episodes most meaningful to believers. Much later, Shaw wrote of John Masefield's *The Trial of Jesus* (1925), "Pilate and Annas carry off the honors. No doubt that is the truth of the matter; but a real madman with a ridiculous delusion cannot be the hero of tragedy." Had he come to that conclusion when he came to conclude his own play?

An outspoken unbeliever, Shaw was nevertheless absorbed, through a long lifetime, by religion. Although he declared in the 1890s that he would enter a church only for its art and architecture, he remained fascinated by the reason for the church's very being—Jesus. The two books in the home of every Irish Protestant in his childhood, Shaw recalled, were the Bible in the King James Version and John Bunyan's *The Pilgrim's Progress*. Both continued to resonate in his writings.

Introducing Shaw to initiate a lecture series in London late in 1914, St. John Ervine, then a young writer, remarked jokingly—as Bernard Shaw was then the most famous playwright in the world—that he sometimes passed on to GBS ideas for plays that he was unable to write himself, including a play about God. "The suggestion that I write a play about God," Shaw bantered back, "is one I rather resent, because I have never written a play on any other subject; and as a matter of fact that is the subject of these lectures, as you will find out when you get to the end of them."

2 · *Who's Afraid of Bernard Shaw?*

His first attempt for the theater, Shaw confessed soon after his early stage successes, was "a Passion Play in blank verse," with the mother of the hero a tempestuous scold—"but I never carried these customary follies of young authors through. I was always, fortunately for me, a failure as a trifler." Twenty-one in February 1878, and still new to London, he was so naive an admirer of Shakespeare that he determined to write his play in the Bard's own blank verse. Only half-educated, as Shaw would put it, he had left school in Dublin at fifteen. In England he had already ghostwritten some musical criticism and attempted some mediocre poetry and fiction, including a biblical offshoot (lost in the post to a publisher), "The Burial of Cain."[1]

Although the Lord Chamberlain's censorship placed an absolute ban on the theatrical impersonation of Christ or the Deity which survived into 1966, the Chamberlain's royal writ did not extend to Ireland, which could have given Shaw hope that if he could bring his Passion play off, it could be produced in his native Dublin. Seeking the most challenging subject he could imagine, he invented an encounter of Jesus with Judas at a time unaccounted for in the traditional Gospels. It is possible that Shaw had read, in his untraditional university, the British Museum Reading Room, that there had indeed been a "Gospel of Judas," as it had been condemned by Irenaeus, the bishop of Lyons, in 180 A.D., but no manuscript surfaced until 1978—post-Shaw—in a burial tomb in Middle Egypt. A partial restoration and translation of the papyrus was published only in 2006.[2]

Striking echoes of the four canonical Gospels emerge in Shaw's dialogue. He did his biblical homework, yet his pseudo-Elizabethan blank verse evidences little borrowing from Shakespeare.[3]

The narratives ascribed to Matthew, Mark, Luke, and John differ about the birth of Jesus and his early childhood. All the Gospels are vague about his growing up. Only Luke, who offers a Nativity story about an unlikely Roman census forcing the Holy Family to return to its ancestral town of Bethlehem, suggests the future by portraying Jesus as the

---

[1] On his divine condemnation, for the murder of his brother, Abel, to be a wanderer, Cain vanishes from Genesis. Shaw was inventing an end for him.
[2] Herbert Krosney, *The Lost Gospel: The Quest for the Gospel of Judas Iscariot* (Washington, D.C., 2006). The translator from the Coptic papyrus was Rudolphe Kasser.
[3] An intemperate suggestion by Shaw's Jesus that a wolf might bay at Mary's grave may reflect lines in act 5 of John Webster's *The Duchess of Malfi* about wolves stealing into churchyards and digging up bodies.

now-familiar precocious boy of twelve found by his parents debating with his elders in the Temple in Jerusalem. He had been missing for three days. "Son," his mother complains, "why hast thou thus dealt with us? Behold, thy father and I have sought thee sorrowing" (Luke 2:48–49). Jesus objects angrily, "How is it that ye sought me? Wist ye not that I must be about my Father's business?" In Luke, Mary and Joseph do not understand the use of "Father," which could be sarcasm, as Joseph is not characterized as devout. (The King James translators capitalize the word to create the ambiguity of a divine parent, yet in Judaic prayer a temple is everyone's father's house, with the Deity addressed as "our Father.")

After the Temple episode, Jesus (Greek for Joshua, his actual name) again disappears in the Gospels until he is discovered, when about thirty, preaching in Galilee about repentance and the forgiveness of sins. The empty years are Shaw's opportunity to imagine the metamorphosis of the carpenter's son from a reluctant journeyman, bored by the drab occupation and impatient with his family, into the intense missionary foreshadowed by the childhood episode in the Temple.

Very likely recalling popular engravings of the most famous of Pre-Raphaelite paintings, John Millais's *Christ in the House of His Parents* (*The Carpenter's Shop*) of 1849–50, Shaw began his draft as "The Household of Joseph." Millais's images were warmly sentimental yet visually naturalistic, with Jesus still a small boy who, having hurt his hand on a nail—anticipating the Crucifixion—has the wound kissed by his mother, while an assistant—presaging John the Baptist—brings a bowl of water to wash the wound. The scene resembles a rude carpenter's workroom; the lean, sinewy Joseph even has dirty fingernails, which offended purists expecting an idealized Holy Family. Charles Dickens sanctimoniously trashed the painting as "odious, repulsive, and revolting." The row in the newspapers over the depiction reached Queen Victoria, who had the painting removed from the Royal Academy exhibition for her special viewing. Millais hoped (an irony?) that it would have no "bad effects on her mind."

A decade after abandoning his unfinished draft, Shaw—now making a go of it as a critic—wrote in an unsigned review, "In Five Acts and in Blank Verse," that even when the results languish afterward in an "over-littered and dusty" drawer, the blank verse form "give[s] expression to the Shakespear in us." But his own bardic momentum lost, he "gave in," leaving the draft incomplete. "What is he that he should sit in judgment on [the] others?" he conceded. "Yet there were some fine lines in it, finer than any he has since reviewed." Many of those "fine lines" have close biblical parallels.

Shaw had read the Gospels closely, and more, seeing evidences of a fractious mother-son relationship he was used to at home, and which he would exploit in his later plays. For example, when collecting disciples in Galilee, Jesus attends a wedding in the village of Cana. His mother is also there, and at the nuptial festivities she reports (John 2:1–2) that the guests have run out of wine. "Woman," Jesus snarls, "what is that to you and me?" ("Woman" may not have been as off-putting in a Middle Eastern sense then as it seemed to Shaw, yet it is only used once in that fashion in the Gospels.) As a public figure later, Jesus turns arrogant, reckless and even violent, but that is yet to come when Shaw opens his play in the carpenter shop in Nazareth. Millais's carefully rendered painting could serve as the play's set, but Shaw's Jesus is now a young man. When Mary enters, Joseph is at work with his son James.

"I want my dinner," says Joseph.

"Work for your dinner then," Mary retorts, calling him "a thriftless sot." Too often, she charges, he is "drunken and brutal," leaving her to toil for their living in the "parched fields." Turning on him further, she questions, "Why did I marry thee?"

"God knows, not I," says Joseph wearily if cryptically. As for their "first-born son, . . . him I swear / Thou never hadst by me." Although he refers to their eldest son as a "bastard," his actual parentage is never discussed other than in Mary's epithet "born my shame." Joseph, nevertheless, likes him, praising him above his own children as "No better boy alive." He detests his son John (the name a Shaw invention, as the brothers in the Gospels were James, Judah, Simon, and Joseph), and even kicks out of the way their youngest son, James, whom Mary describes as her precious "pet."

Far from devout, Joseph resents paying a visiting rabbi hard-earned coin to tutor John—"teaching nonsense to a fool." Mary, however, approves, as "'Tis a goodly thing / T'expound the prophets, sit among the wise / And be respected." What follows is the opposite of the warm scene in Millais's painting. Husband and wife heartily dislike each other: indeed, the ill-suited couple seem often to come to blows. Joseph threatens to launch his "jackplane" at Mary, and she warns him, allegedly a "dry and drunken withered palm," not to touch her. Their tiff continues loudly offstage as Jesus enters, casting aside his basket of carpenter's tools. He is apparently in his twenties now, and volubly unhappy at his rejection that evening by Rahab, a pretty village maiden whom he describes as a "fiery devil" with "snaky hair." (Her name seems borrowed from the feisty Canaanite harlot who hid Joshua's spies sent into the alleged land of milk and honey.) Now, as Jesus, too, calls for his dinner, the family wrangling is interrupted by an apparently well-to-do stranger who inquires whether someone in the shop can repair the brass clasps of his damaged traveling cabinet. Slipping in unseen, Mary listens, as Jesus confesses with more than a little irritation at his lot,

> To tell the truth, we are indifferent workmen.
> We can fit stable doors and nail up fences,
> Or hew out feeding troughs and pens for pigs.
> As artists are we none. This ark of yours
> Is, as you say, costly. Better take it elsewhere.
> We would but botch it. . . .
> Mistake me not.
> I do not scorn your hire, but would not injure you,
> By feigning—to the ruin of your ark—
> A craftsmanship to which I have no claim.

Rarely crossed, the stranger, Judas, is as impressed by such ironic honesty as he is put off by it, and asks:

> Art thou a fool?
> Usest thou all thy customers like this?
> How dost thou live?

"By sloth and idleness," Mary breaks in, eager for more business for the shop. She implores Judas not to listen to her son. But Jesus warns her about exaggerating their skills, "Wrong not yourself to buy us bread."

Such candor to a parent is almost unheard of. Mary excoriates Jesus to the stranger as "the very worst / Of sons since Cain." Joseph, John, and James join in obsequiously to pander for Judas's trade, extolling Jesus for his alleged mastery in "moulding knobs and carving images" and suggesting him for the work. Surprised by their claims, Judas tells Mary and Joseph that their eldest had professed himself as being incapable.

"It is his modesty," Joseph retorts. "He's somewhat strange. Oft speaks he in this wise."

In a bitter aside Joseph mutters, "Plague on his conscience."

As John (nine Johns are in the New Testament, but not this one) had carped to Mary, Jesus is more talker than worker. John recalls seeing his brother in a field now stripped of grain, amidst a group of dawdling reapers who "applaud" Jesus "with their lewd large eyes" as he lies on his back in the stubble "pouring forth volumes of delusive words" that are, John alleges, little more than "heathen tales." Such contempt for traditional values causes Mary to "doubt the wisdom of the gleaning law" (in Leviticus 23:22), in which God had decreed that scraps from the "gleaning of thy harvest" be left for "the poor, and to the stranger," in "the corners of thy field." Angry with Jesus, she explodes at him (adapting both Numbers 6:4 and Luke 15:16), "Thou pig, thou shalt eat husks which the swine revolt from."

Although Shaw also draws clues for the contentious mother-son relationship from the Gospels themselves,[4] it is hardly the picture purveyed by believers, then and since. His Jesus, Shaw insisted later, was "not mine at all, and not one and indivisible, but the three Jesuses of the gospels: the hard, bigoted, vituperative, haughty Jesus of Matthew, the charming, affable, woman-beloved Jesus of Luke, and the restlessly intellectual debater, poet, and philosopher-genius described by John."

His curiosity about Jesus piqued, the play's Judas persuades the carpenter's son to come the next day to his dwelling place. As soon as Judas exits, Mary and Joseph return to brawling in the shop, and Mary falls, at least pretending to be injured. "Mother is dead," cries John. Of course she is not, and Jesus nastily describes her obsessive domesticity as "a hell." Disparaging her as witch as well as shrew, he shouts, "Hence to thy broom!" (Saul, David's predecessor, had consulted the Witch of Endor—but the broom imagery is Shaw's anachronism, which he might have observed was no different than Shakespeare's unhistorical usages, as in *Julius Caesar*.)

As the scene closes, Mary grumbles that "never since the world was made / Was woman so ill used as I by Jesus," and young John agrees that his brother had again violated the biblical commandment to honor thy father and thy mother: "In him is a stiffnecked doubting devil." John believes that the Temple priests could reason with his rebellious brother and employ "their stern authority." A skeptic, Joseph sees only mischief "where priests are found."

---

4 When Jesus responds with hostility to Mary's observation about the lack of wine at the wedding in Cana with "What is that to you and to me, woman . . . ?" (John 2:12), it is the only time in the Bible that a biological son addresses his mother so coldly.

In the second scene, Judas passes by the voluptuous Rahab in a field as he turns homeward. At first not noticing her, he pauses to gaze at the harvest moon and, a self-styled philosopher and poet, extemporizes a purplish ode to the sublimity of what he sees as "a wanderer 'midst / The radiant stars." As much nihilist as narcissist, he is devoid of any faith. "Better believe in nothing," Judas contends, "Than old wives' tales and murder-stained Jehovahs." (In a book review in 1919, Shaw would suggest, "The alternative to believing silly things about God seemed to be blank materialist hedonistic atheism.")

As Rahab wonders whether "the fool [will] stand muttering there all night," Judas finally notices her. Although he scornfully considers women as "mere brood cattle" he proposes, unsuccessfully, what Shaw implies are sexual intimacies. His wealth can be hers under the right conditions. "No longer," the shifty Judas entreats, "shall a hard and vulgar pallet / Receive those goddess limbs."

While Rahab refuses to be bought, she agrees cautiously to let him accompany her toward her village. Identifying himself vaguely, he is "of any place," Judas explains as they walk on, and he has been "everywhere." They continue together in the moonlight, only to encounter Jesus approaching them. When Jesus jealously accuses Rahab of being "shameless," Judas, to demonstrate their innocent intentions, invites Jesus to join them. Rahab indignantly rejects them both, insulting Jesus as a mere carpenter, and stalking off alone.

"Why did'st though let her go?" Jesus asks Judas, who retorts, "I value her more justly than thou dost." Jesus, he implies, idealistically sees in Rahab "unimaginable things" that are only in his fantasy—a "divine something" that Rahab would not understand, as it seems not to be love. Yet, fascinated by the carpenter's brash son, Judas, beguiling Jesus into a sense of self-esteem, which he lacks, assures him that no woman "could boast / Half of thy worth."

"I know naught / Of the great world beyond this wretched village," Jesus confesses, and admits that Rahab's scorn had, for him, "turned the sky black."[5] Until his rebuff, Jesus had thought that he rose "above" common things by striving to be emotionally remote.

Enjoying some titillation in playing puppeteer, the manipulative Judas offers a way out for Jesus, a rebel without a cause, that might stir the young carpenter's potential:

---

5 In Jeremiah 4:28, "the land will mourn and the sky above will grow black."

> . . . Enough of her.
> Thou art no common man, why dost thou rot
> In this forgotten corner?

Jesus must learn, Judas goads him,

> . . . to stand absolutely by thyself,
> Leaning on nothing, satisfied that thou
> Can'st nothing know, responsible to nothing,
> Fearing no power and being within thyself
> A little independent universe.

If Jesus thought seriously about the world outside, Judas admonishes, "the great God will seem a silly idol," and the prophets only "raving and hysteric madmen." The "Riddle inexplicable" of Creation, beyond easy religious explanations, would "retire behind a veil."

That is atheism, Jesus protests. "Behold the world. Somebody must have made it."

"Somebody must have made this somebody," says Judas.

"Some cause must have existed from all time," Jesus insists.

So has the world, Judas blandishes. Inevitably, he contends, the uneducated young villager, limited in his experience, reasons like a carpenter:

> Thou makest coffers; ergo, all visible coffers
> Must have been made by hands intelligent
> As thine are. But behold you sheaves of wheat.
> They were not planed nor sawn; from a small grain
> They grew, containing in themselves the principle
> That thou would'st force on an eternal craftsman.

The background of the scene lay in Shaw's own experience. The enticing young woman he named Rahab seems to be drawn from his infatuation with a "bewitching" Irish lass in 1875, the year before he left for London. In a poem, his "Calypso" was a "blackeyed enslaver" with "black tresses." As Shaw seemed very innocent and with no future, she married someone else that year. Rationalizing his coming off second best as a good thing after all, Shaw wrote in "Calypso," again reminiscent of Rahab,

> I was too young
> To shun the bait, although I saw the snare.
> I freed myself at last, and felt as though
> I had left half my soul behind.

Only twenty, he had been employed as a bookkeeper, detested his dull job although he was good at it, and had quit. For his Irish Calypso he had nothing to offer.

In London, he lived frugally off his mother's earnings as a music teacher while seeking a future as a writer. The question of First Causes was often disputed among inquiring Victorians, as was the case then and since for Intelligent Design. (Don Juan would challenge the nihilist and sharp-tongued Devil in *Man and Superman's* dream scene, "Has the colossal mechanism no purpose?") Shaw recalled being at "a bachelor party of young men" in the year he began his play, at the home of a young physician in Kensington, Kingston Barton. When their discussion, introduced by "the most evangelical" of the group, turned to likely divine vengeance upon blasphemers, a skeptic noted that the most controversial atheist then on the lecture platform, Charles Bradlaugh, had taken out his large pocket watch publicly and challenged the Almighty, if such a being existed, to strike him dead in five minutes. Nothing happened. Even if Bradlaugh hadn't really done that, Shaw ventured, it was an experiment worth trying. "And with that I took my watch out of my pocket. The effect was electrical. . . . In vain did I urge the pious to trust in the accuracy of their deity's aim." Several cowered until the five minutes passed and no thunderbolts struck. Was the world, Shaw mused, "a manufactured article and . . . the private property of its Manufacturer"?

At much the same time, Shaw was wearing a religious medal given to him by a pious Roman Catholic girlfriend who insisted as the price of continuing their relationship that he try it for six months to encourage his spiritual alteration. When he perceived no change, she implored him, still seeking his conversion, to visit her priest, Father Addis, at the Brompton Oratory in South Kensington. The same issue that upset Dr. Barton's party emerged:

"The universe exists, said the father: somebody must have made it. If that somebody exists, said I, somebody must have made him. I grant that for the sake of argument, said the Oratorian. I grant you a maker of God. I grant you a maker of the maker of God. . . . but as an infinity of makers is unthinkable and extravagant: it is no harder to believe in number one than in number fifty thousand or fifty million; so why not accept number one and stop there . . . ? By your leave, said I, it is as easy for me to believe that the universe made itself as that a maker of the universe made himself: in fact much easier; for the universe visibly exists, whereas a maker for it is a hypothesis. Of course we could get no further."

Shaw seems to have adapted his "robust callousness of youth" (his later description) about the appealing chain of causality into "The Household of Joseph," but at that point in the play the young artisan has left the shop for good, to become a rather obstreperous disciple of Judas. "Till this day," Jesus tells his new friend, "I never met a man / Who believes less than I." Yet, Jesus confides, "I could not face / A stony blank of vegetable life." He must believe in a "grand, ineffable, benevolent Power" that gives humans "all that's noble in our nature / . . . Death is to me the portal to this presence."

Judas sees in the callow carpenter's refusal to accept disbelief only "a craving for perfection" and "the snare of self delusion." After dreams, there is only "my very dust." Yet "I do not often meet a man like thee / and fain would be thy friend. . . . What are thy plans?"

He hasn't any, Jesus confesses. "I am not learned. Carpentry I hate. / The people will not listen to my preaching."

Offering to find listeners for him, and relishing the idea of playing a Pygmalion role, Judas invites Jesus to Jerusalem to meet a persuasive preacher known as John the Baptist, who has stirred the mob and "dropped / Hints of one who shall soon come after him." Jesus agrees to meet Judas at dawn, and in a brief third scene they ride from Nazareth on donkeys in early morning, offstage, but to the catcalls of bystanders. Onstage, Rahab sees them go, and weeps. "Where's my apprentice gone?" Joseph cries. Mary calls out in an echo of the Hebrew Bible, "My son! My son![6] . . . He will never come back." And she faints.

Shaw never completed his act 2, which opens in Jerusalem after some passage of time during which marvels attributed to Jesus have occurred. The open interior of the Temple resembles a bazaar. Barabbas and others are selling their goods, very likely acquired by plunder. Merchants and onlookers, including a Roman soldier, pass the time in gossip. The odd immersion rite of John the Baptist comes up in the chatter, and Barabbas dismisses him as a surly preacher of hellfire soon to be out of fashion: "The newest man is [now] entering Jerusalem," Barabbas contends. A utopian dreamer, Jesus has already acquired a rock-star reputation. Young girls are allegedly mad about him and strew garlands about him and his donkey, for he comes amid reports, which Barabbas

---

6   "Would God I had died for thee, O Absalom my son, my son!" 2 Samuel 18:33.

distrusts as overblown fantasies, that Jesus has conjured up miracles along the way:

> Yet he is but a paltry Nazarene
> Who has made a fortune by a great picnic.
> They say he fed ten thousand followers
> Upon a dozen loaves, and at a wedding
> Turned water into wine. Amongst the Gadarenes
> He played the devil with two thousand pigs
> And is—to boot—a potent quack. He cures
> All ills, from warts to blindness.

Others in the throng claim that "men of the first credit" have vouched for the events which no one present has actually witnessed. "Marvels and ghosts will ne'er lack witnesses," Barabbas scoffs. Such trickery, he contends, makes "a fool of God."

Judas, with whom Barabbas is acquainted, and shares some philosophical affinities, is among the crowd in the Temple setting. The Judas-Jesus relationship has already become a pairing of realist and idealist, the first of what would be many in Shaw's plays. Judas seems also to foreshadow David Hume's skepticism about philosophical systems. Shaw had already read in the British Museum Hume's sardonic *Of Miracles*. Only "fictitious characters," Shaw would write in his preface to *Androcles and the Lion*, can withstand Hume's unbelief. "My pride / In reason's empire," says Shaw's Judas, "made me a philosopher." Judas's earlier "Riddle inexplicable" of Creation suggests Hume's oft-quoted phrase from *The Natural History of Religion* that "the whole is a riddle, an enigma, an inexplicable mystery."

Two young followers of Jesus, Peter and John, are with Judas, and Peter refers to Jesus as "our Lord"—a leader of "sheer virtue," espousing good works and penitence, who is to be obeyed without question. Yet despite such pacific words, the scene suddenly becomes violent. An unruly mob breaks into the Temple. The merchants attempt to defend their stalls. Inflamed by his wild reception en route, a "hotheaded" Jesus rushes in, vowing to cleanse the unauthorized "pushers" from the "house of prayer." A money changer whose table is thrown over berates the excitable Jesus as a "daylight drunkard." In the confusion, Barabbas steals a purse, and, seized by a soldier, kills him with a mace before being taken into custody. Jesus volunteers to go to prison in the thief's place, confessing that the riot is his fault. "Let me suffer," he offers; but a centurion answers dismissively, "At some other time."

The crowd follows as the body of the dead soldier is carried out. Jesus is left alone with Judas, who muses, cynically, "How very easy / It is to knock the life out of a man, / Considering how tedious 'tis to make one," but Jesus is distressed. "Is murder mirth to thee?" he asks. Having abandoned his craft of carpentry—"mending sticks," he belittles it—what does he have in its place?

> His friend an atheist, his flock a rabble,
> Himself an ignorant bastard. Bitter lesson!
> Torturing rebuke!—But I am cured of madness.
> I will go forth and wander with the lepers.

Judas challenges his companion's squeamish search for personal absolution. The soldier—who was not "immortal"—would have died in some other affair; the thief Barabbas was overdue for arrest; and the corruption in the Temple needed housecleaning. The "fits of gloom" are irresponsible. Jesus concedes that he has "too much boy left in me" and agrees to go with Judas to Bethany, on the eastern slope of the Mount of Olives, where he has arranged lodging with two attractive sisters, Mary and Martha, who keep house for their wealthy brother, Lazarus. (Shaw conflates Mary of Bethany, who in the Gospel of John [20:17] anoints Jesus's feet, with Mary Magdalen of Galilee.) Judas confesses that he was once involved with the seductive Mary. ("I am none the worse, and almost think the dream / Was worth the waking.") "If she softened thee," Jesus retorts, "She is a wonder."

Into the scene comes Pontius Pilate, the Roman governor, walking with his soldiers, musicians, and a mob of the curious, including Saul, one of Pilate's officers, alongside a litter in which Mary Magdalen, now Pilate's mistress, is being borne. They see Peter and John arguing—even brawling—over who better keeps their master's doctrines. When Pilate orders them seized, Mary intervenes and asks to judge the quarrel. Saul explains that the rowdies are followers of Jesus, which puzzles Pilate as his understanding is that the "newly risen" preacher disapproves of "fisticuffs."

"Send them away," Mary Magdalen proposes—protecting the handsome younger man, the disciple John. Pilate agrees, but he condemns the mob as "vile rabble" and orders them all to leave, threatening, if they misbehave, to tear up their streets, burn their temple, and offer their daughters to his soldiers. "Fairest, forgive my wrath," Pilate apologizes to Mary, and confesses that governing rude Jerusalem is "kennel keeping," which he endures only to be close to her. They are expected at a grand feast at midnight. "We will dance and sing / And drink the stars asleep."

The scene shifts to Bethany at sunset. Judas and Jesus arrive and find Pilate's guard, Saul, there to entreat Mary Magdalen on behalf of Pilate, to "grace his banquet," but she has bridled at his savage talk to the mob, and refuses Saul's offered jewel. "Take thy bribe back," she barks. Apparently altered by the very presence of Jesus, who waits within, she rails in remorse to Saul that she will no longer be Pilate's slave. She wants to see him dead, along with the "unwholesome horde of revellers." Until then dressed immodestly, as befits her life, Mary vows, "I will sit covered in the city gate / And shame them publicly."

There, after forty-nine manuscript pages and 1,260 lines, Shaw's draft ends. Where could the play have gone? Inevitably, as we are in Lazarus's house, and he is described, although still offstage, as a compulsive drunkard, a scene should follow in which he is revived by Jesus from an alcoholic stupor in which he appears dead: another miracle. Jesus is still an appealing, if moody, visionary who attracts followers because of his innocent unselfishness and reputed marvels. But he has only an untested purity, and he is not yet, and may never be, in Shaw's counter-gospel, the driven, even dangerous, preacher gathering believers and hinting at his symbolic death.

Death may come for him, nevertheless, for Mary Magdalen has abandoned Pilate to become, it seems, a follower—or more—of the earnest and attractive newcomer with apparently unlimited potential. A word from Pilate would turn off the magic. The carpenter's son may be trapped by his successes, some of which, if they are the inflated rumors of passionate admirers, he does not even know he has achieved. If Jesus requires his own martyrdom to conclusively prove his reputed powers, someone has to manage that violent end for him. If not Pilate, it might be Judas, forced by his own accomplishment—in creating a charismatic prophet from an unpromising carpenter's son—to conspire at his undoing.

In Shaw, that end would not have been arranged for thirty petty pieces of silver, for his Judas is already wealthy; nor would it have been an act of treachery, for the martyrdom would be at Jesus's own bidding. But Shaw, whose creative thrust would always be satiric, would not have closed with anything that does more than foreshadow a death ordained for the wrong reasons. Endings for him would always be paradoxical, and unfinished. Audiences were often left to contemplate an unwritten next act.

A rebel and unbeliever at twenty-one, Shaw could not have written a "Passion Play" (as he described it) in the conventional sense. If he were planning an ironic use of *passion*, with love reentering the life of Jesus, even if too late, Mary Magdalen was waiting.

In his preface to *On the Rocks* (1933), Shaw explained why he thought a modern Passion play was "impossible." After repeated suggestions from admirers of his trial scene in *Saint Joan* (1923) that he repeat the effort with Jesus—which Shaw had stopped short of doing in 1878—he explained that Jesus was a "dumb prisoner": he would not defend himself. There was no drama in that. The accounts in the Gospels were the equivalent in music of "an unresolved discord." Only in the account attributed to John was there anything to build upon—and Shaw wrote a dialogue (more a debate) between Jesus and Pilate to illustrate the dilemma, turning Jesus into something of a feisty and more philosophical Joan, and Pilate into a sharply intellectual opponent on behalf of Rome.

"I am no mere chance pile of flesh and bone," Jesus contends, standing before his inquisitor, who remains seated: "if I were only that, I should fall into corruption and dust before your eyes. I am the embodiment of a thought of God: I am the Word made flesh."

Pilate, unimpressed, is derisive: "There are many sorts of words; and they are all made flesh sooner or later. . . . How am I to distinguish between the blasphemies of my soldiers reported to me by my centurions and your blasphemies reported to me by your High Priest?"

"Woe betide you and the world," Jesus warns, "if you do not distinguish!"

Pilate is not frightened, although Jesus claims, "I have it from God." Pilate trumps him, maintaining, "I have the same sort of knowledge from several gods."

Jesus warns further, using a term that long was a favorite of Shaw's and perhaps drawn from Goethe and *Faust*, "The kingdom of God is striving to come. . . . Slay me and you go blind to your damnation." But Pilate is determined. "I am to spare and encourage every heretic, every rebel, every lawbreaker, every rapscallion, lest he turn out to be wiser than all the generations that made the Roman law and built the Roman Empire on it? . . . I must make an end to you whilst there is still some law left in the world."

That Pilate will do so wills an eventual end to Rome, for civilization, Shaw concludes, "to save itself from stagnation and putrefaction," must progress through criticism, even that which "shock[s] the uncritical as obscene, seditious, blasphemous, heretical, and revolutionary." Its embodiment, in that context, repellent to Pilate—was Jesus. GBS had finally, in this indirect fashion, finished his dispassionate Passion play.

Bibliographic Essay

The text of *Passion Play: A Dramatic Fragment*, British Library Add. MS 50593, was first published in 1971 (Jerald Bringle, ed. [Iowa City: Windhover Press]), with the date of composition ascribed to 1878. The text was reprinted in Dan H. Laurence, ed., *Bernard Shaw: Collected Plays with Their Prefaces*, vol. 7 (New York and London: Dodd, Mead & Max Reinhardt, 1974). The Jesus-Pilate exchange in Shaw's preface to *On the Rocks* (1933) is drawn from *Complete Plays,* vol. 5.

Many lines beyond those quoted and identified above closely parallel biblical texts. Young John's blandishment of Judas, "Peace, corn and wine for ever be thy portion," echoes Deuteronomy 33:28; and Judas's "Ere thou see the crooked straight / And the rough places plain" recalls Isaiah 30:4. Rahab's "Thou stinging adder, / 'Tis thou hast driven him hence" suggests Proverbs 13:31. Mary Magdalen's retort to Pilate, "Bridle thy tongue, oh saucy governor" seems drawn from James 1:34.

Shaw's declaration about churchgoing is found in "On Going to Church," *Savoy*, January 1896, reprinted in Stanley Weintraub, ed., *The Savoy: Nineties Experiment* (University Park: Penn State Press, 1965). Dickens's violent reaction to Millais's painting of the Holy Family, and Queen Victoria's response, are from Malcolm Warner, *The Victorians: British Painting, 1837–1901* (Washington, D.C.: National Gallery, 1997). Shaw's recollection of representing Mary in the aborted play "as a termagant" in his "failure as a trifler" is from "Who I Am and What I Think," *The Candid Friend*, May 18, 1901, reprinted with revisions in *Sixteen Self Sketches* (London: Constable, 1949). His retort about writing a play about God is quoted in Stanley Weintraub, *Journey to Heartbreak* (New York: Weybright, 1971). Shaw's comment about blank-verse plays is from his anonymous review reprinted from the *Pall Mall Gazette,* July 14, 1887, in Brian Tyson, ed., *Bernard Shaw's Book Reviews*, vol. 1 (University Park: Penn State Press, 1991). The 1919 book review cited is "Samuel Butler: The New Life Reviewed," *Manchester Guardian,* November 1, 1919, reprinted in Brian Tyson, ed., *Bernard Shaw's Book Reviews,* vol. 2 (University Park: Penn State Press, 1996). Shaw's "three Jesuses of the gospels" is from his "Quot Homines, Tot Christi" (As many men as there are Christs), *New Statesman,* June 17, 1916, untitled there but given its heading when Shaw prepared the piece for collected works, for a volume that never appeared. It was reprinted in Warren S. Smith, ed., *Shaw on Religion* (London: Constable, 1967).

The suggestion that Shaw had already read Hume comes to me from Michel Pharand, and it is established from Shaw's writings. I am also indebted to the close reading and suggestions of Rev. Alexander Seabrook, Lois Potter, Michael Lipschutz, Jay Halio, Alan and Eileen Hanley-Browne, Ann and Brian Panter, and Philip Winsor. Quotations from the Bible are from the King James text in the Revised Standard Version.

· 2 ·

A Shavian Caesar

When Bernard Shaw provocatively titled a part of his preface to *Caesar and Cleopatra* (1899) "Better than Shakespear[e]?" he included the question mark to assure readers that he wasn't really challenging the sacred Bard. Although he had no fear of Shakespeare's shade, to make doubly certain that he was forestalling any comparison he set his play in a period predating both *Julius Caesar* and *Antony and Cleopatra*. Caesar has not yet set sail for Rome to be murdered (in 44 B.C.) by Brutus, Cassius, and accomplices, and Cleopatra is still an unruly yet bewitching girl metamorphosing into a woman—a kitten into a cat—rather than the aging Shakespearean beauty who at thirty-eight covets the ambitious hunk that is Mark Antony.

Approaching the close of his controversial first decade as a dramatist, Shaw was setting out his credentials as a serious writer for the stage, making his case with a modern chronicle play echoing the Shakespearean style in his own quirky manner. Confident that he had succeeded, only four years later when his new German translator, Siegfried Trebitsch, attempted to compliment him by writing that he didn't know ten plays as good as *Caesar and Cleopatra* produced in the previous fifteen years, Shaw thundered back (September 18, 1903), "Who are those 9 imposters who pretend to have written anything comparable to my masterpiece?"

To lure established players for box-office reasons, Shaw would employ familiar themes, although in his paradoxical fashion, and create roles—"vivid personalities," he told Trebitsch—that would entice actors like the then-famous Sir Johnston Forbes-Robertson. To ensure a parallel dimension of modernity while inserting burlesque anachronisms (like a primitive steam engine) to spoof Shakespeare's clock striking in

Julius Caesar, he invented his own presentational unreality. The audiences were to recognize from the start that they were sitting in a theater at a play, not at the representation of what passed for historical truth.

Almost from his beginnings as a playwright in the early 1890s, Shaw felt that accepted facts were to be exploited creatively. He knew that many ostensible facts were creative in any case. As a subject, the historical Caesar, as early as Shaw's third year in writing for the theater, already lurked in the back of his mind. "Historical facts," he contended in the London newspaper *To-day* in April 1894, "are not a bit more sacred than any other class of facts. In making a play out of them you must adapt them to the stage, and that alters them at once." Yet, he conceded, "Invented facts are the same stale stuff in all plays, one man's imagination being much the same as another's in such matters, whilst real facts are fresh and varied. So you can judge exactly how far my historical conscience goes. If I were to write a play about Julius Caesar, it would not really be historical; but I should take care not to let him appear with a revolver and a field-glass all the same."

Writing *Caesar and Cleopatra* five years later would test his theory by his practice. This was a modern play on a platform, Shaw suggested at the start, not a photographic glance into the open fourth wall of a room, nor a glimpse outward at the external world. Ironically, that Shavian prism gave him the opportunity for mocking Shakespeare's use of history, which he satirized even more strikingly than in his original script when he trimmed his text for a later production. As an optional alternative to the first scene, he wrote a wry prologue to be spoken by the Egyptian sun god Ra, whom Shaw imagined from long-familiar hieroglyphics as a hawk-headed man wearing a solar disk. He surveys the audience "*with great contempt*" and refers to them (presuming a British audience) as "quaint little islanders" curiously attired in their evening garb and unable to prostrate themselves before him, "for ye are packed in rows without freedom to move." He asks not for worship but silence: "Let not your men speak nor your woman cough; for I am come to draw you back two thousand years over the graves of sixty generations."

As he explains the setting and the time, Ra interjects a warning not to sleep "while a god speaks" and to be wary of those who make war to achieve empire, for "the impossible" seems always to come to pass, "even as the power of imperial Spain crumbled when it was set against your fathers in the days when England was little, and knew her own mind, and had a mind to know instead of a circulation of newspapers.

Wherefor look to it, lest some little people whom ye would enslave rise up and become in the hand of God the scourge of your boastings and your injustices and your lusts and stupidities."

As Ra senses, commanding the stage, the audience is uncomfortable. Their squirming earns his rebuke: "Are ye impatient with me? Do ye crave for the story of an unchaste woman? Hath the name of Cleopatra tempted ye hither?" (One of the staples of the late-Victorian stage was adultery among the privileged classes.) "Ye foolish ones," he admonishes; "Cleopatra is as yet but a child that is whipped by her nurse." (Her teenage innocence would become one of Shaw's improvements upon history.) However it is time for the Shavian chronicle to unfold, and Ra warns his listeners (deplored as "dull folk") to settle silently into their seats, "for ye about to hear a man speak, and a great man he was, as ye count greatness. . . . Farewell, and do not presume to applaud me."

Shakespeare's courtly one-man Chorus in *Henry V* would not insult his "groundling" audience, the Elizabethan theater's bread and butter, but Shaw's listeners would have felt it out of character to be regarded with mere approval. GBS was out to change the world as he saw it; the Bard intended only to reflect it. Yet that required his rousing presenter, once he described the "wooden O" in which the play was performed, to exhort audiences to "entertain conjecture of a time" when the scenes to be depicted imaginatively took place. A fleet would be sailing to France only in men's minds, and the Battle of Agincourt would be fought with Shakespeare's ringing rhetoric. While the Bard knew that his hints of relationships between past and present would be savored, he also realized that his lines had to be politically attuned, or the play could not be lawfully performed.

Shaw had other constraints from the Lord Chamberlain's stage censorship then in force. To be licensed for production (until the Theatres Act of 1968) a play had to refrain from open sexuality, criticism of the Crown and portrayals of living Royals, and direct attacks on the government. Still, like Shakespeare, Shaw could insert sly political inferences signifying his own time. "Allow me," Shaw offers in his preface, referring to hard-nosed realists like the Victorian historian Thomas Carlyle, "to set forth Caesar in the same modern light, taking the platform from Shakespear[e] as he from Homer." Britain's acquisition of Cyprus in the Treaty of Berlin in 1878 would be suggested by Caesar's offering it to Cleopatra's young half brother Ptolmey, whose adviser, Pothinus, scorns it with "Cyprus is no good to anybody."

"No matter," says Caesar, "you shall have it for the sake of peace." And Caesar's trusty slave, Britannus, another unhistorical Shavian invention, adds, "*unconsciously anticipating a later statesman*," Shaw writes wryly in his stage directions, "Peace with honor, Pothinus." His "later statesman," as his audiences knew then, was Victoria's favorite prime minister, Benjamin Disraeli (1804–81). The post-conference claim was ever after credited to him although he had echoed a predecessor, Lord John Russell. We are in 48 B.C., in a mid-Victorian Egypt.

Britannus also afforded Shaw the opportunity to ridicule Victorian prudery. Caesar, who (according to his *Gallic Wars*) had twice traveled across the Channel, described Briton warriors who had dyed their skin with blue woad to strike terror into their enemies, and when Cleopatra questions the guileless Britannus about it, his Shavian response, mocking Victorian propriety, turns the practice on its head. "Blue," he explains, "is the color worn by all Britons of good standing. In war we stain our bodies blue; so that though our enemies may strip us of our clothes and our lives, they cannot strip us of our respectability." And when Caesar prepares to swim away from the besieged Pharos lighthouse, Britannus cautions him, "Do not let yourself be seen in the fashionable part of Alexandria until you have changed your clothes." The stuffy Victorian empire in its sunset years was Shaw's ironic lens upon the Roman Empire of circa 46 B.C., soon to begin sinking into post-Caesar decadence.

To Shaw's audiences at the turn of the twentieth century, the girlish Cleopatra VII, who ascended the throne as a teenager and was taken in hand by Caesar to consolidate Roman control of Egypt, suggests Victoria's becoming queen at eighteen in 1837 and being groomed for her role by her avuncular yet attractive prime minister, Viscount Melbourne, fifty-four at the time, as was Caesar in Egypt. However devoted to Melbourne at the start, Victoria would later thrive in her independence from him, while Shaw has Cleopatra plot to rid herself of external impediments to her own rule, Caesar among them.

For Cleopatra, both impediment and accomplice are joined in the person of a loyal slave who is paradoxically her most powerful courtier. In the play there is grim drama in the duel of wits between Caesar and the queen's obsessively loyal nurse and servant, a formidable foe whose life only has meaning, and is fully used up, in fealty to Cleopatra. Again there are Victorian resonances, since Ftatateeta is not historical, but only a Shavian invention suggesting the imperious and utterly devoted personal nurse and servant to the queen, Louise Lehzen. The future Baroness Lehzen would do, and did, anything for Victoria—at least until the young queen married Prince Albert in 1840, after which he contended with Lehzen for courtly power, finally having her exiled. Coming to the throne when barely eligible to reign, Victoria in her inexperience had depended upon Lehzen, who acquired a proliferation of duties and responsibilities in the royal household. As London gossip knew, Lehzen (prior to the arrival of Albert, who called her the "House Dragon") had a bedroom in Buckingham Palace adjacent to Victoria's suite, with an entrance cut through the wall during the summer of the queen's accession. As George Grenville, the clerk of the Privy Council, remarked in his diary (published posthumously to Victoria's indignation), when the members of the queen's Cabinet came to see her, "The Baroness retired through one door as they enter[ed] at the other, and the audience over, she returned to the Queen."

Mid-Victorian England was also preoccupied by religious ritualism and its opposite, rationalist doubt, as well as by a frenzy for spiritualism, which briefly made a mockery of both. In echoing such aspects of the departing century, Shaw furnishes with dramatic economy a fictitious Egyptian parallel. Spiritualism as practiced in spooky seances and covert table-turning mesmerized many nineteenth-century voyeurs, even Queen Victoria, and retained some believers despite repeated exposures of fraud and trickery. Shaw was even a member of the Psychical Research Society, which sent its skeptical members to expose allegedly haunted houses. In the fourth act of the play, Cleopatra entertains Caesar at a pseudo-birthday party (he invents birthdays for strategic reasons) in which she summons in the semi-darkness, as the god's priestess, Father Nile: "Perhaps he will rap on the table."

"What!" exclaims Caesar—"table-rapping! Are such superstitions still believed in this year 707 of the [Roman] Republic?" But rather than the voice of the Nile deity, the queen's guests hear the stricken cry of someone not far off being murdered—at, it turns out, Cleopatra's instructions. When Shaw was in his nineties, in 1949, the year before his death, Lilli Palmer, who was planning to portray Cleopatra in a new production in New York, came to visit him at his country house north of London to talk about the part, and ask for his blessing. "Anyone can play Cleopatra," he said confidently. "The role plays itself."

Miss Palmer asked about the first London production, in 1907, when Gertrude Elliott was Cleopatra and her husband, the famed Shakespearian actor Sir Johnston Forbes-Robertson, for whom Shaw had written the lead, played Caesar. Humanizing the historical Caesar was less easy, for on his return to Rome the Senate had voted him dictator for an unprecedented ten-year term, conferring on him absolute power over the state. By dealing with Caesar before that—he would be assassinated in 44 B.C.—Shaw could portray an avuncular Roman, full of stories to tell, uneasy about his baldness, worried about aging—yet tough and even cruel when necessity required it. The crucial offstage murder of Pothinus, the conspiratorial prime minister, Shaw recalled, was a shortcoming in the performance. The death scream must ring out in all its fear and agony, shaking the unprepared audience to the very marrow. Without that effect, the confrontation that follows between the feline Cleopatra and the suddenly grim Caesar fails to achieve its dramatic impact. "One night I went backstage," Shaw said, his wintry blue eyes sparkling, "and I told Pothinus to hold his tongue when the cue came. Then *I* gave such a cry!" He pounded his bony knees in ecstatic memory. "Forbes-Robertson said to me [afterwards], 'If we asked the actor to yell the way you do, he'd be hoarse and we'd have to engage a different man every night just for that yell. That's simply beyond our budget.'" Shaw struck his knees again. He wanted his lines to be played full-throttle.

The times—in particular the 1890s, when the play was written—were also enlivened by controversy over the social role of the arts, with the contemporary buzzword "art for arts's sake" denying that the arts had to do more than be themselves in order to justify themselves. Artists of the first class were now respectable, and even knighted, but selling anything, including art, was still under suspicion. Although the social elite had long purchased art, "commerce" was beneath propriety. It was Shaw's opportunity to have Caesar defend the glib, itinerant Sicilian art dealer, Apollodorus, another invented Shavian character, to the prissy Britannus as a gentleman—"a patrician amateur." It was not the heyday of English culture. Just as its best drama was being produced by Irishmen, its best visual art was imported from France and Italy or created by expatriate Americans. "I leave the art of Egypt in your charge," says the departing Caesar to Apollodorus. "Remember: Rome loves art and will encourage it ungrudgingly."

"I understand, Caesar," he responds, suggesting imperial, late-Victorian Britain. "Rome will produce no art itself, but it will buy up and take whatever the other nations produce."

"What!" Caesar objects, "Rome produce no art! Is peace not an art? Is war not an art? Is civilization not an art? All these we give you in exchange for a few ornaments. You will have the best of the bargain." It was Shaw's pragmatic Caesar at his most pithy.

Apollodorus is also in the scene to validate the famous carpet episode from Plutarch. The dealer in carpets and associated collectibles haughtily reproves a Roman sentinel, "I do not keep a shop. Mine is a temple of the arts. I am a worshipper of beauty. My calling is to choose beautiful things for beautiful queens. My motto is Art for Art's sake." Yet art in Alexandria has its unexpectedly practical aspects, and Apollodorus has been summoned to smuggle Cleopatra to the besieged lighthouse at Pharos despite orders to keep her away from Caesar's presence (and likely hazard). He does so by concealing her in an ornate, rolled-up rug, an episode which demonstrates the impact art can have on history— and not merely in Shaw's spin on Plutarch and classical Egypt. In October 1943, during World War II, then on the verge of being lost by the Axis powers, Adolf Hitler ordered a parachute commando unit led by Lieutenant Colonel Otto Skorzeny to rescue the hapless Italian dictator Benito Mussolini, who had been taken captive by partisans. The success of the mission (although Mussolini proved burdensome) prompted Hitler to order Skorzeny a disastrous year later to take hostage the son of Hungarian strongman Nikolaus Horthy, to forestall the doomed puppet regime's threatened armistice with the Allies. In "Operation Panzerfaust," Skorzeny, who knew Shaw's *Caesar and Cleopatra*, flew secretly to Budapest, wrapped the boy in a carpet—Apollodorus style, as he recalled—and spirited him away. Admiral Horthy buckled under.

Shaw not only "made" history while depicting it, but consulted historians past and present in order to establish authenticity. As he told his early biographer Archibald Henderson, who was also one of Mark Twain's first biographers, a chronicle play like *Caesar and Cleopatra* was a way to "arrange history for the stage. The value of the result depends on your grasp of historical issues—whether your history is a big history or Little Arthur's history." *Little Arthur's History of England* in eight small volumes, which Shaw had encountered as a boy, was an 1830s schoolbook text that oversimplified events for novices. Shaw intended to evoke character in order to reveal motive, and, to explain Caesar, drew upon what he described as "original morality." His Caesar is not only "a prodigy of vitality" but possesses a "special quality of mind." Rather than live as most do, by inherited or borrowed principles, the play's Caesar evinces "an air of frankness, generosity, and magnanimity by enabling him to estimate the value of truth, money, or success . . . quite independently of convention and moral generalization. . . . Hence, in order to produce an impression of complete disinterestedness and magnanimity, he has only to act with entire selfishness."

One of Shaw's contributions to the presentational stage—where the audience remains aware on one level that it is seeing a play—is the self-conscious character, one who is aware of himself as actor and as character. In the first-act soliloquy, Caesar is aware of his uniqueness among men, his originality. Soliloquies, which reached their acme in Shakespeare (GBS must open with one to challenge the Bard), are, as spoken thoughts, a theatrical convention beyond reality. Although Shaw has Caesar address his musings to the Great Sphinx looming in the desert, in whose paws young Cleopatra sleeps (is the play also her dream?), the rhetoric, suggesting the Shakespeare's cadences, reveals Caesar's sense of his uniqueness. "I have wandered in many lands," he confides to the silent Sphinx, and although he has encountered "creatures such as myself," he has found "no other Caesar, no air native to me, no man kindred to me, none who can do my day's deed, and think my night's thought."

In the elaborate program that Shaw prepared for the copyright performance of the play on March 15, 1899—a legal quibble of the time to protect stage rights—Shaw listed all the historians he claimed to have studied, from Herodotus, Strabo, and Plutarch to James Froude, Theodor Mommsen, and Gilbert Murray. Then professor of Greek at the University of Glasgow (and later at Oxford), Murray was very much alive and active, and would be Shaw's prototype for Adolphus Cusins, the young professor of Greek who falls in love with Major Barbara in GBS's Salvation Army play of 1905. He read the script for Shaw, who then, Murray said, "modified accordingly." However, Shaw would not alter his characterization of the feline heroine, who develops through the acts from a kitten to be stroked into a cat with menacing claws. (She tells Caesar in almost her first lines, and in all seriousness, "My great-grandmother's great-grandmother was a black kitten of the sacred white cat; and the river Nile made her his seventh wife.") "I am not quite convinced that I have overdone Cleopatra's ferocity," Shaw defended his characterization to Murray. "If she had been an educated lady of the time I should have made her quite respectable & civilized, but what I was able to gather . . . led me to draw her as I did."

Agreeing with Froude (because Shaw preferred it that way) that Cleopatra as a mere child of sixteen, kept innocent by her entourage, would not have had a sexual liaison with Caesar, Shaw seized upon

Mommsen for further support. GBS could hardly have escaped Mommsen's immense reputation, and Oscar Wilde had already claimed in *The Decay of Lying* (1889), "It is a question whether we have ever seen the full expression of a personality.... Caesar, says Mommsen, was the complete and perfect man." His *Römische Geschichte* in five volumes (1854–56) was at Shaw's side at he wrote the play. Surviving pages of GBS's notes from Mommsen, including a rough map of the lighthouse scene, are dated by him from Haslemere, Surrey, where he drafted *Caesar and Cleopatra*, and two leaves of the manuscript have his page references to Mommsen.

A fascinating debt to him is Shaw's exceedingly youthful Cleopatra. The deceptively girlish queen who flowers under Caesar's tutelage reflects the mentor-and-disciple theme which recurs through the Shavian canon: Cleopatra is a precursor, for example, of Eliza Doolittle in *Pygmalion* (1914). But nowhere in Roman chronicles is there an excuse for the Shavian sixteen as Cleopatra's age at the time of Caesar's arrival in Egypt. (Nineteen is more likely.) Mommsen recorded the young queen's accession to the throne to become joint ruler with her young brother as having taken place when she was sixteen and Ptolemaeus Dionynsius ten. On the same page in the William P. Dickson translation of 1894 which Shaw used—but placed with events of three years later—Mommsen records Caesar's entry into Egypt and his recall of Cleopatra, who had been exiled by her brother's overseers. Shaw either misread the two age references—or managed, for his purposes, a puritanical evasion.

Cleopatra's exaggerated innocence and youth as the play opens became a Shavian device by which the conqueror could be humanized by being seen through the irreverent eyes of a child. Caesar's chaste dalliance with her then becomes a strategic device rather than an erotic attraction, and her infatuation with him, alleged by Ptolmey's chief minister, Pothinus, is rejected by Cleopatra, who intends to rule when Caesar returns to Rome, with the challenge, "Can one love a God?" Shaw leaves the glamorizing of sex to Shakespeare in *Antony and Cleopatra*, which depicts the love-obsessed pair when the queen was aware of her fading beauty.

Although Plutarch explicitly relates that Caesar's adventure with Cleopatra had concrete issue—"a son ... whom the Egyptians call Caesarion"—Mommsen, happily for Shaw's purposes, ignores the event. It leaves Shaw free to close his chronicle with a colorful yet ironic farewell scene between Caesar and Cleopatra that offers little hint about their relationship beyond his overly successful tutelage. He even pretends—so it seems—not to notice the queen at the quay where his ship is about to depart for Rome, although she is the most striking figure onstage, clothed amid the exotically costumed throng strikingly and histrionically in black, in mourning for the zealous, assassinated Ftatateeta. (Does a queen mourn a servant? Victoria openly and almost scandalously mourned her faithful, doglike John Brown in 1883.) Onstage, Caesar appears not even to miss Cleopatra. When she asks him what role she has in his leave-taking, the omission dawns on Caesar: "Ah, I knew there was something." He plants a decorous farewell kiss on her forehead. Dalliance is not for those who aspire toward the ultimate possibilities of men. But even Caesar's reach will prove beyond his grasp.

Shaw wrote the play in late 1898, shortly after his marriage to Charlotte Payne-Townshend, a union that was almost certainly, at her insistence, unconsummated—a relationship echoed in Caesar's chaste involvement with Cleopatra. The play received its first full production, by the great German director Max Reinhardt, in March 1906. To shorten the play somewhat, Shaw wrote the "Ra" prologue for the Forbes-Robertson production of October 1912 as substitute for act 1, scene 1, afterwards labeled "Alternative to the Prologue." In some early productions, act 3, the lighthouse scene, was cut to economize playing time. In other productions, both prologues have been staged. A film version was directed by Gabriel Pascal, with Claude Rains as Caesar and Vivien Leigh as Cleopatra, in 1945, under war constraints in production.

Caesar and Cleopatra seems in its visual extravagance almost to have been written with cinema in mind, although Shaw in 1899 was foreshadowing rather than anticipating the still-primitive medium. Ancient Egypt had tremendous appeal for a pre-cinematic, Bible-familiar public, and cheap color lithographs of "Eastern" scenes were a popular commodity. Society painter Sir Edward Poynter (later president of the Royal Academy) achieved his first successes with enormous scenes from the times of the pharaohs, with one crowded and carefully researched ten-foot panorama, *Israel in Egypt* (1867), typical of the genre. Not long before Shaw began his play, Sir Edward triumphed again with his *Visit of the Queen of Sheba to Solomon*, which suggests Shaw's concept, and Sir Lawrence Alma-Tadema, knighted by Victoria in 1899, the year of Shaw's play, was famous for his colorful, often lubricious, canvases of Roman scenes. A striking production of *Caesar and Cleopatra* at the Shaw Festival Theatre at Niagara-on-the-Lake, Canada, was designed to suggest a series of Alma-Tadema paintings.

The visual arts were important to Shaw, an art critic in the late 1880s. His "rug scene" seems based on Jean-Léon Gérôme's painting *Cleopatra Apportée à Caesar dans un Tapis* (1866), and he recalled having the first-act Sphinx scene "suggested" by an engraving of Luc Olivier Merson's *Répos en Egypte* (1879). As he insisted (August 16, 1903) to Siegfried Trebitsch in sending him some crude sketches, "Barbarous as my drawings of the scenery are, a great deal depends on them. Even an ordinary modern play . . . depends a good deal on the author writing his dialogue with a clear plan of stage action in his head; but in a play like Caesar it is absolutely necessary. The staging is just as much a part of the play as the dialogue. It will not do to let a scenepainter & a sculptor loose on the play without a specification of the conditions with which their scenery must comply." Always the complete artist, when Shaw had a character sing a fragment of song, as Apollodorus with a barcarolle, and sailors a chanty in *Captain Brassbound's Conversion* (1898), he composed the music and the lyrics.

Although *Caesar and Cleopatra* can be conceived as a comedy foreshadowing a tragedy—Shakespeare's *Antony and Cleopatra*—and the feline heroines are the same woman at very different stages in the queen's extraordinary life, the men who are the intruding forces that shape the play are of a different magnitude. The offstage Antony, who overwhelms Cleopatra's reason, and who is promised to her by Caesar at the close of Shaw's play, is the precipitant of the catastrophe that Caesar's mentoring cannot avert. Heredity is fate. The Egyptian queen remains the impulsive daughter of the Nile. In *Caesar and Cleopatra*, however, she is primarily the means for revealing not her nature, but the character of Caesar, a Shavian being, like his future Joan of Arc, ahead of his time, and ours.

The irony embedded in every production emerges in the festive, colorful closing scene. Caesar is going off, lightheartedly, it seems, to Rome, and, as every reader of Shakespeare, and almost every schoolchild knows, to his violent death. The tragedy in the comedy, both for Caesar and for Cleopatra, comes after the curtain.

Bibliographic Essay

The text of the play is from Dan H. Laurence, ed., *Bernard Shaw: Collected Plays with Their Prefaces*, vol. 1 (New York and London: Dodd, Mead & Max Reinhardt, 1973). Shaw's manuscript notes from Mommsen are in the Harry Ransom Humanities Research Center, University of Texas at Austin.

Shaw's letters to Siegfried Trebitsch about the play are in Samuel A. Weiss, ed., *Bernard Shaw's Letters to Siegfried Trebitsch* (Stanford: Stanford University Press, 1986). George Grenville's diary is quoted in Stanley Weintraub, *Victoria: An Intimate Biography* (New York: Dutton, 1987). Shaw's letter to Gilbert Murray, July 28, 1900, about Cleopatra's "ferocity" is in Dan H. Laurence, ed., *Bernard Shaw: Collected Letters, 1898–1910* (London: Max Reinhardt, 1972).

The "rug scene" and Alma-Tadema's Egyptian spectacles are described in the preface to Stanley Weintraub, ed., *Bernard Shaw on the London Art Scene, 1885–1950* (University Park: Penn State Press, 1986). Shaw's sea shanty music is in an appendix to Rodelle Weintraub, ed., *Captain Brassbound's Conversion: A Facsimile of the Original Manuscript* (New York: Garland, 1981).

· 3 ·

Schiller's *Die Räuber* and Shaw's *Don Juan in Hell*

Was it a slip, or only a coincidence, that as Bernard Shaw was anticipating the publication of *Man and Superman* in January 1903, he addressed a letter to his new German translator, the Viennese journalist Siegfried Trebitsch, as "My Dear Trebitsch-Spiegelmann"—or "Mirrorman"? It seems a brief glimpse into the complexities of the creative mind, for the play was announced by Shaw as his reworking of Mozart's *Don Giovanni*, with some Mephistophelian adaptations from Goethe and Gounod. Something seems missing. "Spiegelmann" suggests a recent reading of Friedrich Schiller.

Possibly the most striking character in Shaw's play, emerging in act 3 and metamorphosed in its "Dream Interlude" into a quick-witted, Faustian Devil, is Mendoza, the brash and cosmopolitan Jewish brigand, who seems to echo the scruffy but boastful Jewish highwayman Moritz Spiegelberg in Schiller's first play, *The Robbers* (1781).[1] Perhaps to deflect such suspicions that Mendoza and much else is borrowed from Schiller, Shaw offers an alternative confession in the preface to his play: "The theft of the brigand-poetaster from Sir Arthur Conan Doyle is deliberate." But for Mendoza's operating out of the mountains of Spain, rather than Germany, the Conan Doyle connection seems superficial. His bourgeois poet-brigand El Cuchillo appears in *The Exploits of Brigadier Gerard* (1896). "I thought nothing of Sherlock Holmes," Shaw claimed to his biographer Hesketh Pearson in the 1930s, "but the Brigadier Gerard stories were first rate."

---

1 The rather stilted 1875 translation utilized here and very likely known to Shaw would have been easily accessible in London, where it was published. He also knew some German.

Advising young Golding Bright, source of the only "boo" from the audience at the premiere of *Arms and the Man* in 1895, on theatrical matters, Shaw had suggested, among other recommendations, "Read all of Goethe's plays and a lot of Schiller's." Presumably he had already taken his own advice, but as a prodigal son melodrama, *Die Räuber* seems not to have generated any special interest in Shaw.[2] He had long read Schiller, and referred to him often, sometimes unfavorably. The only play by Schiller that Shaw saw onstage was *Maria Stuart* (1800), starring the great Adelaide Ristori, in a performance which impressed him enough that decades later he was still quoting its lines and recalling some of its scenes.

More negatively, Shaw would claim that his *Saint Joan* rescued the Maid from Schiller's "romantic nonsense" in *Die Jungfrau von Orleans* (1801), "which has not a single point of contact with the real Joan, nor indeed with any mortal woman that ever walked this earth." (Schiller's improbable Joan dies on the battlefield and is resurrected.) Yet Shaw admired Schiller's powerful *Wallenstein* (1799), and would write to Trebitsch a week after his earlier letter, much as he often referred wryly to Shakespeare, "Remember that though we may be no bigger men than Goethe and Schiller, we are standing on their shoulders, and should therefore be able to see farther & do better. And after all, Schiller is only Shaw at the age of 8, and Goethe [only] Shaw at the age of 32. This, by the way, is the highest compliment ever paid to Goethe." It seemed no compliment to Schiller.

Shaw owed something to Goethe in *Man and Superman*, as he made clear in his preface to the play. His leading lady, Ann Whitefield, intended as an embodiment of vitality, was his *Ewig-Weibliche*, or Eternal Feminine, out of Goethe, and his concept of Man at his best as endlessly striving for an unattainable but insistent perfection was his equivalent to Goethe's sense of unending quest in *Faust*. "As our German friend put it in his poem," Don Juan quotes Goethe to Ana, the dream equivalent to the frame-play's Ann, "the poetically nonsensical here [in the luxurious Shavian Hell] is good sense; and the Eternal Feminine draws us upward

---

2 Shaw's paradoxical prodigal sons are Dick Dudgeon of *The Devil's Disciple* (1896) and "Black Paquito" Brassbound of *Captain Brassbound's Conversion* (1899). Although Maurice Valency in *The Cart and the Trumpet* (New York, 1973) claimed that such brigands, including Blanco Posnet of *The Shewing-Up of Blanco Posnet* (1909), "seem to trace their ancestry more or less directly to Karl von Moor in Schiller's *The Robbers*," no echoes from Schiller are evident.

and on—without getting us a step further." In the opening dialogue between God and Mephistopheles, in *Faust*, the Lord sees humanity as an imperfect creation, for "Man ever errs the while he strives." Still, to strive is to live more intensely, and although all action is inherently reckless, the goal of Goethe's Mephistopheles, to which Shaw subscribed, is to stir humankind from overcautious passivity.

The apparent Schiller dimension in *Man and Superman* drawn from *Die Räuber* is multifarious and intricate. Some of what seems Schiller-like may have come, rather, from John Milton, who as early as the opening scene of *Paradise Lost*, "struck the popular fancy," Shaw wrote as a drama critic early in 1896, "by changing the devil into a romantic gentleman who was nobody's enemy but his own." There, also, Satan convenes a motley parliament of subordinate devils he has recruited much as does Mendoza (transformed into the Devil in the dream scene) in his bleak Sierra Nevada hideaway, where his buffoonish brigands, largely failed political radicals who claim to be anarchists, accost the few travelers crossing through Spain. The rhetorical echoes suggest Schiller, who wrote his play when he was a deeply disaffected cadet in the military academy at Württemberg, and combined his attraction to Shakespeare's tragedies with his rejection of army discipline, as reflected in the squalid and argumentative rascals collecting in a forest hideaway in Saxony.

The brigand captain Mendoza, whose surname (he has no forename) recalls a family line of Sephardim who either fled the Inquisition or retreated into Catholicism as *conversos*, is a romantic visionary, an execrable poet, and a rejected Romeo. His feistiness is largely verbal, unlike the admired early-nineteenth-century English pugilist of Sephardic background, Daniel Mendoza, whose reputation in the ring Shaw, an amateur boxer in his twenties, knew well. The Shavian Mendoza's wit recalls a line from Heinrich Heine (a contemporary of the historical Mendoza), who quotes a legendary Spanish anarchist challenging a persistent Christian missionary, "How can I believe in your religion when I don't even believe in mine, which is the only true one?"

Schiller's band of bandit amateurs led at first by Moritz Spiegelberg may be the earliest of the "desperado" romances now remembered more for Verdi's *Hernani*, Bizet's *Carmen*, Gilbert and Sullivan's *Pirates of Penzance*, and Offenbach's *Les Brigands*, all of which Shaw saw and, as a critic, reviewed. In his notice of *Les Brigands* in the *Star* (September 20, 1889), Shaw joked (or confessed), "What are brains for, if not to be picked by me and the rest of the world? In my business I know *me* and *te*, but not *meum* and *tuum*."

Anticipating Gilbert and Sullivan comedy, Schiller's band of thieves, in addition to arguing over radical catchwords, sing,

> To rob, to kill, to wench, to fight,
> Our pastime is, and daily sport;
> The gibbet claims us morn and night,
> So let's be jolly, time is short. . . .
> And, when with Rhenish and rare Moselle
> Our throats we have been oiling,
> Our courage burns with a fiercer swell,
> And we're hand and glove with the Lord of Hell,
> Who down in his flames is broiling.

Shaw's brigands merely quarrel over radical political slogans, all meaningless given their remote setting ("such wonderful fine speeches," according to Schiller's Spiegelberg), and it is Mendoza himself who recites to his hostages, Tanner and his chauffeur, rueful singsong verses about his longing for his lost Louisa. Yet Shaw almost never metamorphosed a single source into a scene in his plays. The absurd political arguments of the brigands were also drawn from his experience of the Marxist Second International Congress in Zurich in 1896, as it amused him to have the crafty Mendoza dominate the excessively talkative and ineffectual socialists and anarchists.

Schiller's futile gang of desperadoes is the only one in drama until Shaw's to feature an obvious Jew. Shaw's absurdly sentimental rogue Mendoza had been a waiter at the posh Savoy Hotel in London. His self-exile followed his rejection by Louisa Straker, about whom he writes passionately bad verse, because, he mourns, "she objected to marrying a Jew." Once a cook for a Jewish family, Louisa, her admirer claims, could not "eradicate the impression it made on her mind"—she has a "highly strung temperament"—that their "elaborate" dietary code made Jews "contemptuous of the Gentile. . . . My entreaties were in vain: she always retorted that she wasn't good enough for me, and recommended me to marry an accursed barmaid named Rebecca Lazarus, whom I loathed."

The only woman in Schiller's play, something of a Mozartian Donna Ana figure, is Amelia, a pretty, plucky cousin of Charles (Karl) von Moor and his malicious brother Francis, a rival whose unwanted attentions are rejected much less diplomatically than those of the lovelorn Octavius by

Ann Whitefield in *Man and Superman*. Amelia wants only the outcast Charles, telling Francis spiritedly after one plea, "Go—You have robbed me of a precious hour; may it be deducted from your life."

In Spain, Mendoza confesses to Tanner, he has formed a "syndicate" of hopeless misfits to hold up motorcars—an expensive new invention guaranteed to be owned and utilized by the rich. "I became leader, as the Jew always becomes leader, by his brains and imagination. But with all my pride of race I would give everything I possess to be an Englishman."

More than a century earlier, Schiller's satiric robber scenes seemed no lighthearted spoof to playgoers. Wild locales in Germany were home to runaway conscripts and aggrieved serfs, fugitives from justice, failed students and defrocked clergymen, younger sons with no inheritance prospects, and vagrant Jews whose legally protected parents could not afford residence permits in the restricted cities for all their adult children. In Schiller's day, bands of Jewish highwaymen were said, exaggeratedly, to roam Westphalia, Brandenburg, and Hesse and were rumored to maintain some pious, if token, customs, observing what they could of a kosher diet, robbing only on weekdays, and resting from labor on their Sabbath.

Mendoza introduces himself proudly to the wealthy traveler John Tanner as a brigand who lives by robbing the rich. Tanner, an upper-class socialist, responds, "I am a gentleman. I live by robbing the poor." (Perhaps William Morris, to whom Shaw was devoted, was an earlier reader of Schiller, as in his "A King's Lesson" a captain explains his "craft" to the king, "As the potter lives by making pots, so we live by robbing the poor.")

In Schiller the upper-class rebel is Charles von Moor, a brigand in self-exile in Saxony. Although von Moor leads the brigands by his wits and his pride, it is his accomplice, Spiegelberg, who proposes issuing a manifesto, worldwide, calling on those "who do not eat pork" to move with him to Palestine and restore its glory. More than a century later, Mendoza upbraids a rowdy accomplice who charges him with not being a Christian, "*I* am an exception to all rules. It is true that I have the honor to be a Jew; and when the Zionists need a leader to reassemble our race on its historic soil of Palestine, Mendoza will not be last to volunteer." Spiegelberg boasts of his "teeming wit"—that "Great thoughts are dawning in my soul! Gigantic plans are fermenting in my brain." Von Moor attributes such "swaggering" to "wine," but the Jew has a plan—to "force hoarded coin into circulation" by relieving "rich misers" of it, ostensibly "to restore the equalization of property." Mendoza appears to echo his German predecessor. "We intercept that wealth," he explains. "We restore it to circulation among the class that produced it and that chiefly needs it." Persuaded less by Spiegelberg's specious idealism than by his audacity, one of the libertines, Roller, offers his hand, declaring, "Thus I consign my soul to the devil."

Proud of his recruiting successes, Spiegelberg tells the libertine Razmann, "I think I must be endowed with some magnetic property, which attracts all the vagabonds on the face of the earth towards me, like steel and iron."

On its face, the Mendoza dimension of *Don Juan in Hell* suggests Shaw's close reading of Schiller, while Charles von Moor's grandiose aspirations suggest the philosophic flights of fancy of Don Juan Tenorio, who in Shaw's dream interlude is paired with Mendoza's mythic extension as the Devil. "Am I to squeeze my body into stays," von Moor declares, "and straightlace my will in the trammels of law? . . . Never yet has law formed a great man; 'tis liberty that breeds giants and heroes."

There is much talk among the would-be robbers of "the very devil himself" and that "the devil is in you!" And "Trust not the devil, although he be of your own raising." Schiller utilizes just about every contemporary cliché his audiences would have recognized in which the devil is invoked. There is also much talk of heaven and hell, the transitory and metaphorical venues of Shaw's interlude. "Give the devil his due," says Spiegelberg of himself. "When the honest man is once ousted from his stronghold, the devil has it all his own way—the transition is then as easy as from a whore to a devotee." Francis von Moor, the evil brother, threatens Daniel, Charles's still-loyal servant, "According to all calculations, you will sup tomorrow with old Beelzebub. In these matters all depends upon one's view of a thing." So, too, will the Statue of the Commander direct Juan at the close of the dream interlude.

"Satan must know his people right well," says Razmann to Spiegelberg, "to have chosen you as his factor."[3] But social rank intervenes, and the band is soon led by Charles von Moor himself, whose two tirades about hypocrisy directed at the conventional Father Dominic, a monk out to "save" the brigands with pardons if they accept "the holy church," foreshadow the paradoxes of Shaw's Devil as well as their striking, balanced, cadences:

---

3 Factor: agent.

> Is it possible for humanity to be so utterly blind? . . . They thunder forth from their clouds about gentleness and forbearance, while they sacrifice human victims to the God of love as if he were the fiery Moloch. They preach the love of one's neighbour, while they drive the aged and blind with curses from their door. They rave against covetousness; yet for the sake of gold they have depopulated Peru, and yoked the natives, like cattle, to their chariots. They rack their brains in wonder to account for the creation of a Judas Iscariot, yet the best of them would betray the whole Trinity for ten shekels. . . . You are not ashamed to kneel before crucifixes and altars; you lacerate your backs with thongs, and mortify your flesh with fasting; and with these pitiful mummeries you think, fools as you are, to veil the eyes of Him whom, with the same breath, you address as the Omniscient, just as the great are the most bitterly mocked by those who flatter them while they pretend to hate flatterers.

Mummeries is not a term easily employed onstage, but Shaw's Devil refers to the "mummeries" of old-fashioned, expensively mounted funerals, which add a new terror to death, and suggests that the investments are not to speed the deceased to his godly reward but to satisfy the social requirements of the bereaved. Shaw's mockery of ritual without religion is given, in their separate ways, to both Don Juan (Tanner) and the Devil (Mendoza). "What is his religion?" asks the Devil about mankind. "An excuse for hating me. What is his law? An excuse for hanging you. What is his morality? Gentility!" But Juan calls the Devil's domain a "Palace of Lies," and using balanced, almost operatic, cadences close to those Schiller gives von Moor, explains:

> Your friends are all the dullest dogs I know. They are not beautiful: they are only decorated. They are not clean: they are only shaved and starched. They are not dignified: they are only fashionably dressed. They are not educated: they are only college passmen. They are not religious: they are only cowardly. . . . They are not artistic: they are only lascivious. They are not prosperous: they are only rich. They are not loyal, they are only servile; not dutiful, only sheepish; not public spirited, only patriotic; not courageous, only quarrelsome; not determined only obstinate; not masterful, only domineering—

and on Juan goes off, aspiring to the workshop of the blest he associates with heaven while seeking a way out of the torment of unending bliss that is, paradoxically, the Shavian hell. "Why must I alone," Charles von Moor cries out to his obtuse band of libertines, "inhale the torments of hell out of the joys of heaven?"

Although Schiller makes no claim that his melodrama of rival brothers and a band of brigands to which one brother is driven plays out as a dream, Charles asks one of the libertines, Kosinsky, "How do you know that I am not haunted by terrific dreams?" Also haunted is the satanic Francis, intent on inheriting Charles's patrimony yet disturbed by dreams that his brother is not dead, and will return to stake his claims to the Count's estate and to Amelia. Francis feels increasingly ill—and illness, he confides to Daniel, "bewilders the brain, and breeds strange and maddening dreams." He refuses to trust them as they intimate what he refuses to accept. "What signify dreams? Dreams come from the stomach, and cannot signify anything." Just as Shaw's brigands and their captives wrap their coats about themselves and in the darkness of the Sierras, go to sleep and stir the dreams of Tanner and Mendoza,[4] Schiller's earlier robbers wish Charles von Moor a good night and *"stretch themselves on the ground and fall asleep."* At first, von Moor cannot sleep, and—foreshadowing Shaw—walks about, soliloquizing at length,

> To end, like an empty puppet-show. But why this burning thirst after happiness? Wherefore this ideal of unattained perfection? . . . No! No! There must be something beyond, for I have not yet attained to happiness. . . . Be what thou wilt, so I but take this inward self hence with me. External forms are but the trappings of the man. My heaven or hell is within.

"The earth," Juan tells Ana (as the Devil listens), "is a nursery in which men and women play at being heroes and heroines, saints and sinners" in "a fool's paradise." In the Shavian hell, its closest approximation, where empty happiness is the goal, "there are no hard facts to contradict you, no ironic contrast of your needs with your pretensions, no human comedy, nothing but a perpetual romance, a universal melodrama."

---

4 Mendoza's dream must be imagined. However, Mendoza asks Tanner on awakening,
"Did you dream?"
"Damnably. Did you?"
"Yes. I forget what. You were in it."
"So were you. Amazing!"

In *Die Räuber*, Charles von Moor tells the libertine Schwarz, "Brother, I have looked on men, their insect cares and their giant projects, their god-like plans and mouse-like occupations, their intensely eager race after happiness; . . . this chequered lottery of life, in which so many stake their innocence and their Heaven to snatch a prize, and—blanks they all draw—for they find, too late, that there was no prize in the wheel. It is a drama, . . . enough to bring tears into your eyes while it shakes your sides with laughter." In the Devil's longest diatribe in *Don Juan in Hell*, he also looks down on the poor creature that is Man, challenging Juan in what seem echoes of Schiller,

> Have you walked up and down upon the earth lately? I have; and I have examined Man's wonderful inventions. And I tell you that in the arts of life man invents nothing; but in the arts of death he outdoes Nature herself. . . . Hell is a place far above their comprehension: they derive their notion of it from two of the greatest fools that ever lived, an Italian and an Englishman. The Italian described it as a place of mud, frost, filth, and venomous serpents: all torture. . . . The Englishman described me as being expelled from Heaven by cannons and gunpowder; and to this day every Briton believes that the whole of his silly story is in the Bible.

At the close of the dream interlude, Shaw's Juan finds his way to the frontier between the two mythical destinations, which, he is told by the Mozartian "Statue of the Commander" out of *Don Giovanni*, "is only the difference between two ways of looking at things." Did Shaw recall that Francis von Moor had told Charles's servant that going to the Devil—or the other place—"depends upon one's view of a thing"?

Out of a more conventional theatrical tradition, Schiller gives von Moor a melodramatic but abortive return to the bosom of his Amelia and the Count Maximilian von Moor, his despairing father. "From this moment," he tells his band of felons on departing, "I cease to be your captain." The robbers call him a coward. "Where are thy lofty schemes? Were they but soap-bubbles, which disperse at the breath of a woman?" Spiegelberg is already dead at the hands of pursuing militia. Yet Charles spurns happiness, giving himself up to "the hands of justice" rather than the arms of Amelia, and the audience is left to wonder whether tragedy will follow—as seems likely—or will he be reprieved to his former state.

In Shaw, a final act follows the dream interlude, in which Tanner (Juan) accepts his fate, a betrothal to Ann. Mendoza (the dream Devil) reappears to advise Tanner, "Sir: there are two tragedies in life. One is to lose your heart's desire. The other is to gain it. Mine and yours, sir."[5]

Shaw's creative uses of some of the rhetoric suggested by Schiller's debates among von Moor and his intellectual brigands, the dream references, the ethereal dimensions of heaven and hell, and much else in *Die Räuber* foreshadow *Man and Superman* so strikingly that Schiller must be added to Mozart among the building blocks of what may have been the first great play of the new century.

Bibliographic Essay

The unidentified translation of *Die Räuber* is from *The Works of Frederick Schiller: Early Dramas and Romances* (London: George Bell and Sons, 1875). Shaw's *Man and Superman*, including the dream interlude in Hell (act 3), is from *Bernard Shaw: Complete Plays with Their Prefaces*, vol. 2 (London: Max Reinhardt, 1971). Shaw's reference to the *Brigadier Gerard* stories (the poetaster-brigand appears in "How the Brigadier Held the King") is in Hesketh Pearson, *Conan Doyle: His Life and Art* (London: Methuen, 1943). The letter to R. Golding Bright, November 11, 1895, appears in Dan H. Laurence, ed., *Bernard Shaw: Collected Letters*, vol. 1 (New York: Dodd, Mead, 1965). His reference to Schiller's *Maid of Orleans* is from the preface to *Saint Joan* in *Complete Plays*, vol. 6. Shaw's letters to Siegfried Trebitsch, January 7, 1903, and January 15, 1903, are from Samuel Weiss, ed., *Bernard Shaw's Letters to Siegfried Trebitsch* (Stanford: Stanford University Press, 1986). Shaw discusses Milton's devil in *Paradise Lost* in a *Saturday Review* drama critique on January 4, 1896, reprinted in Bernard F. Dukore, ed., *The Drama Observed*, vol. 2 (University Park: Penn State Press, 1992). He reviewed Offenbach's *Les Brigands* in the *Star*, September 20, 1889, reprinted in Dan H. Laurence, ed., *Shaw's Music*, vol. 1 (New York: Dodd, Mead, 1981).

---

5 Shaw seems to be deliberately borrowing from *Lady Windermere's Fan*, as the braggart Mendoza is exposed as having no originality. Oscar Wilde's Charles Dumby observes, "There are only two tragedies in life: one is not getting what one wants, and the other is getting it."

· 4 ·

Shaw's "Secretary for America" and General John Burgoyne

Some of Shaw's most provocative stage characters disappeared, in cinema terms, on the cutting-room floor. Immenso Champernoon, his spoof of G. K. Chesterton, failed to make it into *Back to Methuselah* (1920) and survives only in a volume of Shaw's odds and ends, *Short Stories, Scraps and Shavings* (1934). Edward VIII, who relinquished all for love, turns up only in a skit that never made it beyond a newspaper piece. A dramatic dialogue between Jesus and Pontius Pilate survives in a preface—to *On the Rocks* (1933). George III, the last Founding Father, and his Secretary for America, the imperious Lord George Germain, were written into *The Devil's Disciple* (1896) for an early 1930s film version—a scene never filmed and never staged. There are more, but such discards suggest the losses.

Since the playgoing public feared how Shaw would handle British history, in May 1899 he was questioned by the *Daily Mail* about any concerns he might have regarding a London production of *The Devil's Disciple*, set in New Hampshire and excoriating the British for their incompetence in losing America. His first success across the Atlantic two years earlier, it contrasted a patriot militia captain whose public face was that of a New England Presbyterian minister, and an apparent reprobate and dissident who was an embarrassment to his upright Puritan family. Yet stealing the stage was a third-act walk-on, "Gentleman Johnny" Burgoyne, a real-life sophisticated general who is wittily scathing about lackluster leadership in London and endemic mediocrity in the army, that would cost his country its American empire and Burgoyne his reputation. The general would have liked Shaw's spin on him.

That Britain lost the war and the colonies seemed an obvious box-office drawback in the West End. "Oh," Shaw scoffed, "that difficulty can easily be got over. I am preparing a new version of the last act in which the British army achieves a crushing and final defeat of the American rebels. Washington will be shown on his knees on the field of battle, saluting the Union Jack and surrendering his broken sword to the victorious [General] Cornwallis. At the last moment General Burgoyne will arrive as King's Messenger, sent by George III to confer independence on the United States of America as an act of grace. . . . I think you will find that all will go right."

The tongue-in-cheek ending was, of course, never written, but in 1933, when a film version was first considered, Shaw devised a new satiric opening. A brief wordless scene opens in Philadelphia with Thomas Jefferson signing the Declaration of Independence. The camera closes up on his signature. After a dissolve a flagpole is revealed. The British Royal Standard is being pulled down and replaced by an American flag with thirteen stripes and a circlet of thirteen stars.

After another dissolve we are in St. James' Palace in London about a year later, in 1777. George III is fussing at his prime minister, Lord North, unwilling to accept the fact of American separation. For the stage, Shaw oversimplifies, but captures, the king's hands-on stubbornness. "Stuff and nonsense!" His Majesty shouts. "States! What do you mean by States? Colonies are not States: they are part of my State. Crumbs of it. Crumbs. What do you mean by New England? Where is it? Is it an island? Is it Robinson Crusoe's island? I never heard of it."

In reality, whatever the king's short fuse, and the bullying of his ministers, he knew the maps his generals used very well, refused to let the colonies go, and liked to micromanage strategy. If it took increased land taxes to raise more British troops, or lease foreign mercenaries, which seemed more practical given recruitment frustrations at home, King George wanted his unruly colonies retrieved. But the brief scene's purpose is to introduce the name of the ex-general coordinating the putting down of the rebellion, Lord George Germain. Those theatergoers well versed in their kingdom's history of the previous century would recall Germain—a Sackville with only a courtesy title who took a new name in 1770 in order to inherit his childless aunt's estate. Elder male Sackvilles, of legendary (but real) Knole House, with its 365 rooms, became the dukes of Dorset. George Sackville was an ambitious younger son with no dukedom in prospect who made his way almost to the top in the army, yet in 1759, during the wars with the French, he was court-martialed for alleged cowardice. Although the battle was won, Lord George was tardy in bringing his cavalry to the aid of a dilettantish officer he despised. Unfortunately, Prince Ferdinand of Brunswick happened to be the nephew of Frederick of Prussia.

Young and new to the throne, George III pressed the British military tribunal not only to cashier Sackville but to forbid him any further army role. That hampered the disgraced ex-general's career for a decade, but he saw renewed opportunity in putting down the unruly American colonies. When, in 1775, there were few hawks in Parliament eager to oversee a likely quagmire, the dithering Lord North made Germain his Secretary for America. Soon he was managing operations in a country he had never seen, two months or more distant by sail, where orders from the War Office in London were often obsolete on arrival.

"What! What!" expostulates the king in Shaw's new lines. "Let me see. America is important, you know, North, quite important." He looks at a map. "Thats a devilish big place, you know, North, devilish big. I had no idea it was so big."

Lord North agrees, pointing at the right-hand part of the map below Canada. "Very big, sir; and all this side of it is in rebellion."

"What, what! Rebellion. Gone Jacobite! Has that drunken blackguard the Pretender broken out again?"

Patiently, the prime minister explains that the colonists have never heard of the Stuart Pretender. "They are dissatisfied."

"Damn their impudence!" snaps the king. "What about?"

"Taxes," North explains. "And restrictions on their trade. They are actually fighting us: it is most serious. Sir John Burgoyne"—playgoers will actually meet him later in the original Shaw script—"has been instructed to march south from Quebec along the line of the Hudson River, while Sir William Howe will be ordered to proceed north from New York City, to effect a junction."

"What, what! Burgoyne. Thats a clever chap; but I dont like him. I feel that he is always laughing in his sleeve at me. Quite right to send him to North America: quite right."

Sending off generals in bad odor at Court to problematic assignments where they risked having their careers ruined has always been bureaucratic doctrine, but Shaw's king is confusing the penal system of "transportation" of convicts to America with the need to have winning generalship where one wants to win. North patiently explains that the two generals, Burgoyne and Howe, are to operate toward each other to cut off the enemy in upper New York. Their victory will be a certainty. "Burgoyne is already on the march. Lord Germain has in hand a special dispatch for Howe."

In reality, Germain already knew that William Howe was intending to move most of his forces south from Manhattan, rather than north, to seize the rebel capital of Philadelphia and bed down with his mistress for the next winter. All Germain could do was persuade him to follow up Philadelphia with a junction on the Hudson with Burgoyne—an unlikely move, given Howe's lethargy—and his letch for Mrs. Loring. Bawdy songs about her cohabiting with Howe had already reached England. But the king in Shaw's spin on history sees the energetic American Secretary as the indolent one. "Take care he sends that dispatch," His Majesty reminds North. "Germain is a lazy, idle, good-for-nothing dog. Never does today what he can put off till tomorrow. But it doesn't matter. Burgoyne can deal with any colonial mob singlehanded. Let me hear no more of it."

Although the stage Lord North helplessly rolls up his map and departs, the king would never have shrugged off an opportunity to intrude into strategy. But Shaw's aim is to fix the blame for Burgoyne's distress at Saratoga on stuffy Whitehall bureaucrats, for he had done so in the play, when the general anticipates his abandonment. Shaw assumed from the inadequate history he had read that Burgoyne only "realized what had happened to the instructions to Howe . . . many months afterward. . . . The scene in which I have represented him as learning it before Saratoga is not historical."

Nothing else, Shaw claimed, departed from fact. "Now it is but the other day," he wrote in a weekly review in 1899 when his mockery of British military skill was condemned as unpatriotic in the midst of the Boer War, "that I called up on the stage the ghost of this very Burgoyne, and was told that he was nothing but my own sardonic self in an eighteenth century uniform." His portrayal of the actual Burgoyne, he insisted, was historical. "Instead of simply putting on the stage the modern conception of a British general, half idealized prizefighter, half idealized music-hall chairman,[1] I had taken some pains to ascertain what manner of person the real Burgoyne was, and had found him a wit, a rhetorician, and a successful dramatic author. Also, of course, an eighteenth century gentleman."

---

1 In contemporary usage, the master of ceremonies at an entertainment.

Although Shaw bypasses Howe's gross culpability, his playwriting instincts were actually closer to reality than the history he had researched. Before Saratoga, Burgoyne had actually worried about being abandoned by Howe. "Of the messengers I have sent [to him]," Burgoyne would write to Germain anxiously, "I know of two being hanged [on capture] and [I] am ignorant whether any of the rest arrived. But my orders [from you] are positive to 'force a junction with Sir Wm. Howe.' . . . I do not yet despond."

In *The Devil's Disciple*, the stage Burgoyne spreads the blame further. Replying to Shaw's fictional Major Swindon, who declares that if he were General Burgoyne he would undertake to do "what we have marched south from Quebec to do, and what General Howe has marched north from New York to do: effect a junction at Albany and wipe out the rebel army with our united forces." (Swindon of course knows nothing of Howe's failure to march north.)

> BURGOYNE [*enigmatically*]. And will you wipe out our enemies in London, too?
> SWINDON. In London! What enemies?
> BURGOYNE [*forcibly*]. Jobbery and snobbery, incompetence and Red Tape. [*He holds up the [blue] dispatch [he has just received] and adds, with despair in his face and voice*] I have just learnt, sir, that General Howe is still in New York.
> SWINDON [*thunderstruck*]. Good God! He has disobeyed orders!
> BURGOYNE [*with sardonic calm*]. He has received no orders, sir. Some gentleman in London forgot to dispatch them: he was leaving town for his holiday, I believe. To avoid upsetting his arrangements, England will lose her American colonies; and in a few days you and I will be at Saratoga with 5,000 men to face 18,000 rebels[2] in an impregnable position.
> SWINDON [*appalled*]. Impossible?
> BURGOYNE [*coldly*]. I beg your pardon?
> SWINDON. I can't believe it! What will History say?
> BURGOYNE. History, sir, will tell lies as usual.

In his notes appended to the play, Shaw explains, "Burgoyne's surrender at Saratoga made him that occasionally necessary part of our British system, a scapegoat. The explanation of his defeat given in the play is

---

2 Burgoyne actually had 6,400 men augmented by 700 Indians, but without the promised reinforcements he would be decisively outnumbered.

founded on a passage quoted by [Albany] de Fonblanque [in his 1876 biography of Burgoyne] from [Lord Edmond] Fitzmaurice's Life of Lord George Shelburne." Shaw saw Burgoyne as a victim of bureaucratic "stupidity." Although the London *General Advertiser* lampooned him as "General Swagger," Shaw defended Burgoyne's self-conscious theatricality. His "peculiar critical temperament and talent, artistic, satirical, rather histrionic, and his fastidious delicacy of sentiment, his fine spirit and humanity, were just the qualities to make him disliked by stupid people because of their dread of ironic criticism. . . . The Burgoyne of the Devil's Disciple is a man who plays his part in life, and makes all his points, in the manner of a born high comedian."

To make his point, in the preface to *The Devil's Disciple* Shaw quotes Burgoyne's sharp rejoinders to General Horatio Gates's articles of capitulation. For example, to an article that dealt with confining British officers who might violate their parole, Burgoyne retorted, "There being no officer in this army under, or capable of being under, the description of breaking parole, this article needs no answer." To another, about grounding arms in their encampments, Burgoyne declared proudly that sooner than suffer such humiliation, "they will rush on the enemy determined to take no quarter." But the general's rhetorical flair was just that. Intending to have his jingoistic remarks published in London, he was performing to the gallery at home. "When the actual ceremony of surrender came," Shaw wrote, "he would have played poor General Gates off the stage, had not that commander risen to the occasion by handing him back his sword."

Thirty-two years earlier, long before coming to America, the stocky, plainspoken Gates had been a lieutenant in the same redcoat regiment as Burgoyne. "I am glad to see you," said Gates earnestly.

"I am not glad to see *you*," said Burgoyne. "It is my fortune, sir, and not my fault that I am here." He did offer his sword; it was returned. However Shavian the lines seem, they are historical. Shaw may not have encountered them. There is no surrender scene, and the exchange is unmentioned in the play's preface.

Having done his background homework on Burgoyne's ill fortune in the British Museum Reading Room with the limited resources then at hand, Shaw quotes Fitzmaurice as writing, "Lord George Germain, having among other peculiarities a particular dislike to be put out of his way on any occasion, had arranged to call at his office on his way to the country to sign the dispatches [to Burgoyne and Howe]; but as those addressed to Howe had not [yet] been fair-copied, and as he was not disposed to be balked of his projected visit to Kent, they were not signed then and were forgotten on his return home." (In his rejoinder to critics in *Review of the Week* in 1899, the unnamed "civil servant" who failed his duty "went down to Brighton" rather than to his country house in Kent.)

No one knew of the signing oversight then, Shaw contends, from his sources. "The policy of the English Government and Court for the next two years was simply concealment of Germain's neglect." His spin on events, Shaw claimed at the time, was "authentic history; but like all authentic histories of great events enacted by men not great, its details produced an effect of comic opera on the multitude, who can recognise tragedy only when she brandishes her bow and dagger. . . . My stage Burgoyne convulsed the playgoers of Kennington by asking a rebel who demanded to be 'shot like a man instead of hanged like a dog,' whether he had any idea of the average marksmanship of the British Army, and earnestly recommending him to be hanged. Everybody shrieked with laughter. . . . And yet, like all my wildest extravagances, it was an uncooked 'slice of life.'" Shaw went on to explain that he based the remark on a conversation with a British general who had conducted military executions, and found the quality of firing squad marksmanship "horrible, sanguinary, and demoralising" compared to the efficiency of hanging. More than a century after Burgoyne, Shaw contended, the British army was still not "perfect," although "War Office apologists" still received "a large official salary."

Since Burgoyne's cynical temperament and his parallel career as a comic dramatist both appealed to Shaw, whose contempt for bureaucracy in any case was absolute, he developed his scene with the American Secretary in the abortive prologue accordingly. The king's receiving room at the palace dissolves to Lord Germain's office in Whitehall, where he is dressed for rural travel and striding about the room in a state of agitation:

LORD GERMAIN. Not ready yet! But you know I go into the country on Friday.
SECRETARY. The fair copy will be in order for signature in about an hour, my lord.
LORD GERMAIN. Wont do at all! I want to get down to the country. Have it for me when I return on Tuesday—er—Wednesday.

> [*He pauses for a moment by a map of America on the wall*].
> Whereabouts is Johnny?
> SECRETARY [*pointing*]. General Burgoyne is there.
> LORD GERMAIN. Oh, there! Well, he can stay there until I come back to town. That place is thousands of miles away from New Amsterdam.
> SECRETARY. New York, now, my lord.
> LORD GERMAIN. My grandfather always called it New Amsterdam. Can't get it out of my head, somehow. Doesnt matter, does it? Anyhow, I'm off. [*Exit Lord Germain, whistling Lilliburlero.*]³

The scene dissolves to Burgoyne and Swindon marching ahead of the column, with a fife band playing, and then dissolves again to the opening scene of the original play.

Germain's shrugging off the delay for a lengthy country weekend lasting until Tuesday or Wednesday has seriously greater implications, if true. Further delay could be disastrous. A fast westward voyage by sail would take two months or more, after which messages had to go overland and somehow find the recipient, whose last known location was now several months in the past. Thousands of miles distant, Burgoyne would stubbornly press on, while Howe, if actually uninformed, would neglect a junction with immense strategic implications, going on in ignorance to Philadelphia, which had only political value (and comfortable quarters in which to wait out the winter with Elizabeth Loring).

Had it happened in the way Shaw had imagined it? Had the Secretary for America taken his responsibilities so frivolously? Was the lapse an implicit acknowledgment that the long-distance war could not have been won at all? The accepted version of events fit Shaw's desire to create a warm and witty Burgoyne abused by complacent bureaucracy. A crucial strategic decision (here, by omission) is handled in the way that one would expect a gentleman of privilege with an estate in the country to deal with what seemed distant priorities.

As Shaw's Burgoyne contends, history seems to have told lies as usual. And Shaw seems to have happily bought into them. Accounts from Lord George Germain's many enemies and the cover-ups of lapses by the generals in America, who were rewarded, as is still the bureaucratic fashion, by commendations and promotions, do not portray what happened.

---

3   A soldier's song then popular, ridiculing the Irish—an irony, as Lord George was educated at Trinity College, Dublin, and held various Irish government sinecures.

After the surprise victories by Washington over the new year of 1777 at Trenton and Princeton, General Howe's belated response was to send a field army to occupy the rebel capital. He would avoid possibly hazardous land routes by sailing his army lengthily to the south and landing below Philadelphia. He planned to leave a small garrison under Major General Henry Clinton to maintain New York City. Possibly Clinton would detach a token force up the Hudson to link with Burgoyne.

Realizing hopelessly that his instructions would be ignored and might even arrive too late anyway, Lord George had written to Howe on March 3, 1777, while Burgoyne and Clinton were back in England, and accessible to Whitehall, "I am now commanded to acquaint you that the King entirely approves of your proposed deviation from the plan you formerly suggested, being of opinion that the reasons which have induced you to recommend this change in your operations are solid and decisive." Phrased in the courteous manner of aristocrat to aristocrat, it was an open-ended charter for Howe to go his own way. Burgoyne and Clinton must have been aware that Howe intended to be useless.

Both King George and Lord George understood at the least that Howe's insubordinate intentions were irreversible. By the time he received the message he was likely to be distancing himself from Burgoyne's army. Howe would continue to "deviate" from the strategy devised in London, and claim royal sanction for running his own war. As his operational revisions crossed the Atlantic in the opposite direction from Germain's responses to earlier messages, one from Lord George would take on the mythic dimensions exploited in Shaw's play. On the basis of Burgoyne's plan for a junction at Albany to isolate New England, on March 26, 1777, as Sir John left London to rejoin his forces, and a convoy was in preparation to resupply them, Germain had his undersecretary, William Knox, prepare orders to General Sir Guy Carleton in Quebec.

As royal governor, Sir Guy was ostensibly—but not actually—Burgoyne's military superior. (Carleton's brief was limited to Canada.) Although Germain stressed that it was "highly necessary that the most speedy junction of the two armies be effected," and orders appeared to be orders, the message was baffling, as Sir Guy was at best a conduit. He had no responsibility for the rebel colonies, or for Howe. Burgoyne's command was also independent of Carleton, and Sir John had gone over his plans personally with the American Secretary in Whitehall. "I shall write to Sir William Howe from hence by the first [mail] packet," Germain informed Carleton, "but you will endeavour to give him the earliest intelligence of this measure and also direct Lieutenant General Burgoyne"—so that neither would "lose view of the[ir] intended junction." Yet Germain already realized that Howe would be hundreds of miles farther from a junction than he would have been had London stood up to Sir William months earlier.

As Undersecretary Knox was comparing his office draft to the copy to go to Carleton, he recalled later, Lord George, on his way to Stoneland Lodge for a long Kentish weekend, came in to sign letters. It was the primitive era of long, painstakingly inscribed "fair copies" of documents. Knox reminded Germain that no message directly ordering Howe to do anything had yet been prepared "to acquaint him with the plan or what was expected of him in consequence."

Lord George reacted to the omission with surprise. To that date, all of Howe's "deviations" had been condoned. When his deputy secretary, Christopher D'Oyley, was also startled by the afterthought, Germain offered to "write a few lines" to accompany the fair copy to Howe. Only a few lines, he insisted impatiently, as "my poor horses must stand in the street all the time, and I shan't be to my time anywhere." He might be late for tea. The colonies could wait. The dialogue could have been written by Shaw.

According to Knox, D'Oyley, cutting corners, offered to "write from himself to Howe, and enclose copies of Burgoyne's Instructions, which would tell him all that he would want to know, and with this his Lordship was satisfied . . . for he could never bear delay or disappointment, and D'Oyley sat down and wrote a letter to Howe, . . . and if Howe had not acknowledged the receipt of it, with the copy of the Instructions to Burgoyne, we could not have proved he ever saw them."

D'Oyley's dispatch written for Lord George, with a copy of Burgoyne's orders, was endorsed as "No. 6" to Howe for 1777, and went off on the fast warship *Somerset*, arriving in New York on May 24. Howe would deliberately neglect to register its receipt until July 5 to fake its lateness, but even at that his laggard armada south did not weigh anchor until July 23. Having received the instructions about an "intended junction" early enough to implement them, he ignored the language as pious wish rather than outright command, for only Burgoyne was explicitly commanded. Sir William was intent upon comfortable Philadelphia. The remote American rabble in upper New York would be easy pickings for Sir John anyway.

The Burgoyne of *The Devil's Disciple* was right, in Shaw's imaginative leap, that Howe was still, then, in New York, but not about Howe's lack of mail from the American Secretary in London. And Howe would soon receive much more. Yet Lord George had to concede to Howe, who could not be controlled in Atlantic sailing distances, in message number eleven on May 18, 1777, that "As you must, from your situation and military skill, be a competent judge of the propriety of every plan, his Majesty does not hesitate to approve the [further] alterations which you propose, trusting however that whatever you may meditate[,] it will be executed in time for you to cooperate with the army ordered from Canada and put itself [when the troops linked] under your command." Howe would evade those orders, too. "Meditate" was hardly a strong injunction.

Always assuming hopefully the existence and ardor of more loyalists than would identify themselves riskily in any colony, Germain saw "every reason to expect that your success in Pennsylvania will enable you to raise from among them such a force as may be sufficient for the interior defence of the province and leave the army at liberty to proceed to offensive operations [in Burgoyne's direction]." Since that seemed more prayer than prescription, Howe gave it no notice. In an office memorandum to William Knox on June 24, a month before Howe obdurately took his fourteen thousand troops south by sea, Germain wondered in frustration, "I cannot guess by Sir William Howe's [last] letter when he will begin his operations, or where he proposes to carry them on."

Nearly a month later, when Howe's army had debarked along the Chesapeake, and was already in Delaware, moving north toward Philadelphia, Burgoyne, running short of rations, sent a Hessian force into nearby Vermont to scavenge corn from the fields. The Germans were ambushed and routed at Bennington, the beginning of the end for Burgoyne. Had Shaw consulted a map in the Reading Room, he would have found the town of Springfield, Vermont, nearby. He would place his fictional Burgoyne, when predicting his downfall at Saratoga and placing the blame on Whitehall bureaucracy, in a fictional Springtown in adjacent New Hampshire, where the general turns up unexpectedly as spectator at a court-martial, although the real Burgoyne never strayed from the lakes route toward the Hudson. The crucial strategic lapse of the war was not due to the failure of Lord George Germain to send a letter to General Howe, but to the irresponsible Howe's refusal to pay any attention to it.

Burgoyne would be offered in defeat—and refuse, in protest—the red ribbon of the Order of the Bath. For his failures, Howe would eventually be promoted to full general and become a viscount. Germain, who had only a courtesy title as a duke's son, would become a viscount as a royal reward for resigning as discredited Secretary for America, a position that, a few months later, would disappear with the colonies. And while the British were still losing America, Burgoyne would return to writing for the stage, composing a comic opera, *The Lord of the Manor*, and the even more successful *The Heiress*. After these triumphs, Horace Walpole predicted that Burgoyne's "delightful" comedies would be remembered when his military career was forgotten. But beyond history, his verve as a general survives on Shaw's stage.

Bibliographic Essay

Shaw's brief, unproduced 1930s prologue for a film script—also never produced—appears in Bernard F. Dukore, ed., *The Collected Screenplays of Bernard Shaw* (Athens: University of Georgia Press, 1980). His preface to the published play is the "On Diabolonian Ethics" section of the preface to *Three Plays for Puritans* (London: Grant Richards, 1901 and all later editions). With it are the appended "Notes to The Devil's Disciple," in which Shaw concedes that Burgoyne's learning "what had happened about the instructions to Howe" is "not historical" but only the dramatist's invention. Shaw takes much of his information, as he notes, from Albany de Fonblanque's admiring but unreliable biography of Burgoyne (London: Barrington, 1875). What actually happened is described in Stanley Weintraub's *Iron Tears: America's Battle for Freedom, Britain's Quagmire* (New York and London: Free Press & Simon and Schuster UK, 2005).

· 5 ·

Cetewayo

SHAW'S HERO FROM AFRICA

Zululand, the region to the north of Durban and to the east of Johannesburg, hardly seems like Bernard Shaw country, and it is not, although GBS did write his *Black Girl* novella in southernmost South Africa in 1931. In his earliest writing days, when his travels were limited by lack of means to London and environs, he merely moved his Zulu chieftain to England, where, indeed, he had briefly and incongruously turned up in 1882.

In the later 1870s, disputes along the boundary between the Boers in the Transvaal and the Zulus in what is now Natal threatened what tenuous peace there was east of the Drakensberg Mountains. The tribal king was Cetewayo, then forty-seven, who had earlier overthrown his brother, Umbulayo, in a bloody civil war over which should be heir apparent. The British were troublemakers themselves, exercising more and more authority north of the Cape. Cetewayo had been crowned in 1873, an event presided over by the watchful Sir Theophilus Shepstone, British secretary for Native Affairs in Southern Africa, who spoke Zulu and Xhosa and was known to Africans as *Sometsu*, or Mighty Hunter. It was the occasion for extracting assurances from the newly crowned king that indiscriminate shedding of blood would cease, that no one would be condemned without a fair trial for a capital crime, that there would be a right of appeal, and that the death penalty would not be exacted for minor offenses. For Shepstone, the son of a Wesleyan missionary, the goal was, in effect, a Methodist Africa—under British suzerainty.

Cetewayo's failure to keep such Westernized stipulations would become an excuse for a British invasion of Zululand six years later. In the interim, he remained popular among most of his quarter-million people. The scattered kraals in which the Zulu people lived were reasonably orderly and, by African standards, prosperous. Each black dweller on communal Zulu lands had several cattle and several wives, and, Sir Theophilus notwithstanding, adultery and some other civil crimes remained punishable by death. As high priest as well as king of his people, Cetewayo presided over a belief system in which evil spirits who could not be propitiated by magic had to be exorcised by the death of the victim they possessed, and his witch doctors often managed to "smell out" evil in persons who had more cattle than jealous neighbors did. The Zulu army, Cetewayo's other power base, created as a professional force by his late uncle, Shaka, was built upon draftees by age group, who lived celibate in military kraals and could marry only with the king's permission, usually not granted until the warrior was forty, or had killed an enemy in battle ("the washing of the spears"), when by custom he could request any unmarried Zulu woman. Wealth remained measured in women and cattle. War offered almost the only chance to gain honor, women, and cattle. Soldiers without such rewards for service chafed at postponements of their manhood.

Polyglot British and Boer settlements, relentlessly encroaching upon Zulu lands, would furnish Cetewayo both opportunity and motive to halt the occupation. Seeing himself as the Queen's proconsul everywhere in southern Africa, Shepstone considered it necessary to move in the other direction—to force the Zulus, for the sake of order and progress, "to submit to the rule of civilisation." He worried about "a kind of common desire in the Native mind . . . to try and overcome the white intruders," language that hid nothing in euphemisms. The possibility of acquiring firearms from freelance dealers lifted black hopes of reversing land confiscations and made colonial politicians nervous. Shepstone, who had become sixty in 1877, was reluctant to retire before accomplishing his personal mission. A paternalist and imperialist "improver," he viewed the seemingly idle life of the native as a handicap to achieving Christian acculturation. The African had to be persuaded to work for Europeans and for wages rather than to eke out an existence in backward traditional villages.

Attempting to federate colonies under the Union Jack, to which Shepstone included by legal sleight-of-hand Boer-settled Transvaal, which had a vocal British minority, he pushed both the Zulus and the Voortrekkers into taking up arms. Cetewayo attempted to avoid outright war in order to keep the British from seizing an excuse to obliterate the tribal system, but disorders on the undefined frontiers emboldened the new high commissioner, Sir Bartle Frere, operating from Government House in Cape Town, to employ the Raj formula. (He had served in India.) What he described as a "rising of Kaffirdom against white civilisation" demonstrated to his satisfaction the need for a white federal state. Shepstone had long deplored the "terrible incubus of the Zulu Royal family," and Frere needed little urging to mount a campaign. He delayed reporting to London the findings of a Natal boundary commission which might have prejudiced an attack on what he called Cetewayo's "man-slaying human military machine," and on January 11, 1879, began to move against the Zulus.

Cetewayo had thirty thousand warriors but few firearms. For a while, mass attacks with spears held off the redcoats, costing the British heavily at Isandlwana, where there was a gallant but vain attempt to save the regimental colors. Imperial troops were temporarily embarrassed, but as the Zulu king put it, he was in the situation of "a man warding off a falling tree." Reinforcements arrived for the Great White Queen's army, and Cetewayo's royal kraal at Ulundi fell on July 4, 1879. Sir Garnet Wolseley, the British commander, imposed a settlement dismembering the Zulu nation into thirteen "kinglets," each with its own splinter chieftain, several of them both cousins and rivals (one a half brother) to Cetewayo, whose Usuthu tribe lost most of its lands and cattle. Young Henry Rider Haggard (who would write *King Solomon's Mines*), although then Shepstone's secretary, privately called the dictated peace an "abomination and a disgrace to England."

Greed among the Zulu factions inevitably led to cattle-raiding and bloodshed, and insistent calls for the return of Cetewayo, who had been captured at Ulundi and exiled with a few retainers to the Cape. By April 1882 the British resident official in Zululand, Melmoth Osborn, admitted to London that the disorders were such that he could only travel "a mile or two" from his headquarters: "I have no authority." From Cape Town came a pathetic plea from Cetewayo himself, "I do not know what we have done, and I pray the Queen to let me go back . . . for though a man be allowed to breathe, he is not really alive if he is cut off from his wives and children."

Lacking realistic alternatives, the imperial authorities looked to Cetewayo, who had been a model prisoner. "All the Zulus wish him back,"

Osborn appealed desperately if untruthfully. Obviously none of the surviving puppet chieftains wanted a restoration, but in London the prime minister, W. E. Gladstone, who deplored all colonial entanglements, a definition in which he included Ireland, wrote hopefully, "If it should appear that the mass of the people in Zululand are for Cetshwayo, . . . so far from regarding him as the enemy of England . . . I should regard the proof of that fact with great pleasure . . . and that would be the sentiment of my colleagues."

Shaw had begun his fourth novel, *Cashel Byron's Profession*, that April, as talk of Cetewayo's possible restoration reached the English press. Inspired in part by enthusiasm for boxing, which had gone from reading, as a boy, such sporting magazines as *Bell's Life* to sparring with his poetasting friend Pakenham Beatty and even to entering amateur competitions as a light heavyweight, Shaw had begun the saga of a prizefighter. Cashel Byron is a young gentleman, unruly son of a Shakespearean actress, who runs away from school at seventeen, ships out to Australia as a cabin boy, and learns there how to make a living at pugilism. Seven years later he returns to England to compete in the prize ring, where he quickly gains a reputation in his brutal, and still illegal, profession. Training in a corner of a country estate where his manager, who has accompanied him from Australia, has rented a cottage, he encounters its owner, Lydia Carew, a beautiful bluestocking millionairess. However attracted they are to each other, social prejudice against his retrograde occupation keeps her from encouraging his attentions.

Escorted by Henrique Shepstone, eldest son of Sir Theophilus (and his deputy) and three tribal chiefs, Cetewayo, his name variously spelled in the London press, arrived in London in July 1882 as Shaw was halfway through his novel and seeking a strategy to maintain Miss Carew's reluctant fascination with Byron. *Punch* had even published a cartoon in advance of the king's arrival depicting him, dockside, about to embark for England, amid packing cases and black attendants. Prophetically, Cetewayo was attired in incongruous top hat, gold-braided military tunic, tribal skirt, and bare feet, and carried an umbrella sword-tipped at its base. "CETEWAYO'S COMING! read the caption. "WHAT'LL THEY DO WITH HIM?"

Society, Shaw began chapter 7, was much occupied

> with the upshot of an historical event of a common kind. England, a few years before, had stolen a kingdom from a considerable people in Africa, and seized the person of its king. The conquest proved

useless, troublesome, and expensive; and after repeated attempts to settle the country on impracticable plans suggested to the Colonial Office by a popular historian who had made a trip to Africa, and by generals who were tired of the primitive remedy of killing the natives, it appeared that the best course was to release the captive king and get rid of the unprofitable booty by restoring it to him. In order, however, that the impression made on him by England's shortsighted disregard of her neighbour's landmark abroad might be counteracted by a glimpse of the vastness of her armaments and wealth at home, it was thought advisable to take him first to London, and shew him the wonders of the town.

The king's freedom from Western ways, Shaw went on, puzzled him as to why a private person "could own a portion of the earth" and make others pay for permission to use it or live on it, and why others toiled incessantly to create wealth for others, leaving neither laborers nor the class that dissipated the wealth any the happier for it. Even worse,

> He was seized with strange fears, first for his health, for it seemed to him that the air of London, filthy with smoke, engendered puniness and dishonesty in those that breathed it; and eventually for his life when he learned that kings in Europe were sometimes shot at by passers-by, there being hardly a monarch there who had not been so imperilled more than once; that the queen of England, though accounted the safest of all, was accustomed to this variety of pistol practice; and that the autocrat of an empire huge beyond all other European countries, whose father [Czar Alexander II] had been torn asunder in the streets of his capital [in 1881], lived surrounded by soldiers. . . . Under these circumstances, the African King was with difficulty induced to stir out of doors.

Cetewayo had in reality arrived in England dressed in as much civilized garb as he could successfully manage, and was squired about London in morning coat, topper, and bare feet. His appearance, and his many wives left behind in Zululand, both noted in the press, inspired a music-hall song performed as he went about:

> White young dandies, get away, O!
> You are now 'neath beauty's ban
> Clear the field for Cetewayo,
> He alone's the ladies man.

To British officials he spoke of his anticipated new role, the best he could hope for, as a "child" in the service of his "mother," Queen Victoria. At the Colonial Office he nevertheless protested the planned land "Reserve" to be carved out of Zululand as a sanctuary for tribes claiming to be threatened by the restoration of the Usuthu, but he knew that resistance was futile and the best he could compromise for would be a rump state. Visiting Mr. Gladstone, who only noted in his diary, "Interview with Cetewayo at noon for half an hour. I was much interested and pleased," the king was shown as part of his tour of Number 10 Downing Street a portrait of the Radical politician John Bright, described by the prime minister as "our Great Orator." Demurring, Cetewayo insisted that the authentic "Great Orator" was standing at his side. Diplomatic despite his bared toes, and with no more English than Shaw would give him in his novel, Cetewayo was even more winning at Marlborough House, the London residence of the often absent Prince of Wales. "After he had been made known to the young princes and princesses," Gladstone's private secretary, Edward Hamilton, noted in his diary, "he asked where was the Princess of Wales. He declined to believe that the lovely young woman he saw before him was the mother of such tall children."

When Shaw reached chapter 9 he set the scene for a grand Roman-style exhibition that the fictional Cetewayo would attend, in which Cashel would spar with the chief contender for the championship, the ruffianly giant Billy Paradise. Only one fight had been lost by the burly Paradise, Cashel's trainer, Bob Mellish, warns. "Shepstone, clever as he is, only won a fight from him by claiming a foul." Reading the papers, Shaw had found the name, awarding the Shepstone family its only entry in literature. The real Shepstone, meanwhile, guided the Zulu king on a visit to Victoria at her home on the Isle of Wight, Osborne House, across the Solent from Portsmouth and Southampton. "Our Portsmouth correspondent telegraphed last night," the *Times* reported. "Cetewayo and his two native generals of division left Victoria station by special train for an audience with the Queen.... It must... be said of Cetewayo that he has a wonderful command of countenance, and that his equanimity is of the highest character. Nothing appeared to surprise him. The gaping, struggling crowd, the capacious harbour, the gigantic men-of-war, and the other sights of the port never disturbed his imperturbable gravity." Although a lunch would be set out for Cetewayo's party, and it was indeed assumed that the Queen would preside, she limited her brief audience to small talk. ("Will not the Queen spoil our 'fat friend' . . . ?" Lord Kimberley, the colonial secretary, wondered to Gladstone.)

Cetewayo was, Victoria wrote in her journal, "a very fine man, in his native costume, or rather no costume. He is tall, immensely broad, and stout, with a good-humoured countenance, and an intelligent face. Unfortunately he appeared in a hideous black frock coat and trousers, but still wearing the ring round his head, denoting that he was a married man. His companions were very black, but quite different to the ordinary negro. I said, through Mr. Shepstone, that I was glad to see him here, and that I recognised in him a great warrior, who had fought against us, but rejoiced we were now friends. He answered much the same, gesticulating a good deal as he spoke, mentioned having seen my picture, and said he was glad to see me in person. I asked about his voyage, and what he had seen." When she mentioned her three daughters in England the chieftain tried out an English response, which seemed to be "Ah!"

After further commonplaces, "the interview terminated. Both in coming in, and going out, they gave me the royal Zulu salute, saying something altogether, and raising their right hands above their heads." (The tribal salute was "Bayete!") Cetewayo walked about on the terrace to take in the view high above Cowes and the Solent, and indoors again was served lunch with his party. From the Colonnade, Victoria watched them leave. "As they drove away, Cetewayo caught sight of me, and got up in the carriage, and remained standing till they were out of sight."

Afterwards the London correspondent of the *Manchester Guardian* asked Cetewayo his opinion of the Queen. "She is born to rule men," he said; "she is like me. We are both rulers. She was very kind to me and I will always think of her."

Despite gifts of hunting dogs and horses, the visits of Temperance League ladies who exhorted him to eschew beer, and tours of places thought likely to impress him, Cetewayo was bored and eager to take up his restored, if reduced, throne. To further keep him busy he was extended the hospitality of the huge Crystal Palace, since 1853 removed from Hyde Park to Sydenham, south of the Thames. His appearance was advertised by the management for the thirty thousand one-shilling visitors that day along with the Company Band and the Electric Exhibition. The great organ pounded as he paced, unhappily nursing an English cold, and at twilight the nightly fireworks exhibition, for all he knew, was put on specially for him.

Fictionally exploiting the Colonial Office's being at wit's end to devise entertainments to keep the king in good humor until his departure, Shaw devised the Cashel-Paradise spar as part of a military and athletic tournament at the Agricultural Hall in Islington, a real-life venue built in 1862 for cattle shows, and used also for horse shows, military exhibitions, and evening entertainments. There Lydia, persuaded to attend by her stuffy cousin Lucian, a minor diplomat, sees across the arena "a gaudy dais, on which a powerfully built black gentleman sat in a raised chair, his majestic impassivity contrasting with the overt astonishment with which a row of savagely ugly attendant chiefs grinned and gaped on either side of him."

In the main event, despite employing every ring illegality for which he has opportunity, Paradise is badly beaten. But Cashel, first pleased by his victory, turns pale and ashamed when he notices Lydia unexpectedly in the audience. "He seemed in a hurry to retire. But he was intercepted by an officer in uniform, accompanied by a black chief, who came to conduct him to the dais and present him to the African King: an honour which he was not permitted to decline."

Through an interpreter, the king explained that "he had been unspeakably gratified by what he had just witnessed; expressed great surprise that Cashel, notwithstanding his prowess, was neither in the army nor in parliament; and finally offered to provide him with three handsome wives if he would come out to Africa in his suite. Cashel was much embarrassed; but he came off with credit, thanks to the interpreter, who was accustomed to invent appropriate speeches for the king on public occasions, and was kind enough to invent equally appropriate ones for Cashel on this." On the king's authentic departure *Punch* closed its "Adieu to Cetewayo" with lines that Shaw either echoed or paralleled earlier in his episode:

> Good-bye, Great CETEWAYO! I think you'll understand
> That what is right in London may be wrong in Zululand!

Cetewayo, the first major figure out of contemporary history to appear in Shaw's pages, would reappear in one of his plays, but nothing beyond the visit to England would supplement the scenario. Given Shaw's propensity for mixed dramatic modes, the king would be more seriously drawn, yet also more comic. As for Cetewayo himself, nothing even remotely comic would happen to him thereafter. In January 1883 he was returned on board the HMS *Briton* to his shrunken kingdom only to find civil war brewing. "I did not land in a dry place," he said ruefully. "I landed in mud." His situation was precarious. He was no one's chief, rather "an ant in a pond of water." He had to flee for his life into the Nkandla forests, where he was injured when his small force was attacked by rebels who rejected him as an English puppet. He was forced, for his own safety, to go "into Mr. Osborn's armpit" and accept British protection. In Eshowe, in the "Reserve" he had resisted, he died early in 1884, officially of a heart attack. Laughter greeted the announcement of his death during one of the less proud sittings of the House of Commons.

The agents of empire who in the name of the Great White Queen had reduced Cetewayo from warrior chieftain in a relatively stable agrarian kingdom would have years of instability and disorder as Cetewayo's legacy. Although Shaw would make only stylistic changes in his episodes involving Cetewayo when he had the novel reissued in 1889 and again in 1901, in the 1901 edition he included as an appendix a comic dramatic adaptation, *The Admirable Bashville.*

Veteran prizefighters had begun seeking opportunities out of the squared circle to exploit their fading celebrity onstage as Cashel Byron. In December 1900 an unauthorized play version opened in New York at the Herald Square Theatre. (In 1909 the famed James J. Corbett would play Cashel.) In the next month—Shaw claimed it took only a week—, to protect his copyright, he dashed off a farce in mock-Elizabethan blank verse, which he claimed was easy to write. Possibly because of the contemporaneity of the events in 1882, Shaw had not named the Zulu king. Since that reason had vanished into history, he was less reticent in 1901.

Cetewayo remained as unidentified in the play's title as, now, was Cashel Byron himself. Featured instead as part of Shaw's extended joke was Lydia Carew's proud but lovesick butler, Bashville, who in the novel has a brief spar with Cashel. (James Barrie in 1902 would echo Shaw's title in his own comedy about an ambitious butler, *The Admirable Crichton.*) Cetewayo, however, is featured in scene 2, and Shaw recalled thirty years later in an addition to the old preface to the play that "James Hearn's lamentation over the tragedy of Cetewayo"—Hearn played the king—"came off, not as a mockery, but as genuine tragedy, which indeed it also is." The costly Boer War had been in embarrassing progress when Shaw wrote the play, and had ended only on May 31, 1902, barely a year before the first professional production on June 7, 1903.

The episode of the forced visit of the captured Zulu king to encourage his appreciation of the benefits of British civilization would have an ironic subtext in the early years of the new century which Shaw had no need to explicate, although he inserted late in the play a wry dig at jingoism which may have been overly subtle then as now. "The moral position of the Boers and the British," he had already written to a Fabian friend, "is precisely identical in every respect; that is, it does not exist. Two dogs are fighting for a bone thrown before them by Mrs. Nature."

In *The Admirable Bashville*, the second scene is set, as in the novel, in the Agricultural Hall, where Cetewayo asks Lucian Webber about the spectators, "Are these anaemic dogs the English people?" He pours out more scorn about a civilization that requires "a pall of smoke" across the sky for its well-being, but Lucian, who is the government's representative at the exhibition, explains,

> You cannot understand
> The greatness of this people, Cetewayo.
> You are a savage, reasoning like a child.
> Each pallid English face conceals a brain
> Whose powers are proven in the works of Newton
> And the plays of Shakespear.
> There is not one of all the thousands here
> But, if you placed him naked in the desert,
> Would presently construct a steam engine,
> And lay a cable t' th' Antipodes.

Cetewayo sees through the brag to the down side of alleged progress:

> Men become civilized through twin diseases,
> Terror and Greed to wit: these two conjoined
> Become the grisly parents of Invention.
> Why does the trembling white [man] with frantic toil
> Of hand and brain produce the magic gun
> That slays a mile off, whilst the manly Zulu
> Dares look his foe i' the face; fights foot to foot;
> Lives in the present; drains the Here and Now;
> Makes life a long reality, and death
> A moment only; whilst your Englishman
> Glares on his burning candle's winding-sheets,
> Counting the steps of his approaching doom,
> And in the murky corners ever sees
> Two horrid shadows, Death and Poverty.

Further, he sees technology as wresting from "wearied Nature" such secrets as will rocket the brave black "explosively from off the globe," while the "white-livered slaves" of "Dead and Dread" are enabled to overrun the earth. Still, he reminds Lucian,

> Thou sayest thou hast two white-faced ones who dare
> Fight without guns, and spearless, to the death.
> Let them be brought.

But Lucian cautions the king that English warriors of the ring "fight not to death" under the civilized rules of the sport:

> Half of their persons shall not be attacked;
> Nor shall they suffer blows when they fall down,
> Nor stroke of foot at any time. And, further,
> That frequent opportunities of rest
> With succor and refreshment be secured them.

Cetewayo scoffs at codified gentlemanly limits on courage. The land of the Zulus would scorn such "Personified Pusillanimity." But Lucian retorts that only a "rude savage" of "untutored mind" can doubt "That Brave and English mean the self-same thing," and the king taunts,

> Well, well, produce these heroes. I surmise
> They will be carried by their nurses, lest
> Some barking dog or bumbling bee should scare them.

William Paradise enters, "hateful" in appearance to the ladylike Lydia, and the godlike Cashel follows. Cetewayo asks the "sons of the white queen" in turn to identify themselves. Paradise calls himself "a bloke" who makes his honest living by his fists, and the king is pleased:

> Six wives and thirty oxen shalt thou have
> If on the sand thou leave thy foeman dead.

Unimpressed, Cashel challenges Cetewayo

> To name the bone, or limb, or special place
> Where you would have me hit him with this fist.

"Thou has a noble brow," the king warns, but he fears that Paradise, a Goliath, is likely to disfigure it.

They spar violently, and an uppercut followed by a hook cause Paradise to topple on his face and remain "quite silly." While Cashel explains to Cetewayo scientifically what blows were landed, the prescribed ten seconds pass. "I might safely finish him," says Cashel, but he does not, out of respect for "your most gracious majesty." But Paradise refuses to be finished according to the rules, and tears off his gloves, complaining,

> How can a bloke do hisself proper justice
> With pillows on his fists?

"Unfair!" the crowd shouts. "The rules!" Cetewayo, however, is caught up in Paradise's willingness to rise from the floor to fight:

> The joy of battle surges boiling up
> And bids me join the mellay. Isandlwana and Victory!

Cetewayo's chiefs join in and fall upon the bystanders, recalling with their king the great victory of January 22, 1879, over the British encamped on the plain at the base of Isandlwana Mountain when twenty thousand Zulu warriors shouting "Usuthu! Usuthu!" and carrying only shields and assegais advanced against rifle fire and wiped out the Second Warwickshire Regiment and its native adjuncts. Of the European soldiers encamped there only fifty-five escaped Zulu spears. Six months later, at Ulundi, a second invasion succeeded in overwhelming Cetewayo's kraal; but now, in the shouting and the chaos in the Agricultural Hall, his cohorts recall only the victory:

> THE CHIEFS. Victory and Isandlwana!
> [*They run amok. General panic and stampede.*
> *The ring is swept away.*]

Cashel drags Lydia out of harm's way, and in the confusion Lucian calls for the police.

Strikingly, the April 22, 1882, issue of *Punch*, as Shaw was beginning his novel, included a cartoon with a text entitled "MODERN LIFE IN LONDON; OR, 'TOM AND JERRY' BACK AGAIN." It was the second part of a satirical feature that would run through the year, this episode picturing two gloved pugilists going at each other in a crowded indoors setting, while rowdy spectators ranging from toffs in checked trousers to monocled gentlemen in formal morning attire intrude enthusiastically into the glove fight on the sides of their heroes. Could Shaw have remembered it, or returned to it?

In the play, the police arrive, and a mock-heroic parody of the attempted rescue of the colors at Isandlwana ensues:

A POLICEMAN. Give us a lead, sir. Save the English flag. Africa
   tramples on it.
CASHEL. Africa!
Not all the continents whose mighty shoulders
The dancing diamonds of the seas bedeck
Shall trample on the blue with spots of white . . .
and he charges the Zulus.
LYDIA. . . . See: the king is down;
The tallest chief is up, heels over head,
Tossed corklike oer my Cashel's sinewy back;
And his lieutenant all deflated gasps
For breath upon the sand. The others fly.
In vain: his fist oer magic distances
Like a chameleon's tongue shoots to its mark;
And the last African upon his knees
Sues piteously for quarter. . . .
CETEWAYO [*trying to rise*] Have I been struck
by lightning?

The symbolic victory becomes, however absurdly here, an English one. Cashel is victorious but injured—not by the Zulus, but by his white rival—in his throwback crudity now, with a war ongoing with the Afrikaners, perhaps a Boer symbol. When Lydia sees the blood, and discovers that Paradise has taken a bite out of her lover's flesh, she swoons in Cashel's arms. Cetewayo vanishes from the play. "The Queen's peace" prevails.

Ironically, Shaw was finishing *The Admirable Bashville* as the old queen lay dying at Osborne. Two days before her burial at Windsor on February 4, 1901, he posted the completed script to Grant Richards, then his publisher. Almost forgotten in the chaos of African history since, Cetewayo lives on in Shaw's farce and the novel from which he drew it.

Bibliographic Essay

Background throughout on Theophilus Shepstone is from Rupert Furneaux, *The Zulu War* (London: Weidenfeld & Nicolson, 1963). Further background on Zulu history, including quotations from Cetewayo not attributed to other sources, are from D. M. Schreueder, *The Struggle for South Africa, 1877–1895* (Cambridge: Cambridge University Press, 1980).

The music-hall song about Cetewayo is quoted by James (Jan) Morris in *Heaven's Command: An Imperial Progress* (New York: Knopf, 1979). According to E. A. Ritter, *Shaku Zulu: The Rise of the Zulu Empire* (New York: Putnam, 1957), the Zulu head-ring, or *isi-coco*, was the most coveted distinction for a Zulu male, as it symbolized permission to marry.

Punch cartoons referred to are from the issues of July 8, 1882, August 26, 1882 ("Prize Medals"), and September 2, 1882. References to Gladstone and Hamilton are from H. G. C. Mathew, ed., *The Gladstone Diaries*, vol. 10 (Oxford: Oxford University Press, 1990), and D. W. R. Bahlmann, ed., *The Diary of Sir Edward Hamilton* (Oxford: Oxford University Press, 1972); the entries are for August 9, 1882 (Gladstone), and August 19, 1882 (Hamilton).

Queen Victoria is quoted from Christopher Hibbert, ed., *Queen Victoria in Her Letters and Journals* (London: John Murray, 1984), entry for August 14, 1882.

The text of Shaw's *Cashel Byron's Profession* is from its first appearance, in serial form, in *To-Day*, April 1885–March 1886, as reprinted from the magazine plates by Modern Press, London, 1886, in a new edition noting later but minor textual alterations, ed. Stanley Weintraub (Carbondale: Southern Illinois University Press, 1968). Shaw's *The Admirable Bashville* (1901) is quoted from Dan H. Laurence, ed., *Bernard Shaw: Collected Plays with Their Prefaces*, vol. 2 (New York and London: Dodd, Mead & Max Reinhardt, 1973). Shaw discusses James Hearn playing Cetewayo in a 1941 addition to the *Bashville* preface. Shaw's letter to George Samuel on the equivocal "moral position" of both British and Boers is quoted by Michael Holroyd, *Bernard Shaw: The Pursuit of Power* (New York: Random House, 1989).

· 6 ·

Disraeli in Shaw

Shaw would never have identified himself as a royalist, or even as a conservative, yet the most admirable politician in all of his plays is King Magnus of the futuristic *The Apple Cart* (1929), who is both. In some respects, too, his rhetorically gifted Magnus suggests the Conservative and royalist prime minister who dominated British politics in the early years of Shaw's emigration from Dublin to London, Benjamin Disraeli, by then Earl of Beaconsfield. "I could not read his novels," Shaw told Hesketh Pearson decades later, "because they are all about upper-ten ladies and gentlemen, whom I cannot abide." Could he have known that by not reading them? After enjoying Shaw's early novel *Cashel Byron's Profession* (1882), about a half-educated, upwardly mobile prizefighter who marries a wealthy lady and gets elected to Parliament, Robert Louis Stevenson wrote to William Archer that he saw in the novel's ingredients "½ part Disraeli (perhaps unconscious)."

Whatever, Disraeli's artful handling of his political role interested Shaw enough that in 1886 he attended a lecture by the economist H. R. Beeton, the subject described in his diary as on "Beaconsfield." And two years later, when writing an article, "The Transition to Social Democracy," he went to the British Museum to read, as background, the Disraeli entry in the new *Dictionary of National Biography*. Shaw admired Disraeli's pragmatism as a politician. As he claimed in 1901, Karl Marx's *Capital* "was supposed to be written for the working classes, but the working man . . . wants to be a bourgeois. . . . The middle and upper classes are the revolutionary element in society; the proletariat is the Conservative element, as Disraeli well knew." With that understanding of "Tory Democracy," which Shaw told Winston Churchill was Disraeli's "invention," King Magnus handily outwits the fantasy Labour prime minister and his quarrelsome Cabinet who blindly assume that they represent popular will.

The work of governing, Magnus tells them cuttingly, has been abandoned by "anyone with outstanding organizing or administrative ability." What man of genius would exchange rewarding work "for the squalor of the political arena in which we have to struggle with foolish factions in parliament and with ignorant voters in the constituencies? . . . Politics, once the centre of attraction for ability, public spirit, and ambition, has now become the refuge of a few fanciers of public speaking and party intrigue who find all the other avenues of distinction closed to them." Echoes of Disraeli the royalist and Tory democrat arise everywhere in the king's polemic. "I do not want the old governing class back. It governed so selfishly that the people would have perished if democracy had not swept it out of politics. But evil as it was in many ways, at least it stood above the tyranny of popular ignorance and popular poverty. . . . I have no elections to fear. . . . Think of the things you dare not do! Responsibilities which would break your backs may still be borne on a king's shoulders. But he must be a king, not a puppet."

As early as 1888, with Disraeli dead only seven years, Shaw became involved with the South St. Pancras Liberal and Radical Association and got himself elected as its delegate to the Birmingham Conference of the National Liberal Federation. In his diary he registered his disgust at "the sheeplike docility of the delegates and the rottenness and meanness of the wirepullers and leaders." Such democracy, he began to realize, was not only inefficient but a sham and a fraud. And that became even more apparent to him decades later when ineffective parliamentary institutions not only blundered into a popular (at first) world war in 1914 but failed to extricate Europe from its consequences afterward. "Evidently," he wrote then,

> there is something wrong with what we call democracy: that is, giving votes to everybody. We were clearly mistaken in supposing that when we got our majority of votes everything would go smoothly and rapidly. Why did we make that mistake? The explanation lies in our history. Democracy had been one of the most wonderful forces in politics. Looking back over its history in the eighteenth and nineteenth centuries, you are amazed to see this curious force making its irresistible way, breaking down old

institutions, becoming an incentive to statesmen, an inspiration to poets. My memory goes back to the palmy parliamentary days of Gladstone and Disraeli, and of John Bright, that great tribune of the people.... To those men, democracy was a real thing. They said and believed that public opinion in England would never stand any interference with the liberties of the British people. Their pet phrase was that any statesman who proposed such an interference would be out of power in a fortnight. This belief and these phrases made Democracy a living force, a great and beneficent force, and we threw it away by giving [all] the people votes.

Despite his seemingly radical language, Shaw was never a "government by the people" advocate. "Public opinion is a great power," he contended, "so long as you take good care that the public has no opportunity of expressing it.... Finally, when the British Parliament had become the perfect instrument we all boasted of, we overlooked the fact that it was an instrument of inhibition, of prevention, of negation." When democracy was a "phantom," operating as "Public Opinion" and "acting as an artificial political conscience, [it] had restrained Gladstone and Disraeli." With votes for everyone, Shaw warned in his preface to *The Millionairess* (1936), that inhibition upon "any confidence trickster" vanished. He saw the real governing power in the intuition of leadership, not the accumulation of votes. "I no longer address my appeal to the working classes, in whose political initiative I no longer believe," he told the Fabians frankly. "I appeal to the rising parliamentary generation, whatever their class or party. And I believe that only by responding to this appeal will any party in future gain the force, the conviction, the power of interesting and persuading which will be necessary to impose Progress on the tremendous Conservatism of the newly enfranchised working classes."

Writing about the impact of Fabian socialists on the early-twentieth-century beginnings of social legislation like unemployment insurance, mandated health care, and pension plans, Shaw declared, as he neared ninety, that these were actually due

> to the dead Disraeli, who as Conservative leader had taken the first serious step in the enfranchisement of the proletariat, then called the working class, because in his early days as a revolutionist to whom the House of Commons refused a hearing ("The day will come when you shall hear me" was his slogan) he had learnt that the bulwarks of Conservatism were not in frivolous Mayfair but in

poverty-stricken Mile End. The more the franchise was extended the more hopeless the situation became, until at last, when complete adult suffrage was consummated by the enfranchisement of women, votes for everybody made the oligarchical Victorian parliaments of Disraeli and Gladstone seem hotbeds of revolution compared to the parliaments of [Stanley] Baldwin and Ramsay MacDonald.

The Disraelian strategy of extending popular suffrage to entrench conservative government was a paradox that Shaw regularly recognized in his political plays. The Depression-era prime minister, Sir Arthur Chavender, in *On the Rocks* (1933), contends to Sir Dexter Rightside that ordinary people

> are at present sick of being told that, thanks to democracy, they are the real government of the country. They know very well that they dont govern and cant govern and know nothing about Government except that it always supports profiteering, and doesn't really respect anything else, no matter what party flag it waves. . . . They cant set matters right themselves; so they want rulers who will discipline them and make them do it instead of making them do the other thing. . . . Weve known ever since we gave them the vote that theyd submit to anything. . . . As long as we give people an honest good time we can do just what seems good to us. The proof of the pudding will be in the eating. That will be really responsible government at last.

Abandoning his early Marxism while claiming he remained a socialist by conviction, Shaw felt all his life that if people eligible to cast a ballot actually exercised their political instincts, they would inevitably become conservative in their own interests, and that any aspiring "reformer-statesman" had to cultivate that through measured change promoted by shrewd stagecraft. The most successful politicians "are forced to become great actors" in order that they might win back by their performances the ground they lost by their statesmanship. Disraeli was forgiven "for his Reform Bill of 1867, the Nine Hours Act of 1874, the great Public Health Act and the emancipation of Trade Unionism from the penalties of the Conspiracy Bill of 1875, for the sake of his picturesqueness and his effective claptraps about 'Peace with Honour' and so on."

In *Caesar and Cleopatra* (1898) Shaw had Caesar scoff at diplomatic niceties when the turncoat general Achillas points out that the queen and her powerless young brother, who was technically her husband as well as king, had an even younger brother and sister who had to be politically accommodated. Caesar's chief of staff, Rufio, explains, "There is another little Ptolemy, Caesar: so they tell me."

"Well," says Caesar breezily, "the little Ptolemy can marry the other sister; and we will make them both a present of Cyprus."

Impatiently, Cleopatra's prime minister objects, "Cyprus is of no use to anybody."

"No matter," Caesar says: "you shall have it for the sake of peace."

"*Unconsciously anticipating a later statesman*," Caesar's uninhibited valet and slave, Britannus, unawed by rank, adds, "Peace with honor, Pothinus." In an afterword to the play, Shaw notes, "The few topical allusions I have indulged in, including the quotation from [the Earl of] Beaconsfield on Cyprus, have passed unchallenged as grave Roman history." Beaconsfield, as Queen Victoria had elevated him, had returned from the Berlin conference with Otto von Bismarck in 1878 ratifying territorial concessions to Russia from Turkey, which included Britain's acquiring Cyprus for his pains, announcing proudly, "Lord Salisbury and myself have brought you back peace—but a peace I hope with honour." However cynical his statement really was, it did not compare with its self-deluded exploitation by Prime Minister Neville Chamberlain in September 1938, on returning from a one-sided conference at Munich with Adolf Hitler. "For the second time in our history," Chamberlain declared, "a British Prime Minister has returned from Germany bringing peace with honour. I believe it is peace for our time." The sellout of Czechoslovakia would bring dubious peace for eleven months.

Although Disraeli's quip was much quoted in its time,[1] probably few realized, including Shaw himself, that the expression was a borrowing from Lord John Russell in September 1853, some months prior to the outbreak of war between Russia and Turkey in which Britain and France would fight in the Crimea. "While we endeavor to maintain peace, . . . if peace cannot be maintained with honour, it is no longer peace." Shaw may have remembered neither locution from history, but rather from

---

1   Shaw's sardonic use of the Disraeli tag was followed much later by an absurdist one in the immediate aftermath of Chamberlain's defeatist accommodation with Hitler. In the novel *Don't, Mr Disraeli*, by Caryl Brahms and S. J. Simon (London, 1940), the reader finds that "In Berlin it has been raining all day long. Mr Disraeli has just hurried over to bring back peace with honour. The negotiations have gone swimmingly and now the treaty is spread on the table before him. But just as he is about to sign it, he pauses: 'The light's bad,' he says trickily. 'Let's sign the thing in Munich.'" There may be other creative twists on the tag.

his years as an art critic. A decade before he began his play he reviewed an exhibition in a Bond Street gallery that included T. Blake Wirgman's painting *Peace with Honour*, in which Queen Victoria is receiving Disraeli, presumably at Buckingham Palace. The prime minister, standing as custom required, leans forward to offer his report from Berlin. "Her Majesty, mildly self-conscious" in Shaw's description, "sits at one end of a table, and Lord Beaconsfield condescends to her from the other, in a 'genteel apartment' pervaded by peace with honour. The old-fashioned furniture helps to give the picture an air of being a family portrait. If it survives to be an 'old master,' it may find itself described as such in a dealer's catalogue. No one will guess that two such unassuming personages are Empress and Earl."

Disraeli's performance in Berlin was often referred to by Shaw as the sort of spectacle intended to influence opinion. When he wrote *More Common Sense about the War* early in 1915, urging, unsuccessfully, a negotiated peace rather than more years of carnage, he called for another "Congress" of "responsible Governments" with its agents possessing real powers. "Who are our plenipotentiaries to be? Are they, for instance, to be popular party politicians actually in office as members of the Government, and go to the Congress as Disraeli went to Berlin or Castlereagh to Vienna?"

Disraeli was in Shaw's art-critic pantheon in still another image. "The best political caricatures," he wrote in 1889, "are still [James] Gillray's George III as King of Brobdingnag, with Napoleon as Gulliver in his hand; and Mr. [John] Tenniel's Disraeli and the Sphinx [in *Punch*] winking at one another over the Suez Canal shares."[2]

It is possible that Disraeli made his unidentified entrance in an even earlier Shavian play, in the last scene—the very last line—of *Arms and the Man* (1894). As the efficient bourgeois Swiss soldier of fortune, Captain Bluntschli, exits after arranging the postwar dispositions between Bulgaria and Serbia, Major Sergius Saranoff says admiringly, "What a man! Is he a man!" The line can be traced to the conclusion of the Berlin conference, when Bismarck exclaims about the departing Disraeli, who had wound up the peace negotiations with aplomb, "Der alter Jude, das ist der Mann!" Shaw shrewdly gave contemporary resonances to his lines, earlier in the play having Saranoff declare stubbornly, "I never

---

2   Late in 1875 Disraeli borrowed millions from the Rothschilds to finance the coup. *Punch* captioned the cartoon "Mosé in Egitto!!!"

withdraw!" The line had been made memorable in the Commons by the flamboyant Sir Robert Bontine Cunninghame Graham.

The 1890s were the seminal years of apparent Disraelian impact on Shaw's plays. When he wrote to Ellen Terry on May 12, 1897, of his dismay that Henry Irving, for whom *The Man of Destiny* had been written (with Ellen as projected co-star), had defected from performing it, playing a "confidence-trick" on the playwright, Shaw closed with "Vengeance I leave to Destiny. You remember about Beaconsfield's plan." The attribution to Disraeli, who claimed destiny in his own behalf and charged vindictiveness to his archrival, W. E. Gladstone, may have been in the back of Shaw's mind as he wrote his dark comedy about the ambitious young Napoleon on the road to Lodi, the general's openly faithless wife, and a devious "Strange Lady" who knew it all. It may have stuck with Shaw, too, when he wrote *Caesar and Cleopatra* (1899), its principal figure also rejecting vengeance for destiny, and *Captain Brassbound's Conversion* (also 1899), whose dark hero begins with vengeance in mind toward an uncle he blames for his misfortunes, but ends with Brassbound's concessions to destiny. Amidst them was the topsy-turvy comedy *You Never Can Tell* (1897), in which the last character to appear is the domineering Walter Bohun, QC, who tolerates no questioning of his legal advice, and suggests—despite Shaw's claim to have read nothing of Disraeli's fiction—Hugo Bohun in *Lothair* (1870). "My idea of an agreeable person," says Disraeli's arrogant Bohun, "is a person who agrees with me."

It may be a stretch to suggest that Disraeli had an inadvertent hand in Shaw's creation of a character who dominates the opening of *Man and Superman*. Yet young Shaw when new in London used some of his many hours in the British Museum's domed Reading Room to scan the daily press, and would have read about the belated but kindly elevation by Disraeli, although a Tory, of a veteran Radical, then a Liberal MP, John Arthur Roebuck (1801–79), to the Privy Council, to "adorn a long and honourable life." Soon after, Shaw would have read obituary notices of "poor Robeuck" (in the prime minister's words), an early spokesman for suffrage reform, whose career had deteriorated, Disraeli wrote to Lady Bradford (December 1, 1879), into unsuccess. Another Liberal MP, less often in the press but continuously reelected from various constituencies, was Sir John William Ramsden (1831–1914). Disraeli had tried to recruit him to support legislative reform, but found him obstinately unreliable.

Although, but for satirizing politicians and generals, Shaw seldom exploited the name of a living person still referred to in the press, he apparently felt it irresistible to combine to the two MP surnames into Roebuck Ramsden, a "highly respectable" liberal, even a radical in his time, and a former "councillor," whom the self-styled young revolutionary John Tanner calls "an old man with obsolete ideas." Objecting, Roebuck Ramsden counters, "You pose as an advanced man. Let me tell you that I was an advanced man before you were born." Yet his ideas have remained unchanged, as would become clear when he is indignant that a respectable if feisty young woman, Violet Robinson, announces that she is pregnant and apparently unmarried. The two surnames combined into Roebuck Ramsden convey conventional masculinity and, in a bestial pair of puns, stubbornness. Shaw could not have christened him in so Dickensian a fashion without having recalled the parliamentary columns in the press during his early years in London, when Disraeli was prime minister.

That Shaw may have fudged about his reading of and about Disraeli seems obvious from a much later letter to Sir Francis Younghusband, soldier, diplomat, and religious mystic, late in 1934. "Nobody ever mentions the real problems," Shaw wrote. "Here we are, as Disraeli put it, two nations, rich and poor." *Sybil, or The Two Nations* (1845) put the concept into political currency, when Stephen Morley, a socialist editor, responds to Charles Egremont, an aristocratic idealist for the downtrodden, who boasts that the young queen (the setting is 1837) "reigns over the greatest nation that ever existed" with the challenge, "Which nation?"

Baffled, Egremont is silent. "Yes," Morley continues, "Two nations; between whom there is no intercourse and no sympathy; who are as ignorant of each other's habits, thought, and feelings, as if they were dwellers in different zones, or inhabitants of different planets; who are governed by a different breeding, are fed by a different food, are ordered by different manners, and are not governed by the same laws."

"You speak of—" asks Egremont in puzzlement.
"THE RICH AND THE POOR."

Later, Shaw seems to have recycled Disraeli's image in his quip that England and America were two nations separated by a common language.

At the time of Shaw's letter to Sir Francis he had just completed his serious farce (my term for the anomaly) *The Millionairess* (1934), with one of the rare scenes in his plays that takes place in a genuinely destitute setting, a basement sweatshop in the Commercial Road in London's East

End. In it, Epifania, the eponymous millionairess cloaked in elaborately indigent garb, comes to seek employment and is at first rejected by the anxious couple who work under a bare electric bulb hung from a wire. The only evidence her attire reveals of that other "nation" outside leaves the elderly sweatshop proprietress suspicious. "Look at her shoes," she asks her spouse. "Could a woman looking for work at tuppence hapenny an hour afford a west end shoe like that?" Shaw could easily have known of Disraeli's oft-quoted line from *Sybil* from a secondary source, but the coincidence in time between citation (to Younghusband) and scene suggests that he may have intended dramatizing the Sybilline contrast.

The only other scene in Shaw contrasting the pitifully poor with the very rich appears in the second act of *Major Barbara* (1905), in the West Ham Salvation Army shelter. By name, Disraeli appeared only once in Shaw's plays, to reaffirm his point that leaders in a democracy, even a constitutional monarchy such as Britain, govern by manipulating, and accommodating, public opinion. In *Major Barbara*, Lady Britomart sees her super-rich husband, Andrew Undershaft, having sprung from the very poor himself, as an exception to the political rule. Brandishing his industrial clout as a manufacturer of armaments for the world market, he and his corporate partner, Lady Brit deplores, "positively have Europe under their thumbs. . . . He is above the law. Do you think Bismarck or Gladstone or Disraeli could have openly defied every social and moral obligation all their lives . . . ? They simply wouldnt have dared."

It may be no coincidence that when Shaw began *Major Barbara* on March 22, 1905, it was only two months after Disraeli's unfinished novel, since titled *Falconet,* had been published in three installments in the *Times*, on January, 20, 21, and 23, publicized in large capitals as "BEACONSFIELD NUMBERS." Surely Shaw read the *Times* daily, and encountered the nine chapters that were all that the ailing former prime minister had completed by his death in April 1881.

In the eighth chapter a German (but London-born) émigré named Hartmann, heir to his brother's English banking fortune, greets Kusinara, a Ceylonese gentleman of Buddhist faith and philosophical bent he had met only once before. While they discuss two subjects Kusinara sees as related, the power of religions and the equally potent influence of women, Hartmann, a widower of mysterious background, notes, "Here comes my daughter. She wants to give you some luncheon. She is not one of those women who is stronger than armies, but she is a dear girl." Angela, described as a great beauty, although devout in her unconventional way, declined to attend Bible classes or teach Sunday school. Hartmann himself eschewed all observance. When Angela attended Divine service at the parish church, she was never accompanied by her father.

Hartmann and Kusinara had first met aboard ship from Rotterdam. At the London docks, they had shared the only cab going into the City—it was a Sunday—chatting en route. Kusinara evinced surprise at the open excess of Victorian-era Sabbatarianism, "which could only have been equalled in old Jerusalem."

"Manners and customs outlive superstitions," Hartmann noted.

At his home in Clapham Common when they meet again, they discuss a "visionary" philosopher whose new book both had received from the author. "What I really feared about him," Kusinara concedes, "was that he had the weakness of believing in politics, of supposing that the pessimism of the universe could be changed or even modified by human arrangements."

"I heard he was a Communist," Hartmann observes.

"He might as well be a Liberal or a Conservative—mere jargon; different names for the same thing." Human misery, Kusinara contends, can only be ended "by the destruction of the species. . . . You and I hold the same tenets, and we desire the same end. . . . You think that centuries must elapse. . . . All that is happening in the world appears to me to indicate a speedier catastrophe. These immense armies, these new-fangled armaments—what do they mean? In the Thirty Years' War they would have depopulated Europe. . . . I trust more to the disease and famine [in the aftermath] of campaigns than to the slaughter of battles."

Hartmann is skeptical. "Surely these are comparatively slight means to achieve such a result as the total destruction of the human species."

"Not so slight as you may imagine. Besides, we must accept all means. Destruction in every form must be welcomed. If it be only the destruction of a class it is a step in the right direction."

The narrative breaks off after a fragment of chapter ten. We have no idea what Disraeli had in mind for Hartmann and Kusinara—and Angela. Nor did Shaw, but in *Major Barbara* he would include a mysterious multimillionaire, contemptuous of politics, who has inherited an armaments business dependent upon destruction, an earnest young philosopher with an Australian background, and a beautiful daughter with unconventional religious ideals. There is no one-to-one connection, yet Disraeli's abortive novel was fresh when Shaw, an assimilator of ideas, began his play.

Disraeli would seldom come up directly in Shaw, obscuring his actual impact. The *Times* on December 20, 1907, published a report, "Mr. Bernard Shaw and the Jews," adapted from an open letter to Max Nordau in the *Jewish World*. It responded to Nordau's charge of Shavian anti-Semitism in reviewing his *Degeneration*, first in 1895 in *Liberty* (New York), and then more expansively in *The Sanity of Art* (1907). With characteristic irony Shaw wrote about Nordau's alleged self-promotion, "The way to create interest in a man here is to claim for him that he is a Jew. On every April 19 [the anniversary of Disraeli's death in 1881] our Conservatives, our Imperialists, our Court party make a pilgrimage to the statue of the only Prime Minister of England who was a Jew, and heap its pedestal with primroses, his favourite flower."

Shaw's "Don Juan in Hell" dream interlude from *Man and Superman* had been performed separately for the first time, at the Royal Court Theatre in Sloane Square, in June 1907. In it, the glib Jewish brigand Mendoza, an English exile, reappears in the dream quartet as the Devil—a parody, the critic William Irvine suggested, of Disraeli in his most extravagant mode. "The Devil," Irvine wrote in *The Universe of G.B.S.* (1949), "talks very much like an above-the-average Member of Parliament, orating platitudinously when dullness is expected, breaking out into sententious epigram. He is, in fact, a kind of second-rate Disraeli—clever, cynical and witty, yet shallow and for all his wit a little solemn and deficient in humor, with the heart of a Philistine, the imagination of a vulgar romantic, and the attitudes of a melodramatic actor."

Echoes of Disraeli reappear throughout Shaw. He admired George Arliss as a performer, and Arliss starred in a silent film, *Disraeli*, in 1921, voice added in 1929. Arliss received an Academy Award for the later version, in the year Shaw wrote to suggest to Theresa Helburn of the Theatre Guild in New York, preparing to stage *The Apple Cart*, "The King is the principal man and has the sort of part that George Arliss shines in"—a suggestion that Disraeli, or Arliss (who was the striking screen image of Disraeli), may have been echoed in King Magnus. Several years later Shaw wrote to Hollywood producer Kenneth MacGowan suggesting Arliss if a GBS play were to be filmed.

The climax of *The Apple Cart* pivoted upon the king's threat of abdication in order to retain the "popgun" of power left to the monarchy. Disraeli and Shaw were both aware that the sovereign could step down in favor of the next in the line of succession—Robert, the callow, and fictional, Prince of Wales in Shaw's play, and in reality the playboy Prince

Bertie, Victoria's heir presumptive, a frightening prospect to both political parties. During the "Eastern Crisis," when the queen threatened "to lay down the thorny crown" because the Cabinet was dithering about an aggressive response to Russia, Disraeli assured her in error, probably because he understood that she was posturing, "Your Majesty has the clear constitutional right to dismiss them." She did not, and Disraeli knew that they were acting in a private comedy in which they played themselves. In reality the sovereign could veto the appointment of a prime minister (even Elizabeth II would do that in the case of "Rab" Butler) but could not control offices after the fact—but for her own.

When the Conservatives lost their parliamentary majority in 1880, the queen was on firmer ground in withholding assent for a new prime minister (and his likely Cabinet). Disraeli had to remain uncomfortably in office while Sir Henry Ponsonby communicated for her with W. E. Gladstone, whom she despised, and the outgoing prime minister. "She would sooner *abdicate*," she wrote to Ponsonby, who kept Disraeli apprised, "than send for or have any *communication* with *that half mad firebrand* who wd soon ruin everything & be a *Dictator*." But no other Liberal who privately aspired for the role could offer himself if Gladstone wanted it. When the Liberal leadership determined, as Disraeli put it to the queen, to "shrink from the responsibility [to recommend an alternative]," he advised Victoria to send for Gladstone. Again, abdication was an empty threat.

It was not so seven years after *The Apple Cart*. When a real abdication occurred, the play was revived for a post–Edward VIII England. Now that King Magnus's political stratagem was reconsidered as timely and even prescient, Shaw wrote in the theater program, "How natural and reasonable and probable the play is, and how improbable, fantastic, and outrageous the actual event was. There was not a single circumstance of it which I should have dared to invent." If a Disraeli or Macaulay could be raised from the dead to see the play and were asked, "Could this thing happen?" Shaw thought the response would be, "Oh, quite possibly. Queen Elizabeth threatened to abdicate and Queen Victoria used to hint at it once or so." But Shaw added, if you had told either one about the exit of Edward VIII, Disraeli or Macaulay would have warned, "If you put a tale like that into a play you will spend the rest of your days in a lunatic asylum. So much for holding the mirror up to nature."

Shaw's postwar prime ministers in his political plays after 1914–1918 largely satirized the ineffectual Cabinets he saw mishandling the war and misgoverning the anxious interwar peace. But for echoes of Disraeli in the successful—but fantasy—king who manipulates the elected mediocrities in *The Apple Cart*, there was little place for a positive "mirror up to nature."

Bibliographic Essay

Shaw's sweeping assertion to Hesketh Pearson that he refused to read Disraeli's novels was in June 1950, three months before the fall in the garden at Ayot that led to Shaw's death. Pearson published "postscript" chapters to his biography (New York: Harper's, 1942) in 1951. Stevenson's letter to Archer, written early in 1888, is quoted in the introduction to a reprint of *Cashel Byron's Profession*, ed. Stanley Weintraub (Carbondale: Southern Illinois University Press, 1968). Shaw's comments to Churchill were in an undated letter attributed to August 1946 in Dan H. Laurence, ed., *Bernard Shaw: Collected Letters*, vol. 4 (London and New York: Viking and Reinhardt, 1988). Shaw's comments on how "Public Opinion" was a "phantom of Democracy" that had restrained Gladstone and Disraeli appeared in many forms, from lectures to Lady Britomart's assertion to her son in *Major Barbara*, and finally in the preface to *The Millionairess*.

"Disraeli was forgiven . . ." by Shaw in "The Political Situation," British Library Add. MS 50684, folio 162. The paper was first read at a Fabian Society meeting at Essex Hall, London, on October 4, 1895. His diary for 1895 is more crowded with political talks than in any other year, most of them questioning the possibility of change through working-class initiatives. His "palmy parliamentary days of Gladstone and Disraeli" speech was "A Cure for Democracy," presented to the Fabians at Kingsway Hall, London, on November 27, 1930, and published in the *Clarion* in February 1931 (repr. in Lloyd J. Hubenka, ed., *Practical Politics* [Lincoln: University of Nebraska Press, 1976]). *The Malvern Festival Souvenir Book* comment on Disraeli and the abdication was in the 1937 issue.

The Disraelian "peace with honor" reference by Caesar to the acquisition of Cyprus is explained by Shaw himself in the post-play notes to *Caesar and Cleopatra*. Shaw's review of Blake Wirgman's painting of Disraeli and Victoria after the Berlin conference appeared in the *World*, March 23, 1887; his reference to John Tenniel's *Punch* cartoon of December 11, 1875, was in the *World*, June 12, 1889. Both are reprinted in Stanley Weintraub, ed., *Bernard Shaw on the London Art Scene, 1885–1950*

(University Park: Penn State Press, 1986), which includes a frontispiece illustration of the Wirgman painting.

Shaw's Disraelian response to Nordau, in its many manifestations prior to the *Times*, is detailed as item C1622 in Dan H. Laurence, *Bernard Shaw: A Bibliography*, vol. 2 (New York and Oxford: Oxford University Press, 1983). Paradoxically, Disraeli (or Earl of Beaconsfield, as he became) appears nowhere in the index to the *Bibliography* as heading or subject. Laurence's fourth volume of Shaw's *Collected Letters* (1988) includes the two letters referring to Arliss—to Theresa Helburn (February 8, 1929) and to Kenneth MacGowan (April 7, 1933).

· 7 ·

Shaw's Musician

EDWARD ELGAR

In the first year of the post-Victorian century, Edward Elgar composed music for a play by George Moore and W. B. Yeats, *Diarmuid and Grania,* produced at the Gaiety Theatre in Dublin that October. In the next year, 1902, he entered a musical competition for an "Irish Symphony" by expanding on what he had written for the play. He didn't win any prizes, and that ended his music for the theater. But he had made a conquest of the coming man of the English stage. Bernard Shaw had become one of Elgar's admirers, and a few years later he responded to a suggestion by a London impresario, Colonel James H. Mapleson, that he write an opera libretto for the French composer Camille Saint-Saëns by turning the proposal upside down. "Unfortunately," Shaw joked, "I have a prior engagement with Richard Strauss, which is at present hung up by the fact that I want to write the music and he wants to write the libretto, and we both get on very slowly for want of practice. I wonder whether Elgar would turn his hand to opera?"

The implication was that if Elgar wrote the music, Shaw would furnish a libretto—the only time he ever made such an offer. The two would form a mutual admiration society. Shaw, who always wanted to write music, knew he had no talent in that direction and wrote only a few forgotten songs. Encouraging Elgar was his route to musical composition. Elgar, who would become the major British composer of his time, had read Shaw's "Corno di Bassetto" music columns in London newspapers in 1888–89, before Shaw had heard a note of Elgar's early music. "He was a musical critic and a good one," said Elgar later, "in those dull days when the two [Oxbridge] Universities and the Colleges of Music used to do nothing but sit around and accuse one another of the cardinal virtues." Later, once Shaw and Elgar became close, they would discuss setting one of Shaw's plays to music, but, Shaw recalled, "I think we agreed to my view that he could do nothing with a play except what his [symphonic poem] Falstaff did with Shakespeare's."

After Shaw's critic days were over, in 1900, he heard Elgar's symphonic *Enigma Variations* (of 1897) and his oratorio *A Dream of Gerontius*. The haunting *Enigma Variations*, he recalled, "took away your breath. Whew! I knew we had got it at last." He would become a friend, enthusiast, and patron of Elgar's, spurring on his creativity—an essential task, as Elgar was diffident and self-critical to the point of tearing up much of what he had composed. Shaw opened him up with wit and praise and entrée to a new cultural landscape. At first there seemed little likelihood of that. Elgar claimed to have admired Shaw's critical pieces, written when he was trying, in London, to reach beyond a purely provincial reputation, but his first known reaction to a Shaw play was less than enthusiastic. Writing to a friend, the stage set designer Arthur Troyte Griffith, after reading *Man and Superman* in 1904, he responded to it, predictably, as the conservative Roman Catholic he was. "Bernard Shaw is hopelessly wrong," he objected, "as all these fellows are on fundamental things: amongst others they punch Xtianity & try to make it fit their civilization instead of making their civilization fit it. He is an amusing liar, but not much more & it is a somewhat curious p[oin]t that in the Don Juan [in Hell dream] scene he makes his characters 'live in the remembrance' (in figure, age, etc) just, or not just but very like [Cardinal] Newman in Gerontius. Extremes meet sometimes."

It is possible that extremes did meet here, and that Shaw got something out of the dream-vision of Gerontius, which speculated on evolution, extreme age, the loss of Eden, and salvation. Elgar's oratorio referred also to a Devil, and Shaw would have the Devil as a character in his dream interlude, while the other characters in the dream would be, to quote Newman, "out of the body," beyond "space, and time."

More suggestions of Elgar may have turned up in a later play Shaw described as his "metabiological Pentateuch, *Back to Methuselah*—in what Newman called "the garden shade" of Eden. Elgar's early impact may have been more than Shaw ever recognized. The creative process is a mysterious one, and the computer that is our brain may store ideas in the memory for a long time before they emerge transformed. Elgar, for example, was an enthusiastic amateur chemist, with a laboratory erected in his garden that led him into chemical metaphors. In a 1909 University of Birmingham lecture on critics he had defined Bernard Shaw chemically, observing that in Shaw's writings "there was a substratum of *practical matter*, or to put it chemically, to volatile and pellucid fluid, held in solution, matter which was precipitated into obvious solid fact by the introduction of the reader's *own common sense*." Nitrogen iodide, he explained further, is formed "when an excess of aqueous ammonia is added to a solution of iodine in potassium iodide." In Shaw's fantasy *The Simpleton of the Unexpected Isles*, written in 1934, just after Elgar died—which could have awakened dormant memory—is an eccentric character, Iddy—actually named Phosphor—whose father, he claims, was a biological chemist, the reason Iddy grew up as a "nitrogen baby" fed on nitrogen-enriched food.

After *Man and Superman* Elgar would attend other Shaw plays, at first largely to see his friend Troyte Griffith's sets. One occasion was the London revival of *The Devil's Disciple* in 1907, which Elgar found "unconvincing." Apparently he read a lot of Shaw, having singled him out wryly in his Birmingham lecture. Elgar saw *Getting Married* the next year, and pronounced it "fine." In 1912 he and his wife saw *John Bull's Other Island*, with its humane and mystical—but unfrocked—Irish priest, Father Keegan. Moved, to her surprise, the ultra-pious (and Roman Catholic) Alice Elgar, who was a profound influence on her husband, wrote, "Most delightful. The noble & ideal left in instead of the poison of [the] other B. Shaw." In 1913 Elgar saw *The Doctor's Dilemma* and *Androcles and the Lion*. He also saw *Captain Brassbound's Conversion* in a revival, and Shaw's feminist satire *Fanny's First Play*.

Although Elgar was a committed playgoer, the Shaw and Elgar circles of friends did not intersect, and the men did not meet until March 1919, at a luncheon arranged by Lalla Vandervelde, wife of a Belgian Socialist politician who had lived in London during the wartime occupation of their country. An occasional actress, Lalla had played in Shaw's homefront farce *Augustus Does His Bit*, which the Elgars had seen. (They would soon see her again in Shaw's *Arms and the Man*.) The other guests were Elgar and the art critic Roger Fry. Elgar, so Shaw recalled in a letter to Virginia Woolf, confided that he had "enjoyed my musical criticisms when he was a student and remembered all my silly jokes. . . . We two plunged into a conversation into which Roger could not get in a word: in fact we forgot all about him."

Frustrated, and feeling that his hostess expected him to contribute something, Fry pontificated, "After all, there is only one art: all the arts are the same." That was too much for Elgar, who considered his own art the only true one. "Music," he spluttered, "is written on the skies for you to note down. And you compare that to a DAMNED imitation!!!" Fry let the tirade pass with a gentle smile.

Shaw had long liked Elgar's music. When in 1931 Shaw collected his *Saturday Review* musical columns of 1890–94 as *Music in London* he would inscribe on Elgar's copy, "The title is wrong. There was no [English] music until you came." Now Shaw knew he also admired the man. In an address to the Musical Association in December 1910 he had described Elgar as a composer who, rather than produce "second-hand Handel" or "second-hand Mozart," or even "second-hand Mendelssohn," wrote music "as characteristically English as a Shropshire country house and stable are characteristically English." In the *Morning Post* in 1911 he had written that "the history of original [English] music, broken off by the death of Purcell, begins again with Sir Edward Elgar." In an interview at the Glastonbury Music Festival in 1916 he declared that Elgar was "the first musician who, after a century of imitation of Handel, Mendelssohn and Spohr, began to write music like an Englishman. . . . I hold the view that after two hundred years during which our abler men would not touch music, we are now coming into our own again as a great musical nation." He also saw Elgar as a master of dramatic music, suggesting in 1917 that if Elgar took over the conducting of Mozart's *Marriage of Figaro* from Sir Thomas Beecham for only one night, Beecham would exclaim, "And I took this great composer for a mere confectioner!"

Within days of Madame Vandervelde's luncheon, Shaw was a visitor at Elgar's home in Hampstead, 42 Netherhall Gardens, where the composer's Piano Quintet was given a private run-through in the oak-floored music room dominated by a grand piano. Another listener was composer Arthur Bliss, and Elgar's daughter sat deep in the inglenook as a fire burned silently. In a thank-you note the next day Shaw wrote that the music "knocked me over at once," but ever the honest critic he added, "You cannot begin a movement in such a magical way as you have begun this Quintet and then suddenly lapse into the expected." The work did have its problems, as Elgar did not write as well for the piano as he did for strings. Shaw, a good amateur pianist, explained, diplomatically, "There are some piano embroideries on a pedal point that didn't sound like a piano or anything else in the world, but [were] quite beautiful, and

I have my doubts whether any regular shop pianist will produce them: they require a touch which is peculiar to yourself, and which struck me the first time I ever heard you larking about with a piano."

Elgar responded on March 11, 1919, enclosing the score. On the same day he sent another copy to music critic Ernest Newman, enclosing Shaw's letter and suggesting, cautiously, "I think he has mistaken the drift of the *fugato*"—a fugue-like passage. But to Shaw, Elgar confided that "it was a proud moment to see you enter my room," and he closed with praise for "the vast intellectuality of your dramatic work." Putting his own reputation in play for Elgar, GBS used the composer as example in pressing for public subsidy during the postwar curtailment of the market for music "to keep British music in the front rank of culture." To the *British Music Society Bulletin*, which then reprinted his appeal in the mass-audience *Outlook* in July 1919, he insisted on "fine art as an indispensable element in the greatness of States and the glory of God." There was always enough encouragement for bric-a-brac, but not for "music in which British musicians express their British character in . . . international language. When Elgar startled us by suddenly reasserting the British character in music he did it in an idiom which was no more distinctively English than the idiom of Schumann; but Schumann could not, or rather would not, have written ten bars of an Elgar symphony."

Continuing his campaign—the most relentless he ever pursued for a contemporary artist—GBS, now energized as an Elgar missionary, wrote a long piece for *Music and Letters*, published in January 1920, contending, "Elgar is carrying on Beethoven's business. The names are up on the shop front for everyone to read. ELGAR, late BEETHOVEN & CO, Classics and Italian & German Warehousemen. Symphonies, Overtures, Chamber Music, Oratorios, Bagatelles." Earlier, Shaw had been a disciple of Wagner, but now he claimed that Elgar's "musical mind was formed before Wagner reached him," and Shaw didn't find that a handicap, for Elgar wrote "in the Beethovenian sense." If he were king, or Minister of Fine Arts, Shaw declared, "I would give Elgar an annuity of a thousand a year on condition that he produce a symphony every eighteen months."

In September 1921, after moving from Hampstead to the country, Elgar returned to conduct a Promenade Concert at Queen's Hall. The program included his symphonic fantasy *Falstaff*. Shaw was in the audience, and postcarded Elgar that he had never heard it before, and thought it was "perfectly graphic to anyone who knows his Shakespeare." It was, he wrote, "the true way to set drama to music"—perhaps a hint, but Elgar in return only sent Shaw his own program notes to the music. Shaw responded with a long letter with his thoughts about Shakespeare's Falstaff character, and also sent a copy of his new play, *Heartbreak House*, which was in rehearsals in London. Elgar replied in an innocent postscript, "Did you leave the error on p. 12 . . . to see if people really read the book? If so you are, in this instance, not so clever as I am! I leave a glaring mistake somewhere well on or near the end." There was no typographical error on the page. Elgar was unacquainted with Shaw's idiosyncratic spelling and punctuation, which involved dropping the apostrophe from *thats*. But he was reading every Shavian word.

Elgar would see *Heartbreak House* with delight, and take its stage Lady Utterword (Edith Evans) to dinner and to a recital of his music. Soon Elgar would see Shaw's *Pygmalion, Candida,* and even the lengthy *Back to Methuselah*. By this time he and Shaw were good friends, and when Tory critic Sidney Colvin made cutting comments about Shaw to Elgar, the composer diplomatically put Colvin down, observing, "I don't think we shd. have 'liked' Aristophanes personally, or Voltaire (perhaps) but I cannot do without their work. GBS's politics are, to me, appalling, but he is the kindest-hearted, gentlest man I have met outside the charmed circle which includes you. . . . I am still at heart the dreamy child who used to be found in the reeds by Severn side with a sheet of paper trying to fix the sounds & . . . as a child & as a young man & as a mature man, no single person was ever kind to me, so my heart goes out to any man or woman of assured position as G.B.S. who helps others. Enough."

When Richard Strauss, a composer both Elgar and Shaw esteemed, paid his first postwar visit to England early in 1922, Elgar invited him to a luncheon to meet younger British composers, yet he also included Shaw. Acting as host was an effort for Elgar, whose wife, Alice, eight years his elder and long ill, had died, but like Shaw, he wanted to encourage younger artists. GBS added gravitas to Elgar's table.

The British public remained unenthusiastic about British music, and Elgar in particular. They admired little more than his ceremonious "Pomp and Circumstance" marches, which had already become identified as the epitome of modern English music. They were not interested in anything more formidable, which became embarrassingly obvious at a London performance of Elgar's oratorio *The Apostles*—a fund-raiser for the Westminster Abbey Restoration Fund. Almost no one came. Shaw loyally expressed his unhappiness in a letter in the *Daily News* (June 9, 1922), writing, "It would be an exaggeration to say that I was the only person present, like Ludwig of Bavaria at Wagner's *premieres*. My wife was there. Other couples were visible at intervals. . . . I distinctly saw six people in the stalls, probably with complimentary tickets." He was, he confessed, "unspeakably ashamed. . . . I apologize to posterity for living in a country where the capacity and tastes of schoolboys and sporting costermongers are the measure of metropolitan culture."

He would continue in his self-appointed role as keeper of Elgar's reputation. In 1931, responding to a derogation of the composer in a new edition of the *Handbuch der Musikgeschichte*, Shaw joined seventeen other composers and critics to attack the "unjust and inadequate treatment of Sir Edward Elgar." The *Handbuch* in its article on English music had devoted sixty-six lines to Hubert Parry, forty-one to Villiers Stanford, yet only sixteen to Elgar. The deflation, by musical journalist E. J. Dent, dismissed Elgar's orchestral works for their "pompous style" and "too deliberate nobility of expression," and downgraded his chamber music as "dry and academic." Both were assessments with much truth in them. Elgar, however, was far beyond the forgettable Parry and Stanford, and the respondents, who included William Walton and Philip Heseltine, declared that Dent "cannot go unchallenged." The Press Association was offered the collectively signed letter, and for the *Manchester Guardian* (February 6, 1931) Shaw added a postscript, to ensure that the letter was published, suggesting that "Elgar holds the same position in English music as Beethoven in German music"—an assessment that was reasonably parallel without differentiating between the qualitative levels of the musical traditions in which they established their primacy. Dent, Shaw carped, "should not have belittled his country by belittling the only great English composer who is not dwarfed by the German giants."

The middle 1920s, after the triumph of *Saint Joan*, were a fallow period for Shaw, and even more so for Elgar, whose wife had managed him and his professional life. His last major work, and one of his finest, his Cello Concerto, now a staple of the repertory, found few instrumentalists willing to risk it. He was now writing little except for the wastebasket. Shaw sent him his between-plays book, one unlikely to find a convert in the conservative Elgar, *The Intelligent Woman's Guide to Socialism and Capitalism*, turning it into an encouragement to his friend to keep composing. Responding to a letter about it on the subject of consumers and the economics of consumption, Shaw wrote (May 30, 1928), "Your products have the extraordinary quality of being *infinitely consumable* without diminution or deterioration. I should have done a chapter on the economics of Art; but it would have been too long." Elgar had been complaining that his music brought him little money. The only financial gain from orchestral performances had been that music lovers bought piano arrangements as they would now buy recordings. Yet Shaw knew that Elgar lived in comfort and style despite financial disappointments, and that he recognized in the years before the recording industry became big business that a serious composer had to live on commissions, which meant that he had to compose.

Frustrated at beginning anything new he wanted to keep at long enough to complete, Elgar confided as much to Shaw, who replied on a postcard that after a hiatus in writing for the stage he had been at work again, and had completed a political fantasy, *The Apple Cart*. It will seem, after *Saint Joan*, he confessed, like "a hideous anti-climax. It is a scandalous Aristophanic burlesque of democratic politics, with a brief but shocking sex interlude." The play would be, he added, performed at the new summer festival at Malvern, not far from Elgar's Worcestershire home. "Your turn now," Shaw cajoled. "Clap it"—that is, in the sense of concocting something hastily—"with a symphony." He kept pressing Elgar to write something for Malvern, and at the least to turn up as invited guest. The producer at Malvern, Birmingham impresario Barry Jackson, Shaw wrote, although it was clearly Shaw's own idea, "In his first enthusiasm . . . was bent on getting from you an overture for The Apple Cart, but on obtaining from [conductor Adrian] Boult a rough estimate of the cost of an Elgar orchestra, and letting his imagination play on the composer's fee, . . . went mournfully to his accountants."

His own view, Shaw teased, was that "six bars of yours would extinguish (or upset) the A[pple] C[art] and turn the Shaw festival into an Elgar one; but that it would be a jolly good thing so. So I demanded overtures to Caesar, to Methuselah (five preludes), and a symphonic poem to Heartbreak House, which is by far the most musical work of the lot." He was only half teasing. Had Elgar warmed to any musical introduction to, or interpretation of, Shaw, very likely GBS would have found some subterfuge to furnish the money himself. The closest they would come to a joint work was when, in Malvern days, Elgar did ask Shaw to write an opera libretto for him. Evasively, he replied that his plays had a verbal music of their own "which would make a very queer sort of counterpoint" to Elgar's music. He suggested to make his point that Elgar take *Androcles and the Lion* and try setting a single page. "You will find," said

Shaw, "that you cannot make an opera of it, just as you could not make an opera of Shakespeare's *Henry IV*. But you may make another *Falstaff* of it. That is really your line."

Elgar did go to Malvern. It was arranged that he would open a Shaw exhibition at the Malvern Public Library. On September 19, 1929, his informal opening remarks, as he did not have a prepared text, were taken down as he wished only in the third person. To introduce anything about his friend Shaw, he began, was one of the greatest honors he ever had. He had the best of all qualifications, Elgar claimed. He had read Shaw's works "from beginning to end." Some of them may have been "rather shattering to the nerves" of his audience. He often thought that Shaw offered the British public his plays "in the spirit in which Sterne gave the ass a macaroon"—to find out "what the dickens it was going to do with it."

Shaw responded that Elgar was one of the finest living composers. "I am seriously and genuinely humble in his presence. I recognise a greater art than mine and a greater man than I can ever hope to be." Tartly, the September issue of the *Musical Times* observed that it was "apparently the only public utterance in which Mr. Shaw has acknowledged himself to be second to any creative artist, living or dead."

In the later 1920s Shaw encouraged Elgar to join him in fighting a new copyright bill, under which a composer would be permitted to charge only two pence for the right of each performance, and Elgar, who had never been a political activist, suddenly saw his livelihood threatened. With other composers he joined the opposition as its most visible practitioner, and in the *Evening Standard* (December 17, 1929) editorial cartoonist David Low published a cartoon showing Elgar playing a Salvation Army harmonium with his *Gerontius* on the music stand, and Shaw standing beside him trying to evade a parsimonious "Labour Concert Favourite" who chucks a tuppence at them. Next to the musical boor is another representing "Cheap Music for the Caledonian Choral Society," who asks his partner, "For why did ye no mak' it a penny?" The bill was defeated. It was Elgar's second brush with official discouragement of the arts in as many years, as his musical dilettante friend Frank Schuster had died, leaving the composer a legacy from which the Chancellor of the Exchequer's office extracted a death duty of £700. Shaw had commiserated (April 4, 1928), "Why don't they make us [artists] duty-free instead of giving us O.M.s and the like long after we have conferred them on ourselves?"

Despite Shaw's obvious political radicalism and Labour Party connections, Elgar remained, more quietly when with GBS, an unreconstructed reactionary, and when during the general election of 1929, rallies for candidates wanted to exploit his "Land of Hope and Glory" anthem, Sir Edward let it be known that it was available only to Stanley Baldwin's Tories. (Baldwin, who lost to the Labourite leader Ramsay MacDonald, was also a fellow Worcestershire man.) To Lady Rennell of Rodd, wife of the Conservative MP for Marylebone, Elgar he wrote, warning, "Don't let any blasted Labour rogues or Liberals use the tune!" He may never have put his political opinions otherwise on paper, but as early as 1902, when he was even more rigidly Tory, he had resigned from his club, the Athenaeum, when MacDonald was elected, although composers Sir Hubert Parry and Sir Villiers Stanford were his sponsors.

Shaw's promotion of Elgar also took the form of planting a piece in the *Radio Times*, August 30, 1929, puffing a performance by Albert Sammons on station 5GB of Elgar's Violin Concerto on September 12. "Bernard Shaw has recently been giving his friend, Sir Edward Elgar, a public pat on the back: his music, Shaw says, is among the greatest of our time. It is not Shaw's way, as everyone knows, to be redundant; and he knows a thing or two about music. Elgar has never been accorded the wide reception that his admirers claim to be his due."

For the 1930 Brass Band Festival at the Crystal Palace—a national competition still ongoing, but now at the Albert Hall—Elgar was commissioned to write the test piece, which had to be performed by each of the many competitors. From earlier sketches he put together his attractive *Severn Suite*, which he dedicated to Shaw. Elgar planned to attend with Shaw, but back trouble kept him at home. Loyally, GBS attended, and sent the composer a long typewritten report on September 28, 1930, using his red ribbon (here italics) for suggested musical directions:

> My dear Elgar
> I heard the Severn Suite yesterday only eight times, as extreme hunger and the need for catching the 5.10 train at King's Cross forced me to surrender before I ceased to find new things in it. [He missed the eventual winner, Foden's Motor Works Band.]
> If there is a new edition of the score I think it would be well to drop the old Italian indications and use the language of the bandsmen: For instance
> *Remember that a minuet is a dance and not a bloody hymn;*
> or

> *Steady up for artillery attack;*
> or
> *NOW—like Hell.*
> I think that would help some of the modest beginners. . . . It is a pity you did not hear them. . . . Nobody would have guessed from looking at the score and thinking of the thing as a toccata for brass how beautiful and serious the work is as abstract music.

Shaw went on for pages, clearly delighted to be part of the occasion, but when the Columbia Records staffers there to record the winning performance asked him "to do three minutes chin music as an introduction," he said no, explaining to Elgar that he would have needed three hours. Quite obviously he did not want to intrude on Elgar's moment. On the flyleaf of his inscribed copy of the score, Shaw wrote that Elgar had dedicated the work "to me; so my name may last as long as his own." Only once otherwise did he evidence such humility about a living artist—when he declared that he might in future be known only as subject of a bust by Rodin.

Always now seeking a way to get attention for Elgar, in the first days of 1931 Shaw suggested to Elgar's daughter, Carice, and then to Elgar himself, that he compose a singable version of his orchestration of the National Anthem. Shaw had already written a striking replacement stanza, with alternative feminist language:

> O Lord our God arise
> All our salvation lies
> In! Thy! Great! Hand! (la Elgar)
> Centre his/her thoughts on Thee
> Let him God's captain be (Let her God's handmaid be)
> Thine to Eternity
> God save the King/Queen.

Although an open secret, he suggested that the contributor of the lyrics remain anonymous as "the least suspicion" of its real origin "would spoil everything." Reaction in the *Times* did not give Shaw away. The original lines, Shaw claimed to Elgar, "are hard for any Christian to stand." But Elgar saw no chance for change, and wrote to the Dean of Worcester Cathedral, to whom Shaw had tried out the idea, that he did not think "this National address to the Almighty" would have any effect—"if the Almighty ever took notice of anything, which of course he never did, does, or will do." It was a remarkable shift in Elgar since he had first encountered Shaw's works, and then Shaw. Elgar had moved from a traditionally religious composer to something of a Shavian skeptic—except to friends to whom he had to appear as of old. Yet Shaw persisted, canvassing other cathedral deans, who saw nothing but trouble in the idea. (One of those who saw a religious reversal in Elgar was the retired actress—and Roman Catholic—Mary Anderson de Navarro, an old friend of Shaw's as well as Elgar's. "I pulled him up soundly," she recalled when she realized that his faith was fading, "saying that he was making a new religion by taking all the *nots* from the Commandments & putting them into the Creed, but that was when he was very intimate with Shaw.")

When the critic H. C. Colles returned from a memorial service for Elgar in Worcester Cathedral in 1934 he shared seats on the train to London with the crusty first violinist of the London Symphony Orchestra (LSO), William H. Reed, who commented unhappily, "After Lady Elgar's death he"—Elgar—"took up with a set of people who were not those of his old life at all and who made him think it was smart or up-to-date or something to be irreligious." Colles guessed at Shaw. "Exactly," contended Reed; "he was awfully flattered because instead of lampooning him Shaw gave out that he [Elgar] was the only great composer.... It was not a real friendship. Elgar liked Shaw's brilliant talk.... I always knew that that sort of thing was not Elgar's real self." Yet Elgar had become over the years far less dogmatic about religion, and when, in December 1932, Shaw had sent him the jeu d'esprit that would become a surprise Christmas season best-seller, *The Adventures of the Black Girl in Her Search for God*, Elgar coupled his thanks with regret that GBS and Charlotte were leaving for months on "a devastating world journey"—devastating to him for their absence from his life. The religious parable, however, prompted his own fable, which he intended as his own Christmas and New Year greeting to friends.

Elgar fancied "a gorgeous, illimitable, golden corridor" in which "several of the Higher-Beings were in waiting," apparently disappointed with the new world that God had made. Then a "vast Purple Shadow filled he space and Lucifer sat [there]," pleased with his possibilities among the inhabitants and their religions. The onlookers become even more despondent, until a "pleasant and not unmirthful" sound is heard, identified only when the Archangel Michael draws a curtain and whispers, "He is pleased—He laughs—He has made—a Puppy!" Now Lucifer's hopes are disappointed, for he realizes that "through the ages Man could be serenely happy with his Dog." The widowered Elgar's companions were his dogs. And his own jeu d'esprit had downgraded God.

Despite back pain that was early warning of the spinal cancer that would be fatal, Elgar was attempting to be more active. For one thing, he needed the income. He was to open the new EMI recording studios in Abbey Road by conducting some of his own works. Among the guests was Shaw, and the occasion was filmed by Pathé for a newsreel. An Irish journalist, Herbert Hughes, interviewed Elgar, and he talked of his friendships with Richard Strauss and Shaw, and of Shaw's amazing musical sensibility. A Mass in D minor by Cherubini had been rediscovered, and before it had been performed at a music festival—and Elgar played a few bars on the piano for Hughes—he tried a passage from it, he said, "on several musicians of my acquaintance, asking if they could identify the composer. They thought of Mozart, of Beethoven, of Weber, dismissing each after a moment. Then I tried it on Shaw, and Shaw—who knows more about music than most people—though puzzled, immediately said, 'What about Cherubini?'"

In the summer of 1932, as the Malvern Festival was preparing to premiere Shaw's newest comedy, Elgar appealed, "Can't you engineer that I sit with you for the first performance of *Too True to be Good*—my last chance," he confided, feeling his years. (Elgar was seventy-five, a year younger than GBS.) He remembered, so he reminded Shaw, "the glory of being with you for *The Apple Cart*." Elgar not only received a prime seat: just before the opening, Bernard and Charlotte Shaw visited Elgar's home, Marl Bank, to hear a new recording of the Violin Concerto just produced with the sixteen-year-old Yehudi Menuhin, and brought with them the offstage star of the new Malvern play. The "Private Meek" of the comedy spoofed Lawrence of Arabia, who came in his Royal Air Force uniform. An Elgar friend, Vera Hockman, described listening to the test pressings—how they "all sat, spellbound at the glorious sounds, G.B.S. with bowed head, sometimes softly singing with the music, Aircraftman Shaw serious and silent, looking straight ahead with those unforgettable blue eyes which seemed to see into the life of things." Lawrence—now legally T. E. Shaw—was a devotee, like GBS, of Elgar's music, and had an Elgar record collection at his Dorsetshire cottage that would soon include the HMV disc by Menuhin and the LSO.

Shaw's own record collection of Elgar would reach thirty-four works, evidence of a late-years interest in contemporary British music that would also include fifteen of Frank Bridge, thirteen of Arnold Bax (another GBS friend), twelve of John Ireland, and nine of Vaughan Williams, as well as compositions by Havergal Brian, Rutland Boughton (yet another friend), Lord Berners, and William Walton, who would compose the score for the film of *Major Barbara*.

While Elgar was musically silent, Shaw had visited South Africa (where he conceived and wrote the *Candide*-like *The Black Girl*) and exploited his fame to induce W. J. Pickerill, conductor of the Cape Town Orchestra, to invite Sir Edward to visit and conduct his own works. Elgar's lifestyle required more income than his dwindling royalties from performances and recordings produced, and Shaw was trying to conduct some pounds Elgar's way. Through much of 1932 a frustrating correspondence went on between Novello, Elgar's publishers, and Pickerill, the composer feeling it inappropriate as a gentleman to conduct his own negotiations. However, Elgar remained intrusively in the middle, writing Novello on June 1, 1932, "I received the enclosed letter to-day; you will see that the writer, whom I do not know, repeats what he said to Bernard Shaw. I wish you would write [for me]." Sir Henry Clayton of Novello took the matter up and deflated the puzzled Pickerill, who expected, on Shaw's confident assurance, that Elgar, although elderly, would be enthusiastic at being lionized and even paid for it. The composer's fee for performance of a work would be seven and a half guineas each (as gentlemen cited fees in guineas, thus gaining an additional shilling in each pound). Further, Sir Edward would only appear himself if his expenses were fully paid, plus "a substantial fee for each Concert at which he would conduct his works." A "cut and dried scheme, giving the fullest possible details," had to be "laid before him." After that firm and less than sympathetic response, the proposal foundered. Elgar told Clayton that it was "business like." Very likely GBS never knew the details. He might have quietly subsidized the arrangement.

Elgar's seventy-fifth birthday got his creative juices flowing a bit. He thought of setting Ben Jonson's seldom-produced comedy *The Devil Is an Ass*, and asked Shaw to help him reduce it to a libretto he could score, which he intended to call *The Spanish Lady*. Shaw told him to stick to what he could do best, and suggested an orchestral fantasy like *Falstaff*. But Elgar's search for a subject gave Shaw what he considered a far better idea. On September 30, 1932, he wrote to the imperious John Reith, the director of the BBC, whom he knew well. Shaw was on the

BBC's Committee on Spoken English, and his own talks on the air were popular broadcasts. He offered a "suggestion":

> In 1823 the London Philharmonic Society passed a resolution to offer Beethoven £50 for the MS of a symphony. He accepted, and sent the Society the MS of the 9th Symphony. In 1827 the Society sent him £100. He was dying; and he said "God bless the Philharmonic Society and the whole English nation."
>
> This is by far the most creditable incident in English history.
>
> Now the only composer today who is comparable to Beethoven is Elgar. Everybody seems to assume that Elgar can live on air, or that he is so rich and successful that he can afford to write symphonies and conduct festivals for nothing. As a matter of fact his financial position is a very difficult one, making it impossible for him to give time enough to such heavy jobs as the completion of a symphony; and consequently here we have the case of a British composer who has written two great symphonies which place England at the head of the world in this top department of instrumental music, unable to complete and score a third. I know that he has the material for the first movement ready, because he has played it to me on his piano.
>
> Well, why should not the BBC, with its millions, do for Elgar what the old Philharmonic did for Beethoven? You could bring the third symphony into existence, and obtain the performing right for the BBC for, say, ten years, for a few thousand pounds. The kudos would be stupendous and the value for the money ample....
>
> He does not know that I am meddling in his affairs and yours in this manner; and I have not the faintest notion of what sum he would jump at; but I do know that he has still a lot of stuff in him that could be released if he could sit down to it without risking his livelihood.

Reith immediately invited Elgar, through the composer-conductor Landon Ronald, who was also (like Novello) handling Elgar's musical business for him. And Shaw duly postcarded Elgar as if the idea were a surprise, "Ronald has told me the gorgeous news. Nobilmente." (GBS sent a similar note to Reith. "Nobilmente" was Elgar's favorite direction in a score.) On December 9, Elgar signed an agreement with the BBC, and eleven days later the *Times* published a letter from Shaw trusting that the next great British composer would not have to wait until he was past seventy to have his bread and butter guaranteed while he was scoring his "Eroica." And "T. E. Shaw" wrote to Elgar that the news about the Third Symphony "was like a week's sunlight."

Cribbing from his letter to Reith, Shaw wrote to the *Times* (December 20, 1932) that he had "occasionally remarked that the only entirely creditable incident in English history is the sending of £100 to Beethoven on his deathbed by the London Philharmonic Society; and it is the only one that historians never mention." He went on to thank Sir John Reith for commissioning a work from "the first English composer to produce symphonies ranking with those of Beethoven"—as if GBS had nothing to do with it. "I suggest," he closed, "that we make a note not to wait until our next composer is seventy before guaranteeing his bread and butter while he is scoring his Eroica."

Inevitably, Elgar learned that the idea was GBS's—"the wonderful plan which you invented," he wrote to Shaw when the £1,000 commission was formalized. "I am overwhelmed by the loftiness of the idea & can only say *thank you*." Shaw prodded him to produce it. "Remember," he wrote, answering an Elgar letter, "you have to catch up to Beethoven." But early in the next year it became obvious that Elgar could do little if anything to further the 141 pages of musical notations, drafts, and scribbled directives for the new symphony, and he wrote anxiously to John Reith before hospitalization for exploratory surgery that if the music did not "materialise" he would return the "sums you have paid on account." The operation revealed inoperable cancer. Elgar's removal to a nursing home was doubly appalling to him, as he worried that he could not afford the £50 a week it cost, and he sent Shaw a note apparently to ask assistance in withdrawing from the commission. Shaw seems to have destroyed it after paying a visit to Reith, following which Elgar's financial concerns were dismissed. Shaw had made a gift to Elgar earlier in the 1930s of £1,000, and now may have quietly paid additional hospital and nursing expenses, although he could not tell the proud composer that. He had once proposed to Elgar an autobiographical Financial Symphony— "Allegro: Impending Disaster. Lento mesto: Stony Broke. Scherzo: Light Heart and Empty Pocket. All[egrett]o con brio: Clouds Clearing."

He was sending, Shaw wrote on December 5, a copy of *Too True to Be Good*, just published with another play, *On the Rocks*. Don't bother about the plays, he urged, "but read, or get Carice to read to you the part [of the preface] about Socrates, Jesus, Joan [of Arc] and Galileo, because it ends with a dialogue between Christ and Pilate which you will have to orchestrate and vocalize for the Gloucester Festival [in September 1934]. It ends with a quotation written expressly for you. . . . Meanwhile trust to your mighty Life Force and damn the doctors."

The BBC commission, Elgar responded in a letter the next day which he had to dictate, was his "greatest worry & disappointment," and he confessed being "low in mind." Before the day was out, having turned the pages of the new book, his mood had improved. He dictated a follow-up note, delighted that he had seen through the name of Shaw's gullible mediocrity of a prime minister in *On the Rocks*, Sir Arthur Chavender. Shaw's character tags, he said, pleased with himself, were "always . . . precise & inevitable," and he recalled Chavender—as critics would not—from his own "earliest Isaak Walton days." An angler from boyhood, he recognized chavender as another name for the small fish known as chub (or chevin), easily deceived and often used for bait. He may have also seen, although there is no hard evidence, a tip of Shaw's hat in the comedy *Village Wooing*, which had been published in *Nash's Pall Mall Magazine* in November 1933. In the playlet the male wooer, "A," talks of listening to "the wireless echoes of Beethoven and Elgar," a reference to the BBC and another Shavian linking of the composers.

Village Wooing was a Shavian playlet beginning aboard ship, with a writer trying, amid distractions, to write. It was a farce that Shaw had begun on his round-the-world voyage. He had kept in touch with Elgar on his travels as well as after with suggestive musical prodding, and to keep the composer's spirits up. "At Tientsin," he wrote May 30, 1933, "they had a Chinese band for me. It consisted of a lovely toned gong, a few flageolets . . . which specialized in pitch without tone, and a magnificent row of straight brass instruments reaching to the ground, with mouthpieces like . . . brass saucers quite flat, with a hole in the middle. They all played the same note, and played it all the time, like the E-flat in the Rhinegold prelude; but it was rich in harmonies, like the note of the brasses in the temple."

When the musicians paused, Shaw asked them to play other notes as well, to demonstrate the range of the brasses, but they explained that they "had never played any other note; their fathers, grandfathers and forbears right back to the Chinese Tubal Cain, had played that note and no other note, and that to assert that there was more than one note was to imply that there is more than one god. But the man with the gong rose to the occasion and proved that in China as in Europe the drummer is always the most intelligent person in the band. He snatched one of the trumpets, waved it in the air like a mail coach guard with a post horn and filled the air with flourishes and fanfares. . . . We must make the B.B.C. import a dozen of these trumpets to reinforce our piffling brasses." Shaw also described to Elgar how Chinese choruses "produce harmony" without "your laborious expedient of composing a lot of different parts to be sung simultaneously." Although they sang "in unison," they managed their voices "in some magical way that brings out all the harmonies with extraordinary richness, like big bells."

In a shaky hand, Elgar worked into the new year on the slow movement of his symphony—its opening and closing—but he could do little more. He died on February 23, 1934, having extracted a bedside pledge from Carice that no one would be permitted to "tinker" with his far-from-complete symphony. Shaw conceded in a letter to "Billy" Reed (August 17, 1934) that "no completion or reconstruction" was possible. "Like Beethoven's tenth, [it] died with the composer." Yet enough of it had survived for it to be completed more than half a century later by Anthony Payne, and performed by the BBC Symphony in 1998 to critical kudos.

"Having friends like you," Charlotte Shaw had written to Elgar for her husband as well as herself in 1932, "is the one thing in life worth having when one reaches the age of GBS & myself." Elgar would respond that "the world seems a cold place to me when you are both away." At the Gloucester Festival in the summer of 1934, for which Shaw had suggested, knowing fully well that Elgar wasn't up to it, the setting of his Christ and Pilate dialogue, an earlier Elgar work, *The Kingdom*, was performed, and both Shaws were there. "I cannot tell you how we all miss Edward Elgar," Charlotte wrote to Nancy Astor. "We loved him . . . & when another man got up into the Conductor's Chair it was hard to bear."

When GBS lay dying at Ayot St. Lawrence in 1950, Lady Astor was one of the few old friends he permitted to visit. He told her that he wanted two pieces of music at his funeral, "Libera Me" from Verdi's *Requiem* and Elgar's "We Are the Masters." Very likely he meant "We Are the Music-Makers," but a friend upon whom Lady Astor depended upon for musical expertise suggested that Shaw may have meant "We Are the Ministers" from Elgar's *The Apostles*. The selection was hardly in character for Shaw, or even the later Elgar, but it was appropriate in any case that the music of Shaw's countryman should play him out.

Bibliographic Essay

Early on, Elgar saw *Man and Superman, Arms and the Man, John Bull's Other Island, The Doctor's Dilemma, Candida,* and *Androcles and the Lion;* his comments are documented in Jerrold Northrop Moore, ed., *The Windflower Letters: [Elgar's] Correspondence with Alice Catherine Stuart Wortley and Her Family* (Oxford: Oxford University Press, 1989).

The inscription on Elgar's copy of *Music in London* is quoted by Ronald Taylor, who recalled having seen it, in his "Shaw and Elgar," in *Elgar Studies,* ed. Raymond Monk (Aldershot: Scolar Press, 1990), 221. Elgar's letter to Troyte Griffith on July 14, 1904, is quoted in Jerrold Northrop Moore, ed., *Edward Elgar: Letters of a Lifetime* (Oxford: Oxford University Press, 1990). Further Elgar letters to Shaw are from this edition.

W. H. Reed is quoted from his *Elgar as I Knew Him* (London: Trafalgar Square, 1936). Shaw edited this volume for Reed after encouraging him to write it. Shaw's letter to Virginia Woolf, May 10, 1940, was written to her to assist her biography in progress of Roger Fry. He then recycled it in a recollection he contributed to Hesketh Pearson, then writing his biography *G.B.S.*

Shaw's pitch for subsidy of composers appeared in "The Reminiscences of a Quinquagenarian," reprinted in Dan. H. Laurence, ed., *Shaw's Music,* vol. 3 (New York and London: Dodd, Mead & Bodley Head, 1981). Other Shaw musical journalism is also from this edition. Brian Trowell describes the trying out of Elgar's Piano Quintet, which Shaw attended, from the account of Canon H. T. Gardiner, and from Shaw's and Elgar's exchanges, in "Elgar's Use of Literature," in *Edward Elgar: Music and Literature,* ed. R. Monk (Aldershot: Scolar Press, 1993).

Shaw's promotion of English music as crucial to its culture appears in "The Future of British Music," *British Musical Society Bulletin,* June 1919; and again in the *Outlook,* July 19 and 26, 1919, as "Starved Arts Mean Low Pleasure." It also appeared in *Harper's Bazaar* (New York), April 1920. His and Elgar's remarks at Malvern, and the tart comment of the *Musical Times,* appear in *Borrow's Journal and Musical Times* in Monk, ed., *Edward Elgar.*

Elgar's letter to Lady Rodd, April 17, 1929, is from the facsimile of Elgar's letter reproduced in the catalog of *John Wilson (Autographs), Ltd.,* December 1997. Shaw's explanations to Elgar of his proposed rewriting of the lyrics of the national anthem appear in a letter to Associated Press correspondent Russell Landstrom, December 27, 1943, reproduced in catalog 111 of manuscript dealer Robert F. Batchelder, Ambler, Pennsylvania, 1998, as item 65.

The BBC *Radio Times* references are indebted to the notes of Leonard Conolly. BBC director John Reith's account of the symphony commission to Elgar is from his memoir *Into the Wind* (London: Hodder & Stoughton, 1949), supplemented by Andrew Boyle in *Only the Wind Will Listen* (London: Hutchinson, 1972).

Elgar's dictated letter from his sickbed to Shaw, December 6, 1933, is British Library Add. MS 50520, f. 227, quoted in Stanley Weintraub, "Elgar: Shaw's Musician," *SHAW* 22 (2002). The first London performance of Symphony no. 3, constructed by Anthony Payne from Elgar's notes and sketches, is reported by Warren Hoge in "A Change of Heart, and a Work Is Born," *New York Times*, March 12, 1998. Andrew Porter reviewed the "forceful" work as "Sketches of a sketch for a sketch" in *TLS*, London, February 27, 1998.

Also played at Shaw's obsequies in November 1950, on a large pipe organ, was the "Nimrod" section from Elgar's *Enigma Variations*.

· 8 ·

Shaw's Goddess

LADY COLIN CAMPBELL

"When I got home in the afternoon," Shaw noted in his diary on October 17, 1889, "I did a thing that has been in my mind for some time—[I] wrote to Edmund Yates asking him to give the art-criticship of *The World* to Lady Colin Campbell, as it is no longer worth my while to do so much work for so little satisfaction, not to mention money." As Shaw was not only the art reviewer "GBS" in the *World* but also, as "Corno di Bassetto" in the *Star*, the most readable music critic in London, and busy in myriad other ways, he was eager to relinquish what had become a bore. Yates admitted that in salary Shaw had been "cavalierly treated."

Decades later he would write to Frank Harris, "From Lady Colin Campbell onward, I have been familiar with celebrated beauties and with what is by no means the same thing, really beautiful women." Yet, although she had filled in for him on occasion, and he had seen her at galleries and plays and concert halls, when he gave his art columns over fully to Lady Colin he had yet to meet her.

A vivid presence and an authentic celebrity, the statuesque, dark-eyed Irishwoman, born Gertrude Elizabeth Blood in May 1858 in County Clare (and thus two years younger than Shaw), already had her own column in the *World*. In the mid-1880s she was one of the most glamorous, and most disreputable, women in England. Inauspiciously, Shaw had first encountered her on canvas. On December 8, 1886, he covered an exhibition that included a full-length portrait of her in a white bouffant satin gown by Worth of Paris, *Harmony in White and Ivory*, by James

McNeill Whistler—"which, being unfinished," GBS dismissed, "has no business in the gallery." Since Whistler was then the dictatorial president of the Society of British Artists (SBA), he got his way, although he had failed to capture her for enough sittings before her scandalous divorce court appearances ended them.

Her lawyer, Sir George Lewis, was then cross-examining one of her alleged (and actual) lovers, Lord Blandford, young Winston Churchill's unsavory uncle, who denied everything but acquaintance. Over the protests of scandalized SBA members, the publicity-seeking Whistler also exhibited in their annual show, which opened on November 19, 1886, a landscape by Lady Colin, *Glimpse of the Thalassa*. He had asked no one's consent. Whether or not she had any artistic talent was no matter. Whether or not her picture belonged in the show, *she* was a beauty.

A striking subject, portraitists sought her out. Gertrude Atherton, an expatriate American novelist who first met her in the 1890s, called her "one of the most beautiful women I have even seen; quite six feet tall but perfectly made, poised, and balanced; she reminded me of a spirited clean limbed race horse. Her eyes and hair were black, her skin of a luminous ivory hue; she had no color save her lips and used no-make-up. Unexpectedly, she had a great deal of animation, and a keen satiric, brilliant, mind."

Although Whistler made a sketch of his unfinished portrait, published in the *Pall Mall Gazette* on November 30, 1886, he was frustrated by his inability to complete it, and apparently destroyed the canvas after the exhibition. Although he had called her his "lovely leopard" and confessed that he was "heartbroken" that her "superbly sitting" for him had exhausted her, Lady Colin did not return after the trial. Another engraving of *Harmony in White and Ivory*, by Bernard Partridge, who would later do a memorable drawing of Shaw rehearsing *Arms and the Man*, appeared in the illustrated magazine *Judy* on December 8, 1886. Whatever its variations, Lady Colin's striking portrait was all Shaw would see of her until April 29, 1890, by which time she had assumed most of his art assignments, and Shaw had moved his music columns, signed now "GBS," from the *Star* to Yates's *World*.

Always known by the aristocratic courtesy title of the husband she had left in 1884, suing then for a legal separation on grounds of cruelty, Lady Colin in 1886 had further petitioned for a divorce, citing their housemaid. Lord Colin Campbell countersued, naming four corespondents, one the womanizing Lord Blandford, heir to the Duke of Marlborough (and elder brother of the politician Lord Randolph Churchill) and already divorced because of his very public affair with the Countess of Aylesford. After eighteen days of scabrous testimony, the jury rejected both petitions. Lady Colin's career as a society ornament was over. But with her connections, she fashioned a career as a journalist that could cash in on her notoriety.

Lady Colin remained as much reviewed as the pictures at elite gallery openings she attended, and she was often noted as the most striking embellishment. In the year of the sensational divorce trial she was seen at the Grosvenor Gallery, "in historic black, relieved only by a yellow flower." She had learned that device from other Whistler portraits. At the New Gallery, a critic wrote, "No show is complete without Lady Colin Campbell, who looked wonderfully well in dress and daring green hat." At the Royal Academy private view she "stood waiting, splendidly turned out"—again—"in historic black, set off by an exquisite spray of yellow orchids, looking secure in her beauty."

With two beautiful daughters to marry off, Gertrude's ambitious mother had visited friends at a country house in Scotland to gain access to the aristocracy, and angled for an heir to the eighth Duke of Argyll. At a country house party in September 1880 the Duke warned Mrs. Blood that his playboy youngest son was unfit to be a husband, and paid midnight visits to the beds of Argyll's maidservants. She assumed that the Duke was merely rejecting her dowryless daughters, who had no social standing.

Nonetheless, Gertrude intended to be a Lady. Lord Colin Campbell considered himself engaged to her three days after they met. Since she was an elderly twenty-two and further handicapped by being Irish, time was running out for her. Despite objections from his family that delayed the nuptials, they married on July 21, 1881.

Lady Colin quickly discovered his infidelities. She amused herself in return, confident in her beauty and in the cover of her husband's affairs. As Mrs. Atherton put it, men succumbed "like grain before the reaper." When, to tame her, Lord Colin resorted to what the newspapers reported happily as cruelty that "would not bear printing," she sued for a judicial separation, which was granted in March 1884.

Two years later she sued for divorce on grounds of infidelity and cruelty, alleging that he had knowingly infected her with syphilis, a word the sensational coverage in the newspapers had to eschew. He countersued, identifying four co-respondents: Lord Blandford; General Sir William

Butler (husband of the famous battle painter Elizabeth Thompson Butler); the fashionable surgeon Thomas Bird; and Eyre Massey Shaw, the chief of the Metropolitan Fire Brigade and famous enough to be satirized in Gilbert and Sullivan's *Iolanthe*.

While W. T. Stead exploited the trial in his *Pall Mall Gazette* (much boosting its circulation), he also deplored it as "the filthiest case ever reported." The staid *Times* published twenty-six columns by its zealous court reporter, while the *Chronicle* offered seventy-four. One newspaper charged her with having "the unbridled lust of a Messalina and the indelicate readiness of a common harlot." In her defense, her attorneys noted charitable activities, ranging from helping out in an East End soup kitchen to teaching factory girls in evening classes, that would have left little opportunity for gross dalliance. Sanctimoniously, despite his own coverage, Stead charged that the *Morning Chronicle* gave the trial only 1,258 fewer words than were in the entire New Testament.

When the jury denied her a divorce, Lady Colin was left with little more than a twice-shattered reputation. With few material assets after her trial other than her jewels, her clothes, and herself, she had only her court-ordered separation allowance. Deftly, she put her literary verve to further use as a journalist. She was already a published writer. A children's book set in Italy, *Topo*, embellished with illustrations by the ultra-respectable Kate Greenaway, had been published in 1878 as by "G. E. Brunefille" (a self-description), and in *Cassell's Family Magazine* she had published travel pieces about Italy, Turkey and Egypt.

Clever pseudonyms were the fashion. And it helped to have editors who had fattened their circulation figures on her court proceedings. Among those who exploited the judicial record was Frank Harris, who had been indicted for obscene libel for publishing verbatim what was openly cited in court testimony. Although he lost his job as editor of the *Evening News*, which had doubled its readership during the trial, he landed on his feet as editor of the *Fortnightly Review*. When the libel case had come up before Mr. Justice George Denman, Harris defended himself by pointing to his most respectable competitor. "The standard of what is becoming [acceptable in print]," he explained, "varies in every country and age. I could do no better with a half-penny paper than keep within the limits established by *The Times*. This I have done." He placed the two accounts side by side before Justice Denman, who dismissed the case.

Filing new objections into mid-1887, Sir George Lewis, Lady Colin's eminent society attorney, held off her husband's plea for a new trial to clear himself. In the end Lord Colin never paid the required deposit of £125 as security for his wife's costs.

Urged by the formerly smitten (but now vanished) Lord Blandford to find Lady Colin gainful employment, Frank Harris offered her work. His own taste for tarts, and for crude talk about his exploits, precluded any other interest in him on her part. Downplaying to intimates (including Shaw) her physical assets unavailable to him, he referred to her characteristically as a "fat-arsed bitch." (She disdained corsets). Writing years afterward to Harris, down on his luck, in a letter intended for Harris to publish or sell, Shaw joked that Lady Colin was "someone you used to describe in your best buccaneering English as a lumbarly exuberant female dog."

At the invitation of Edmund Yates of the *World*, she began a regular column, "A Woman's Walks," which exploited her Continental worldliness. Shaw, who also wrote for Yates, described her columns as "impudently amusing." She had grown up in Paris and Florence, spoke excellent French and Italian, and knew art and artists as well as she knew high society. Just as Shaw would pretend in the *World*'s pages to be the musically sophisticated "Corno di Bassetto" (Italian for basset horn), "Vera Tsaritsyn" occasionally invoked her nonexistent Russian heritage. "I suddenly happen," she wrote about exploring the exotica at the Duveen Gallery, "upon a somewhat familiar sight—a small Russian sleigh, with the silver-mounted harness (sadly tarnished by London fog) all complete."

Shaw appreciated her quick wit and admired her cool, confident sexuality. She dismissed Oscar Wilde, he recalled, as "that great white caterpillar." (Although Shaw misremembered the term—she had called Oscar a "Great White Slug"—Wilde bridled at the slur and was not on speaking terms with her.) Rather than disappear in the shadows of scandal, she looked it in the face, and Shaw recognized her obvious courage as a working woman down on her luck. When the Society of Authors gave a dinner at the Criterion Restaurant to honor American writers in England for their support of copyright legislation at home, she was there as a recognized English author—and seated next to Wilde, who protested and was moved farther apart.

Her bravado seems to have been, quite literally, in the blood. An ancestor was Colonel Thomas Blood, once sketched in a "visionary head" by William Blake, one of Shaw's heroes. Blood (1618–81) was a Cromwellian adventurer whose Irish properties were confiscated at the

Restoration by henchmen of Charles II. In 1663 Colonel Blood plotted kidnaping the Lord Lieutenant from Dublin Castle, to ransom back family lands, but was betrayed. Although he evaded capture, his confederates were hanged. Undaunted, in 1671 Blood and three accomplices with rapiers hidden in their canes tied up the Keeper of the Regalia in the Tower of London, stealing the Crown, the Globe, and the Sceptre. When caught, Colonel Blood refused to confess where they were hidden except to the king in a private audience. King Charles agreed to see Blood, was charmed by him, and restored the colonel's estates.

Feistiness was in the family. Gertrude's Galway-born cousin was General Sir Bindon Blood, a decorated veteran of many Victorian colonial wars, who would stubbornly remain on the active list until he was ninety-two.

Shaw enjoyed Lady Colin's colorful columns, which were witty, knowledgeable, and replete with the unexpected. At a time of year when few days were fit for walking she suggested that the rare "fine days might be remembered by name, like the feasts of the saints." She explored Madame Tussaud's waxworks, the barges and houseboats along the Thames Embankment, new plays and old in the West End theater district, the Law Courts at the Inner Temple, the Spitalfields silk weavers off Bishopgate, the workrooms of East London embroiderers, the Zoo in Regent's Park, and the Bond Street arts and antiques showrooms. At least for her readers, and Victorian decorum, she seemed to travel with a companion, perhaps not always the one invented for her column. One was a small boy taken to "breathing on the window-panes and drawing patterns thereon with the end of a button nose." Another is clearly a lady, as "the tic-tac of our heels rang out with resonant rhythm; for, mindful of [Viscount] Palmerston's remark about the unspeakable Turk—'What can you expect from a nation that have no heels to their shoes?'—my friend and I are by no means inclined to discard those excellent contrivances which, like the pattens of our grandmothers, keep us out of the mud." The sweep of her allusiveness for one who, like Shaw, acquired most of her education informally from life and the library, is remarkable.

After examining a refuge for stray dogs "tucked away under the arches of the London, Chatham, and Dover Railway" at Pimlico, she wrote brightly in her next column, "Having gone to the dogs last week, it was clearly indicated by the finger of Fate that I should go to the cats immediately after, and consequently last week found me on my pilgrimage to the Crystal Palace, to see the twenty-first annual Cat Show held by the National Cat Club."

Her social conscience was outspoken. Once she suggested in print that to prevent "the extermination of the silk trade" in England, there should be "a society whose members should pledge themselves to wear no silks, velvets, or brocades that are not manufactured by English workmen for English women." As late as her 106th column, as they became more occasional with the burden of other assignments, she wrote a piece about Dr. Barnardo's homes for "waifs and strays," about which there was an exhibition at the Coliseum in St. Martin's Lane. She even risked embarrassment for good causes, once making an appearance for a fundraiser at the Bermondsey Town Hall, just south of the Thames below Stepney, for the Popular Music Union, established to educate "the industrial classes." Having nothing to fear but the snootiness of others, as through the coaching of composer Paolo Tosti she had a well-trained contralto, she volunteered to sing.

Corno di Bassetto came. The professionals in the announcement were identified in small print, but, wrote Bassetto, who as a lark reviewed the program in the *Star* on April 13, 1889, "The vocalist announced in colossal letters suitable to a star of the first magnitude was Lady Colin Campbell. This piece of snobbery annoyed me to begin with." Then, jokingly referring to his own alleged snobbery (via his pen name) as a distinguished Italian critic, he complained in mock outrage that he was "not formally received, as I should have been, by the Mayor and Corporation of Bermondsey. Further, in spite of my card of invitation, I was only admitted to a seat worthy of my dignity on payment of a sixpence extra. But I never spare money in the service of the public. Bang went the coin without a murmur from me." However, Shaw slipped out at the interval, evading having to review Lady Colin's performance. Forever her admirer, even tongue-in-cheek, he noted in the *Star* on June 14 that a "vulgar and disrespectful ruffian" in the stalls at a performance of *Don Giovanni* blathered while the conductor was taking his place, "'Good old Lady Colin,' as the most divinely tall of the art critics took her place in front of me and extinguished my view of the stage."

"Vera" turned up often where social-minded aristocratic ladies could do some good. The *Star* and the *Sun* sent their society reporters to the grand opening of Mrs. Isabel Cooper-Oakley's first restaurant for West End working girls in June 1889. Celebrities ranged from countesses to Constance Wilde, Oscar's spouse; Shaw's good friend of myriad causes,

Annie Besant; and the theosophist guru, Madame Blavatsky. According to the gushing *Sun*, which singled out Lady Colin, she, "of course, looked charming, as she always does, and all the other women," the reporter lied, "looked charming likewise." A crowd of the uninvited pressed their noses against the windows to watch the more daring of the female gentility smoke cigarettes.

In her own columns, "Vera" displayed a wry sense of humor, describing going "up a stair so steep that I find myself wishing for a hooked nose, that I might climb with, like a parrot, and we emerge through a hole in the upper story." Her Irish Catholic upbringing emerged with the admission, after a lengthy examination at Duveen's Gallery, of "marvellous" Beauvais tapestries by Boucher, "I am not tired, only covetous; but as I believe that is one of the natural feelings we are told to renounce by the Catechism, some remnant of early teaching suddenly bears fruit." Visiting a venerable church off the Strand, she cast her eye upon the sarcophagus of the helmeted crusader Sir Geoffrey de Magnaville—"a most truculent-looking individual, who in default of a better headpiece, has fitted himself into a saucepan." Viewing at Tussaud's a sculpture in wax of Napoleon on his deathbed, she gave way to womanly feeling, describing his face as "one of the most beautiful ever given to man" and as "modelled from the original cast taken from the Emperor himself by [Francesco] Antommarchi, an Italian physician, sent out to St. Helena." Dressed in the chausseur uniform he wore as a youthful general, he was "covered with the cloak he wore at Marengo in 1800." Shaw, who would shortly write a hero-worshiping play about the young Napoleon of the Marengo period, *The Man of Destiny*, may have taken note. Later she collected some of her columns as *A Woman's Walks: Studies in Colour Abroad and at Home* (1903).

Impatient at the time to abandon the art galleries in order to have more time for the concert halls, Shaw proposed to Edmund Yates, his editor, that he drop the art assignments and take on more of the music. Since Yates declared, "I have no idea of loosening my hold on you," Shaw's last *Star* column as "Bassetto" appeared in May 1890 and he became "GBS" in the *World*.

Months after he proposed Lady Colin as his replacement, Shaw met her for the first time when she introduced herself on April 29, 1890, at the New Gallery. In that efficient pre-electronic era, when letters posted in London that morning were often delivered the same day, negotiations could be conducted by mail, and, Shaw recalled, Lady Colin—who disliked coyness—"used to get me to put 'the feminine touch' into her [business] letters to Yates." As late as December 29, 1891, Shaw would write of visiting her at 5:30 as the afternoon waned to help her "redraft" a proposal to the *World*—"and this occupied me until it was time to hurry off to the lecture" he was to give to the Goulburn Liberal Club.

It was the beginning of an unusual friendship. Although Yates did not want to lose Shaw as art critic, Shaw made his preferences clear in a review that appeared on October 23, 1889: "I cannot guarantee my very favorable impression of the Hanover Gallery, as I only saw it by gaslight. This is the fault of Sarasate, who played the Ancient Mariner with me. He fixed me with his violin on my way to Bond Street, and though, like the wedding guest, I tried my best, I could not but choose to hear." As "Q.E.D.," Lady Colin published her first regular art column in Shaw's place on December 11, 1889.

William Archer had secured Shaw his art critic assignment with the *World*, having taken it on to let his unemployed friend write the columns, and then identifying the ghost critic to Yates. To Archer, Shaw wrote the day before his Hanover Gallery valedictory appeared that he had persuaded Yates that "he should hand over the job" to Lady Colin, "who could include the exhibitions in her 'Woman's Walks.'" But Yates also wanted to keep her column going, and offered "to put all the minor exhibitions on to Lady C.C.; to take eight [GBS] articles a year on the big exhibitions at the usual rate, and to pay me besides £52 a year as retainer. After this I cannot complain as to money; but I am hanged if I know what to say." The deal seemed too good to pass up, but in November 1890 he had second thoughts and turned all the art over to Lady Colin.

Shaw's friendship with "Vera," as she was known to intimates, began, it seems, in his admiring a goddess fallen from Olympus. Looking down on people "from her not less than seventy inches" with her unforgettable dark eyes, she was not easy to put out of mind. She rode brilliantly; she swam when it was still unfashionable for ladies; she even fenced. Despite their Irish backgrounds, Shaw's bohemian ambience remained a barrier, although she knew many of his theatrical friends. In any case, more approachable women overwhelmed his amorous life, and some from his socialist set unsuccessfully pursued him. Nonetheless, Shaw would write Lady Colin long letters, send her books, including his own *Fabian Essays* of 1889, and often seemed to deliberately neglect to note their meetings into his diaries—sometimes not even that they happened. Once in December 1890 he received a letter in the morning asking him to be at her flat at 67 Carlyle Mansions in Chelsea early in the afternoon, and his diary notes that there he met Victor Maurel, who had originated the Iago role in English performances of Verdi's *Otello*. Vera thought that the famous baritone's lectures on singing needed some promotion. She arranged a meeting, and Shaw, writing as GBS, published an interview touting Maurel for her.

Henry James, her sometime neighbor in Carlyle Mansions, had little direct association with Lady Colin but became aware through mutual friends of her assistance to his acquaintance Mabel Huntington, who was beset by debts run up by her estranged husband. "Oddly enough," James explained to Francis Boot, "the person who, in combination with the lawyers, is helping and advising her in the matter, is Lady Colin Campbell." James commended her "kindness and sympathy." James was a bit afraid of her. According to Gertrude Atherton, who once was visiting when he called on Lady Colin, "She dropped her broad white eyelids over smouldering eyes, extended a languid hand; her voice was alluring." Before his "precipitate retreat" he chatted "as if every sentence had been carefully rehearsed; every semi-colon, every comma was in exactly the right place."

Few knew of Shaw's visits, although he continued to drum up writing assignments for her. When, in March 1891, Ibsen's *Ghosts* was pilloried in the press as "an open drain" and "a dirty act done publicly," Shaw arranged with the *World* to have Lady Colin do a special article "in which she played up [Ibsen] heroically," he wrote to Charles Charrington, husband of the lead actress, Janet Achurch. Yates did not know of it until he read the column while on holiday at Bath. He was helplessly irate. "Was it his conscientious Puritanism," Shaw wondered to Archer, the play's translator, "or his countryhouse circulation that was imperilled then?"

In print in the *World*, Lady Colin at first sounded much like Shaw. Even later, as Shaw substituted for her under her "Q.E.D." byline when she was away, or was otherwise engaged, it was not easy to tell them apart. Yates objected vainly to paying her for Shaw's ghosting. Once, when she was ill, Shaw dropped drafting his own music column to review a clutch of art books for her, and to go gallery-hopping in her place. Questioning in Shavian fashion the value of "didactic" prefatory notes in exhibition catalogs after reading Frederick Wedmore's introduction to Augustus Weedon's watercolors at the Fine Arts Society in Bond Street, she wrote, "I congratulated myself on having seen the sketches before reading the note, as my enjoyment of the pictures had consequently been unmarred." Was it actually Shaw? Going on to the Dunthorne Gallery to see Wilfred Ball's watercolors, she observed, again much like Shaw, "'Comparisons are odoriferous,' said Mrs. Malaprop, and it is not my intention to make any, for it is somewhat of an absurdity ever to compare work by two different artists, who each see things and effects through different spectacles."

In April 1893 Shaw began his second play, *The Philanderer. Widowers' Houses*, the year before, had lasted only two performances. Inverting all audience expectations, economic as well as romantic, it was attacked in the press even by the usually loyal Archer. The second of what he would call his "unpleasant plays"—there would be still another—would deal again with sex as a cold power game. By mid-June he had finished a draft in several notebooks, completing it outdoors under a warm morning sun on Primrose Hill, just above Regents Park, and taking it that afternoon, June 17, to Carlyle Mansions and Lady Colin, who knew all about philanderers and the social and legal lot of independent-minded women.

Shaw read all the parts stylishly to his audience of one. Even if the script passed the Lord Chamberlain's theatrical censorship office and was licensed, Vera warned when he finished, it would fail with the public. "She pointed out to me," Shaw told his diary, "that the third act at which I have been writing ought to be put in the fire. This opened my eyes for the first time to the fact that I have started on quite a new trail and must reserve this act for a new play." The "new trail" seems to have been the discussion comedy, on which Shaw focused with great success more than a decade later in *Getting Married, Misalliance*, and *Heartbreak House.*

He wrote in the sixth of his shilling notebooks used for *The Philanderer*, at the end of the act, "cancel all the foregoing"—and five days later reopened his notebook and began anew. After putting it down to go to a matinee he had to cover, he returned to Primrose Hill in the long light of a summer evening to work unsatisfactorily on his music review and to finish the last act "as suggested by Lady Colin." The substitute scene was more cautious than the original on marriage and divorce. The earlier acts of the play had focused on Leonard Charteris, a thirtyish philanderer and man-about-town who had divided his attentions between Julia Craven and Grace Tranfield. The original third act had shifted focus to Dr. Percy Paramore, who, in the dining room of his house, is celebrating either the third or the fourth (the manuscript is inconsistent) anniversary of his marriage to Julia, whom Charteris had abandoned for Grace. Paramore now wants a divorce. He had fallen in love with Grace. All the principal characters gather to discuss the dilemma. Love and marriage remain in uneasy imbalance.

In the revised ending, the later years are eliminated, and one character—a comic butler. Paramore proposes to the discarded Julia, and Charteris is rejected by Grace, lamenting to her, "Yes, this is the doom of the philanderer. I shall have to go on philandering now all my life." It is a more mechanical "well-made play" conclusion. Although Shaw preferred his longer original, he had accepted Lady Colin's pragmatism. After reading the new scene to Janet Achurch and Charles Charrington on June 28, Shaw bought some chessmen "to work out the stage positions in my play," but only on August 24 does his diary record returning to read the revision to Lady Colin. She was apparently satisfied, but he would write to Janet about his frustrations in getting the play produced, "I am struggling with an almost overpowering temptation to burn The Philanderer." J. T. Grein, who had little success with Shaw's first play, found the second equally unpleasant from an audience standpoint, and overtures to other producers failed. Only in 1907 was it professionally staged, running for only eight matinees. Decades after Shaw's death, and the end of censorship, the play would be performed restoring the longer last act vetoed by Lady Colin, still surviving in the original notebook. It worked. Perhaps social change had accomplished what she and Shaw had not visualized in 1893.

Actors and acting often surfaced in her columns, and she also risked writing plays and fiction. When the Charringtons (with Janet Achurch in each work) presented a quintuple bill at Terry's Theatre in June 1893, along with short plays by James Barrie, Conan Doyle, Thomas Hardy, and the forgotten Walter Pollock, they included a farce by Lady Colin, *Bud and Blossom*. To promote her playlet, Shaw wrote an imagined interview for the *Star* that he sent to her for approval. Based on their friendship, it was entirely his own invention, in the spirit of the satiric self-interviews he would always enjoy composing.

> The spoof interviewer was frightfully nervous. "You may interview me," said Lady Colin Campbell, "within limits."
>
> Imagine a lady with lightning wit, a merciless sense of humor, a skill in journalism surpassing that of any interviewer, a humiliatingly obvious power of reckoning you up at a glance, and probably

not thinking much of you, a superb bearing that brings out all the abjectness in your nature, and a beauty the mere fame of which makes you fall into an attitude of amateurishly gallant homage that fulfils the measure of your sneaking confusion. The custom is for the interviewer to describe the subject of an interview as his "victim." It is not possible to express how completely the tables were turned on this occasion....

The interviewer's scattered thoughts collected themselves about her voice. The comparatively low pitch, the clear, delicate touch, the rare mixture of decision and tenderness in the tone! Had the interviewer heard something like it before? The pitch and clearness from the Queen, perhaps.... Here the interviewer's hat fell into the fireplace, but such was his nervous incapacity for acting like a man of sense that he pretended not to notice it.

However playful, Shaw's buildup to the mock interview also suggested the authentic awe he always felt in Lady Colin's presence. Still, he could joke playfully about their Irish beginnings, and he quoted her as contending that her playwriting (only a wisp of her work)[1] represented "the Irish School and not the Celtic School; for to describe an Irishwoman as a Celt is about as sensible as to describe Tintoretto as an Italian."

"I always thought of him as an Italian," the interviewer admits sheepishly, revealing a limited sense of history. (Italy as an entity didn't exist in Tintoretto's time.)

"No doubt you did," Lady Colin the art critic admonishes. "In future, think of him as a Venetian. Since I have written a farce, I suppose I must have a school; and I wish you therefore to understand that my school is not the British-domestic, nor the Anglo-Norwegian, nor the Fabian-sociological, but that I am a most humble follower of the great Irish school of Swift, Goldsmith, and Sheridan."

"They're out of date, rather, aren't they?" the interviewer ventures timidly. "Wouldn't it be better to mention Oscar Wilde, and George Moore, and Bernard Shaw? They're all Irish, you know."

He is put down firmly with, "I think you had better confine yourself to what I tell you, as far as you can remember it."

---

[1] In 1902, in collaboration with Clotilde Graves, she would produce, in Brighton, *St. Martin's Summer*, a melodrama starring William and Madge Kendal, which did not make it to London.

"The fact is," the man from the *Star* apologizes, "I am not accustomed to fashionable society."

"You are not in fashionable society. I am a hard-working member of your own profession; and I could have lived on my earnings as a critic when some of the young gentlemen who will patronise me next week as a fashionable amateur were in [public school] jackets and turndown collars. . . . I have also tried my hand at novel writing, but the novel form does not suit me. . . . I have always thought playwriting the only satisfactory and entirely attractive form of literature—far more so than acting itself; for it is so much more manysided. If I acted at all I should want to play all the parts, which might create unpleasantness with the company and would certainly end in carving-knives if had not my own way." Even in creating his cringing reporter Shaw could hardly have been more Shavian, but readers would have assumed only a Lady Colin superiority.

When she rises majestically, indicating that the interview is at an end, and is being thanked obsequiously for her kindness, Lady Colin condescends to a "Very well; put in all the brilliant things you intended to say." And the discomfited newspaperman escapes, to reappear in Shaw's *The Doctor's Dilemma* (1906).

During the "interview" Lady Colin confesses that she had written an earlier play. She (or Shaw) exaggerated. It was a collaborative work, with Shaw's friend Janet Achurch, who had originated the Nora Helmer role in the English production of Ibsen's *A Doll's House* in 1889. Both Shaw and Achurch had used a Maupassant story as the springboard for a play. It was Shaw's third, begun in a notebook in a country pasture three days after he had read the new ending of *The Philanderer* to Vera.

For the new work, Shaw had Janet Achurch in mind to play the formidable young heroine, Vivie Warren, although Janet could no longer be visually convincing as a recent Cambridge undergraduate. As she learned about the progress of the script, she persuaded herself that she could do better, and began, with Lady Colin, her own treatment. Both women would get to know *Mrs Warren's Profession* well. He read it to a half-dozen friends, including Florence Farr (then his mistress), Janet and her husband, and, on December 2, 1893, to Lady Colin. Vera would help Janet to finish her version, *Mrs. Daintree's Daughter*. It would never find a producer, although, unhandicapped by Shaw's hint of incest, it was licensed by the Lord Chamberlain's Office—as Shaw's was not. When a script-in-hand "copyright performance" was acted at Ladbroke Hall on February 14, 1894, Shaw read three of the parts. He does not mention in his diary what role Lady Colin took—very likely Mrs. Warren herself—but only that she returned with him "as far as Edgware Rd." Shaw's own play remained commercially barred from the stage in England, other than in ostensibly private performances, until the 1920s.

Lady Colin's freedom to do as she pleased was largely due to the self-immunity of her style. Possibly the only lady in England quite like her was Lady Randolph Churchill (also Shaw's friend), who sailed superbly through her husband's scandals and her own, and was entirely liberated by his death in 1895. Lord Colin Campbell, who held the family-dominated parliamentary seat for Argyllshire until impending disgrace forced him to relinquish it in 1885, had disappeared to Bombay. He died there of drink and venereal disease—also in 1895. Legally, financially, and emotionally, it freed his widow, but Lady Colin preferred writing to remarrying. She may have realized, too, that her dreaded inheritance from his debauchery was already beginning to gnaw at her, a real-life shadow of Ibsen's *Ghosts*.

In 1894 Lady Colin founded a weekly, the *Realm*, which folded in a year, but, undaunted, took on the editorship of *Ladies' Field* from 1901 into 1903. She wrote a popular novel about a shady journalist and a scheming society dame, *Darrell Blake* (1889), and collected some of her essays in *A Book of the Running Brook, Still Waters*, and *A Miracle in Rabbits*. In *Etiquette and Good Society* (1893), a guide that sold ninety-two thousand copies, she defined a lady in her own terms as one who would "never try, by any means, to appear other than she really is." On occasion Shaw, by then the leading drama critic in London, and finally a successful playwright, still advised her when asked. Twice he noted in his diary visits to her *Realm* offices. Very likely there were more, but his diary, now full of gaps, would soon break off. In November 1897 he wrote to his future wife, Charlotte Payne-Townshend, then holidaying in Paris, that he had just seen Lady Colin, "who wanted to consult me about professional business."

Nearly forty then, Lady Colin had just been painted, life-size, by Giovanni Boldini, who had been made wealthy by his lubricious depictions of Italian models, often in the altogether, and by sensual portraits of wealthy Continental society dames. The canvas of Lady Colin—now in the National Portrait Gallery in London—hung in her drawing room. In contrast to the lost Whistler, it pictured her in a black gown leaning against a plush settee, her dark hair curled and tumbling down her left shoulder. A hint of a smile crosses her face. Beneath the hem of her draped gown her long legs are visible. She seems to have wanted a portrait by which to remember herself before it was too late.

Shaw's last known letter from her, dated from Carlyle Mansions on January 19, 1901, warmly thanks "GBS" for sending her his play collection *Three Plays for Puritans*. (Almost certainly she also shelved the earlier works.) She had "wanted them badly," she confessed, and had made her wishes known. Now she had a suggestion for his next volume: "'Plays for Pagans'? I will graciously accept the dedication. . . . I wish you would come & see me. Why should the joys of matrimony even with so charming a wife as you have . . . make you forget & neglect old friends? . . . So please amend your ways." She promised to be "unfailingly at home," for she was "gruesomely busy" (a telling adverb) and felt at times like the juggler Paul Cinquevalli[2] "racing about the stage." She signed herself, "Yours ever, Vera C."

Shaw's next play, the massive *Man and Superman*, with its "Don Juan in Hell" play-within-a-play, which he began in a notebook that May, could well be the "Plays for Pagans" she wanted. Very likely she never saw the result performed. Would she have recognized anything of herself in it? The feline heroine, a "lioness" in Shaw's notes for the play, suggests something of Vera. Ann Whitefield has "ensnaring eyes and hair," combines "audacity" and "vitality" with "perfect dignity" in what Shaw describes as "brave unconventionality," allegedly "makes you will your own destruction," and contends that "all passions should be moral." But deflecting the interest in art that impelled Shaw to make Lady Colin his successor as art critic, he has Ann declare, as complete philistine, "Beauty is all very well at first sight. but who ever looks at it when it has been in the house three days? I thought our pictures very lovely when papa bought them, but I havnt looked at them for years."

Whether or not Shaw had Lady Colin in mind as a dimension of Ann, his frame-play subplot about Violet Robinson inverts Vera's own background. Lady Colin's ambitious Irish mother had left John Bull's other island to seek an Establishment aristocrat for her daughter to ensnare and wed. In *Man and Superman* the wealthy, Irish-born Hector Malone comes to England (from America) determined to have his son marry a

---

2 "Cinquevalli" (1859–1918), born Emile Otto Braun-Lehmann in Posen, then part of Prussia, ran away from home at fourteen and joined an Italian troupe of acrobats led by Guiseppe Chiese-Cinquevalli. A master of balancing objects, he became the first juggling superstar. Paul Cinquevalli may have inspired Shaw's attributing juggling feats to the Polish aerialist and acrobat Lina Szczepanowska in *Misalliance*.

titled upper-class bride fit for a castle Malone is prepared to buy for the pair.

Shaw did not complete the long play until 1903, and the Hell Scene (his "play for pagans") was not performed separately for two more years. Lady Colin would have especially approved of the preface where Shaw spoke in Bunyanesque terms of the joy in life in consuming one's self in usefulness, for in an interview she had given in 1902 she had spoken of work—Ladies included—as "the justification of living at all, the rent we are bound to pay to Nature for the actual space we occupy in the world." One can only wonder who was echoing whom.

By then, Sir Edward Burne-Jones, near the end of his life, had attempted to paint Vera, but she was showing signs of the painful progressive paralysis that would lead to her death at fifty-three. According to Gertrude Atherton, who loyally visited her, Lady Colin's beautiful hands were becoming distorted, and the fastidious Burne-Jones would neither paint them nor fake them.

Her long-dormant catastrophe, described as rheumatoid arthritis, although it could have had a venereal inheritance from Lord Colin, gradually left her wheelchair-bound and by 1906 restricted to her rooms. The Boldini portrait would overlook what was becoming its real-life grotesque. Certainly no one who visited her then (Shaw left no record that he did) would have reminded her of its fictional inversion in Wilde's ghoulish portrait of the ever-youthful Dorian Gray. Lady Colin's luxuriant hair had turned white; her dark eyes lost their luster; her tall figure thickened with inactivity. She claimed to Mrs. Atherton that she had not looked into a mirror for four years. Yet in the company of her most intimate women friends, almost the only people she would still permit to visit, like the ebullient (and by then socialist) Countess of Warwick, the dreamy poet Alice Meynell, the romantic novelist Marie Belloc-Lowndes, and the faithful Duchess of Sutherland, she struggled to remain as vivacious as she could, her contralto still startlingly echoing her former self.

Toward the end, her devoted French maid and companion, worn out by illness herself and by the strain of Lady Colin's care, predeceased her, and life became even less tolerable. With Boldini's portrait still looking down, she died at Carlyle Mansions on November 1, 1911, and was cremated at her wish at Golders Green on November 5. Cautiously, the *Times* wrote that "rheumatism" forced her retirement from active life and "ultimately crippled her." The mourners included Henry James, Sir

Bindon Blood, her ladies, and a clutch of Shaw's friends, like Sir Robert Cunninghame Graham. But, surprisingly, not Shaw. Like Vera he was a pragmatist who believed in cremation, and decades later, Golders Green would receive him also. However, he was in the country, at relatively nearby Ayot St. Lawrence, and his absence at her obsequies remains unexplained. Perhaps she was now only remotely a part of Shaw's past, although she lives on in his writings, and in her own lively work which he helped make possible.

Bibliographic Essay

A brief biography of Lady Colin by K. D. Reynolds appears in the *Oxford Dictionary of National Biography* (Oxford: Oxford University Press, 2004) and includes references to her children's novel and other early writings. Its only reference to Shaw, in passing, does not suggest any Shavian dimension in her life. The letter to Frank Harris, September 18, 1930, about "celebrated beauties" was intended for Harris's biography *Bernard Shaw* (New York: Simon and Schuster, 1931), where it was published in slightly expurgated form. It appears complete in the *Collected Letters*, vol. 4. Shaw's letters to Lady Colin are *Collected Letters*, vols. 1 and 2. The "white caterpillar" description of Wilde is quoted by Shaw to Frank Harris on January 15, 1917. That and other references to Frank Harris and Oscar Wilde are from Stanley Weintraub, *Shaw's People: Victoria to Churchill* (University Park: Penn State Press, 1996). Diary entries are from Stanley Weintraub, ed., *Bernard Shaw: The Diaries, 1885–1897* (University Park: Penn State Press, 1986). Shaw's art reviews are from Stanley Weintraub, ed., *Bernard Shaw on the London Art Scene, 1885–1950* (University Park: Penn State Press, 1989). Whistler's frustrations with completion of his Lady Colin portrait are described in Stanley Weintraub, *Whistler: A Biography* (New York: Weybright, 1974).

The divorce trial was covered by all the London press from broadsheets to such gossip weeklies as *Town Talk* and *Hawk*. W. T. Stead's claims about coverage of the trial by the London press are from Raymond L. Schults, *Crusader in Babylon: W. T. Stead and Pall Mall Gazette* (Lincoln: University of Nebraska Press, 1972. The quotation about Lady Colin at the divorce hearing from an unidentified newspaper is from the *Oxford DNB*.

Lady Colin's manuscript letter to Shaw, January 19, 1901, is from British Library Add. MS 50516. Shaw's whimsical interview with Lady Colin is from the *Star*, June 2, 1893. Quotations from "A Woman's Walks" by Vera Tsaritsyn and "In the Picture Galleries" by "Q.E.D." are from issues of the *World* as described from 1889 through 1893.

That the last act of *The Philanderer*, cut on Lady Colin's recommendation, was the germ of Shaw's discussion comedies is suggested persuasively by Brian F. Tyson in "Shaw's First Discussion Play: An Abandoned Act of *The Philanderer*," *Shaw Review* 12 (September 1969). Shaw's notebook beginnings of *Don Juan in Hell*, May 31, 1901, are British Library Add. MSS 50735 and 50727. He followed these notes by a scenario, "The Superman, or Don Juan's great grandson's grandson," dated July 2, 1901, eleven leaves now in the Berg Collection of the New York Public Library. This latter manuscript is reproduced by Charles W. Berst in "Superman Theater: Gusts, Galumphs, and Grumps," *SHAW* 16 (1996).

Lady Colin's view of work as the justification of living is quoted from Baroness de Bertouche, "Lady Colin Campbell," *Crampton's Magazine* 19 (1902). Gertrude Atherton is quoted from her *Adventures of a Novelist* (New York: Blue Ribbon Books, 1932) and from Emily Wortis Leider, *California's Daughter: Gertrude Atherton and Her Times* (Stanford: Stanford University Press, 1991).

The *Times* in November 1911 published an obituary of Lady Colin and also an account of her obsequies at Golders Green, with a full list of mourners. In her will she left her portrait by Boldini to the National Portrait Gallery.

· 9 ·

Shaw's Sculptress

KATHLEEN SCOTT

Many years into their long friendship, Bernard Shaw told Kathleen Scott (she had sculpted him, wearing then-unfeminine coveralls or slacks), "No woman ever born had a narrower escape from being a man. My affection for you is the nearest I ever came to homosexuality." Lady Scott, widow of the Antarctic explorer, nevertheless always had trouble deflecting admirers. Nor did she try very hard. Devotees often became subjects for her chisel, and if not then, they became helpless with admiration as they sat for her.

A friend late in her life, who would write Kathleen's obituary in advance (and by request) for the *Times* in 1937, ten years before she died, called her "alleged vamping of distinguished men" empty charges that were "rubbish." Rather, "famous men sought K. out, even those who were not being modelled," and she would claim in pleased vanity that she had "volumes" of letters from them. Shaw's alone would make a small volume.

GBS met Kathleen Bruce in the early 1900s. Born on March 27, 1878, she had studied with Rodin when just out of her teens, preened at Gertrude Stein's salons, traveled with Isadora Duncan, and volunteered in Macedonia with refugees from Turkish brutality. She introduced Shaw to Isadora, who urged him, Kathleen recalled, "to sit beside her and hold her hand," because, although she was no longer "much to look at, I'm very good to feel." Shaw remembered Isadora, who attracted him far less than Kathleen, "clothed in draperies and appearing rather damaged," with a face that "looked as if it had been made of sugar and someone had licked it." Holding out her arms, she appealed, "Come to me, I have loved you all my life!" So they sat on a sofa while Shaw sang an aria from *Tristan and Isolde* and "the entire party gathered around us as if they were witnessing a play." If he called on her, Isadora promised, she would dance for him "undraped." He never did.[1]

Kathleen also radiated unconventionality, but she kept her private life prior to her marriage a mystery. Like other men, Shaw was attracted by what he described as her vitality, but he was hardly the first votary. Occultist and magician Aleister Crowley, who met her in Paris at Rodin's studio, penned outrageously bad poetry urging her to "Whip, whip me till I burn! Whip on! Whip on!" Masochistic fantasy? The repellent Crowley claimed that her "brilliant beauty and wholesome Highland flamboyance were complicated with a sinister perversity.... She initiated me into the torturing pleasures of algolagny[2] on the spiritual plane.... Love had no savour for her unless she was causing ruin or unhappiness to others." Crowley may have merely been frustrated—yet enjoying it. Old Rodin "would flatter me and my work," she wrote, and he would, like so many other admirers, send her fulsome letters. He would call her "Un petit morceau grec d'un chef-d'oeuvre," she recalled, "and I would look at my stalwart arms and legs and not feel at all fragmentary."

In Paris, too, was photographer Edward Steichen, whose wife, Clara, identified Kathleen as "the lovestruck young woman" who had allegedly gazed longingly at Steichen across the tables of a cheap café in Paris in 1902. Clara perceived, suspiciously, a sexual overture, and was jealous of the arty women she viewed as rivals for her husband even if the relationships were entirely innocent. At work in England later, Kathleen mingled with politicians and artistic people in circles that intersected with Shaw's own. Her admiration of Shaw was so complete that when she was hospitalized for surgery on an abdominal cyst, and "half-expected to die," she became even more certain of that when a nurse asked her if she would like to have a clergyman visit. No, she said, she would rather see Bernard Shaw.

---

1 Shaw denied the canard that Isadora had offered to have a child by him in order to produce the perfect offspring—her body matched to his brain—and that he had retorted, unkindly, "What if the child turned out to have my body and your brain?" In his early novel *Cashel Byron's Profession* (1883), the rather frail but intellectual millionairess Lydia Carew marries a handsome prizefighter on the eugenic grounds of combining in their offspring his body and her brain. Their children, according to the wry epilogue, have his intellect and her physique.

2 The *OED* defines algolagnia (the spelling by Crowley in his confessions is his own) as the practice of obtaining sexual pleasure from pain inflicted on oneself or another.

Her personal world found a focus when she met naval captain and explorer Robert Falcon Scott and determined to make him her husband. He was forty and she was thirty. She had waited almost in eugenic Shavian fashion until she had found the man she wanted to sire her sons (she was sure they would be sons). Scott succumbed.

Peter Scott was born before "Con" left to search for the South Pole in 1910; and with Scott gone, Kathleen resumed much of her former life despite the intrusions of her new celebrity. Later she recalled that among her own searches for excitement she had been the second woman in England to fly, going up in a biplane with dual controls accompanying Thomas Sopwith, and getting her now-familiar face—but to her relief, not her name—in an issue of *The Aeroplane*. Shaw's characters were often real-life composites, and she may have contributed to the personality of Shaw's daring aviatrix in his farce *Misalliance* (1910), who flies tandem with a male companion, and turns men into helpless worshipers. In 1911, while Scott was contending with Antarctic extremes that Kathleen could hardly imagine, she went to the opening night of Shaw's next comedy, the feminist *Fanny's First Play*, after which she chatted happily with GBS, who was "awfully hilarious."

Such diary notes were now stockpiled for Robert, to share with him when he was home again, and she planned a voyage to New Zealand to be in the greeting party as he arrived in glory. But Scott, who reached the Pole in January 1912, perished with the team struggling back after the final push. Even making it had been less than a triumph. Arriving at the ultimate ninety degrees south they had discovered that Roald Amundsen, the Norwegian explorer, had beaten them by a month and left the evidence. It was almost as if Scott's party would be dying twice.

For Kathleen it was not the way she wanted to become a titled Lady, but she was authorized by George V to use the style that would have been her own had her husband been knighted on a triumphant return. The wrong kind of fame would continue to come her way. A public subscription for victims' families raised almost £75,000 (a very substantial sum in pre-inflationary years), headed by donations from the king and queen. Since such grants were made in order of rank rather than need, Kathleen in 1913 received £8,500. The widow of a petty officer with a naval pension of £48 a year for herself and three children was awarded £1,250.

News of the deaths at the South Pole reached London on January 11, 1913. Kathleen, at sea somewhere between California and Tahiti, only learned of it a month later, as her ship had been too remote from the nearest, still-primitive, radio signals. The three bodies in Scott's tent, Robert included, had been found on November 12, 1912, long after they were presumed dead, and a fourth, located nearby soon after, was that of ailing Captain Laurence Oates, who had left their shelter in a blizzard to die alone, remarking, memorably, "I am just going outside and may be some time."

London intimates vied to comfort her, although according to Shaw she "never played the grief stricken lonely widow." Kathleen had long since adjusted to the inevitable, but that was difficult for most friends to accept. Spending an evening with Shaw's Adelphi Terrace neighbor, Scottish playwright James Barrie, also a friend of "Con," on October 6, 1913, she was advised, animatedly, to appear unmournful although he could not falsify his feelings. "Shaw has just bought a motor-bicycle. He is so happy and excited. My dear, I wish you could tell me something I could buy that would make me happy and excited for one minute." As Kathleen knew, Barrie's comedies masked his own deep melancholy, and she noted in her diary, "Poor wee soul! I wish I could." She was not feeling sorry for herself.

Sculpting commissions—including an inevitable Scott memorial—increased with her widow's visibility, but when war came the next year she sought more appropriate work. At an electrical apparatus bench in the Vickers armament works at Erith, east of Woolwich, she felt more fulfilled, but it was a long commute from young Peter and their home at 174 Buckingham Palace Road. It also seemed inappropriate for a Lady, especially one who was taken dancing at the Savoy by Prime Minister H. H. Asquith, who doted on her.

Midway into the war Lady Scott was persuaded to take a job with the Ministry of Pensions. She became private secretary to the Permanent Secretary, Sir Matthew Nathan, for whom she was working when, at Christmas 1916, she and Peter visited Apsley Cherry-Garrard for the holidays. Then thirty and still a bachelor, and invalided out of the war for Antarctic-related ailments, "Cherry" had survived the "Terra Nova" expedition, not having been among the four who died short of rescue. Shaw's country neighbor at Lamer Park in Hertfordshire, Cherry-Garrard had lived at the idyllic Garrard estate since he was six, when his father inherited it and accordingly hyphenated his name. Sturdy and athletic, and as always without makeup, Kathleen was a striking figure—although perhaps not to the thick-spectacled and brooding Cherry, who blamed himself rather than circumstances for not having returned in time with supplies for Scott.

Her visits exacerbated his sense of guilt, yet also relieved it. And although Kathleen and Peter took the train to Lamer at least one weekend in the month to bask in Cherry's devoted hospitality, he was either too overawed to be physically attracted, or his sickly conscience got in the way. She coolly found him "a young thing."

Cherry-Garrard invited his neighbors the Shaws to join them for Christmas Eve, and Kathleen noted in her diary, "Shaw was enchanting; told me I had the blue eye of genius, what he called the Strindberg eye."[3] ("He always flatters me a good deal," she confessed.) On Christmas Day 1916 she and Peter (whom Kathleen dressed for the occasion as a miniature Father Christmas) took several books as gifts to the Shaws at nearby Ayot St. Lawrence—less than a mile down the lane. GBS asked them to stay (with Peter as the excuse) so that he could read to them "what he called a children's story, [although] it was a hyper adult story." It imagined an encounter between the Kaiser and a waiflike girl somehow exposed at night on a Flanders battlefield. Shaw had written it for a gift book in aid of a Belgian children's charity, the *Vestiare Marie Josef*. When he had delivered it some months earlier, the charity had bypassed its own book for more ready money, selling the GBS contribution instead, for £400, to the *New York Herald Tribune*. The fantasy had already appeared on the front page of the *Tribune's* Sunday magazine on October 22, 1916, illustrated (above a sentimental caption) by Boardman Robinson.

Kathleen was still fixated on death and sacrifice, as were the many who mourned loved ones lost in the continuing carnage of the war. It may have seemed to her as if Shaw, anticipating Joan of Arc's death in 1431, had suggested what the Maid of Orleans was like when she was a girl. Simple yet shrewd, and irreverent toward authority figures, the child is the Kaiser's intellectual match in their brief exchange, and the blustering Wilhelm II is seen as the helpless pawn of his position. As they debate amid the shellfire, a round explodes nearby, obliterating the child but leaving her disembodied voice, in which fashion she reappears to him as if in a waking dream. Although the bewildered and bespattered monarch remains alive, he is now alone. The child has been "set free by the shell" from the pain and privation of existence much in the manner

---

3 When Shaw met the reclusive August Strindberg in Stockholm in 1908 he was struck by the dramatist's "sapphire-blue eyes; . . . the man of genius was unmistakable."

the lively Joan of the epilogue of Shaw's play to come (in 1923) is freed from the body by her burning.

Sixty, but younger in heart when it came to attractive women, even when he thought of them only as the daughters he never had, GBS was exhilarated by reading the story to Kathleen and her fatherless little son. He would see much more of her through the war years and later. When she learned that he was going to Flanders by army invitation in January and February 1917, which he would write up as "Joy-Riding at the Front," she used her connections to get him a follow-up invitation to visit the Austro-Italian lines. He knew it would disappoint her, but he responded to General Charles Delme-Radcliffe of the British Military Mission that although the Trentino in the spring was a pleasant thought, he would be of no propaganda use there. Few Englishmen were involved in the fighting, and the public considered the war in Italy a sideshow to the main stage.

Kathleen would be among the select few in the Shaws' Adelphi Terrace flat late in the afternoon of June 8, 1917, when he read the opening scenes of his newest play, *Heartbreak House*, taking all the roles himself. "Very, very funny," she noted in her diary about the first act. Halfway through came tea, and the remainder of the play followed, but while others stayed to the end, Lady Scott had to return to her office at the Ministry of Pensions to work late.

The next day Shaw traveled to Lamer with her, and after Peter had gone to bed that evening, GBS read to her and to Cherry parts of what she had missed. She was baffled by it, its dreamlike elements escaping her: "All the people develop as you least expect." On Sunday she and Peter lunched at the Shaws, and afterward as she dozed intermittently in the sunlit garden, GBS completed his reading, more for himself, it seemed, than for her. According to one of her diary entries in May 1917, after lunch at Ayot, GBS walked back with her to Lamer, "and we discussed the propagation of the race." The new play he was planning, the *Back to Methuselah* cycle, would deal in part with longevity and evolution, and he was apparently trying out ideas with her.

He would see a lot of Kathleen. Both in London and in Ayot St. Lawrence he had his work, and nearby in both places (as she often frequented Lamer Park) there was almost always Lady Scott on weekends. She had emerged as a trusted figure in whom he could confide those things he was reluctant to tell Charlotte. Once, encountering Kathleen and Peter on the train, he "descended from first class to third class to play with us."

At Lamer he would turn up for tea, and remain for the evening, telling bedtime stories for Kathleen's son which he would invent on the spot. Ever since he was very little, Shaw explained to Peter, he always told himself a story each night before he went to sleep, some of them continuing as serials over several nights. He repeated his favorite stories, Shaw confided, over and over again.

One evening that November, after Peter went off contentedly to bed, the Shaws and Kathleen had dinner with Cherry, at which GBS confessed for reasons unknown that he had never learned to dance. Kathleen offered to give him a lesson, and he glided across the floor with her to music from Cherry's phonograph, pleased with himself. Following another dinner at Lamer, with the artist pair Charles Ricketts and Charles Shannon also as guests, she urged Shaw to demonstrate his new dancing skills. Again in December at Lamer they danced, and she "gave Shaw a lesson, both practical and demonstrative." While Charlotte watched placidly (she bridled at his attentions to other women, yet never about Lady Scott), Shaw happily went through his paces with Kathleen. "To begin to learn to dance at sixty-one is rather delicious," she had written in her diary two weeks earlier. "I love old Shaw." He wrote to a friend, Henry Salt, "I was found to possess a senile and lumbering diable au corps which made my King David–like gambols amusing to myself and not so utterly unbearable for my unfortunate partner as might have been expected." Given the biblical David's lusty reputation, Shaw may have inadvertently intimated more than daughterly feelings when in Kathleen's arms.

Late in December 1917, she became a war casualty, falling ill from overwork. She had often worked at the Ministry far into the evenings, and loathed the dull job, considering it "very little different from a grave." On January 8, 1918, Shaw visited and sat for hours at her bedside, returning two days later, after which she was able to pen a diary note, "Still in bed, fainting a good deal. Bernard Shaw came, and we discussed dreams, deliriums, and happiness." He often told her his dreams, never revealing them to Charlotte.

Shaw often visited, alone, at Buckingham Palace Road, dining with her and reading scenes from his overly talky new play about characters based on her friend H. H. Asquith and his Downing Street successor, David Lloyd George. "Ll.G. the bouncing rhetorical fraud, and Asquith, the bland, benign old gentleman—very funny, but not quite right," she observed loyally about the ousted Asquith. When she next went to Lamer, this time without Peter, Shaw was again there because he expected her. If the weather proved mild, some of Cherry's overnight guests slept outdoors, and Kathleen uninhibitedly danced barefoot in her nightgown. Shaw "amazed me," she wrote (June 29, 1918). "I have known him for fifteen years, and this was the first time I knew he sang. He went almost through the score of Rheingold on the piano, singing in a charming baritone voice. He plays amazingly well. He is a marvellous man." Alone with her, he often reminisced about his past indiscretions—his affair with actress Florence Farr, whom Kathleen met only after her looks had faded; children's writer Edith Nesbit's failed passes at him; his own frustrations in trying to seduce "Mrs. Pat" Campbell, his Eliza in *Pygmalion*.

What Shaw did not tell Kathleen—if he knew himself—is that he may have put aspects of her into a character in the next futuristic playlet, after the Asquith–Lloyd George segment, in his *Methuselah* cycle, "The Thing Happens." It includes a female Domestic Minister, perhaps a promotion from Kathleen's job at the Ministry of Pensions, who wears a tunic and dresses "*not markedly different from . . . the men.*" Mrs. Lutestring, who, from experience, discusses, among other matters, "Old Age Pensions," is "*a handsome woman, apparently in the prime of life, with [an] elegant, tense, well held-up figure, and the walk of a goddess.*" Among men she inspires "*instinctive awe.*" Although never an artist herself—a cautious deflection from fact—her late husband was "a great painter." Only the smallest of hints, perhaps, but the stately Cabinet Minister may be a Shavian bow to Lady Scott.

For July and August 1918, Kathleen rented Streatley Vicarage in Berkshire, up the Thames from London, using it also as a studio. Shaw agreed to visit and pose for her while she did a statuette—if he did not have to dress "respectably." And while Charlotte went off to visit her sister in Ireland, Shaw paid visits to Kathleen and Peter. His first full day at the Vicarage was July 26, his sixty-second birthday. As he had been about to leave Ayot, a telegram had arrived for him as "next of kin." In the war years one dreaded a messenger at the door. Robert Loraine, who had played John Tanner in the American run of *Man and Superman*, and now was a major in the Royal Flying Corps, had been shot down. To Shaw, who had visited Loraine on the Flanders front, he was a difficult surrogate son, and Loraine had duly listed the Shaws as next of kin. It was not the first such telegram. Loraine had been wounded before, and Shaw returned a hasty note hoping that "it is a cushy one this time."

Brooding over the news, and cold and wet from a soaking rain, he arrived unhappily at Lady Scott's. Shaw was cross, and she was shy and dull, Kathleen told her diary. "I am not good at sustained efforts of niceness." Besides, the food was "bad," and the prospects for improvement, given wartime rationing, were "hopeless." Still, GBS remained at Lamer for ten days, swimming in the Thames when the sun shone, sitting for her statuette when it didn't. And he wondered to her whether an artist's own gender and character revealed itself in the work, guessing that in her androgynous case it did not. Although husbandless since 1912, Kathleen was unconcerned about having Shaw on the premises, whatever her rather remote neighbors might gossip. Their relationship was as much father-daughter as that with Loraine was father-son. She could be just as irreverent as an emancipated daughter, too, as she noted in her diary on Sunday, August 4, when the grave and sober Frederick Watson, a leader in crippled children's causes, whom she knew from the Ministry of Pensions, came to visit for the afternoon.

Watson found himself greeted by the overpowering Shaw, who "at once took up the duties of a host, and behaved through the day in a manner reminiscent of Queen Victoria and the annual Wesleyan Conference." While Watson seemed "extremely promising in occasional asides," he was "instantly submerged and rejected by the reminiscences instantly inflamed in the mind of Shaw." Even at dinner, when Watson hovered "on the point of a joke," the vegetarian Shaw "set up a strident noise for cheese," and poor Watson's moment passed, "never to return."

At Streatley, Shaw received word that Loraine's wound had shattered his knee and that he would be evacuated to an English hospital, possibly for amputation. Preparing a telegram for Shaw to Loraine, Lady Scott quoted Shaw in her diary as advising, "Oh, tell him to be sure not to take any leg they recommend at Roehampton." He was attempting, with whatever humor was possible under the circumstances, to prepare Loraine for the most extreme solution. (Loraine preferred keeping his stiffened leg.)

From Streatley, Shaw was to travel further, by bus and rail, to visit Beatrice and Sidney Webb in Wales. Since that meant lunching en route, Kathleen asked her cook to pack cucumber sandwiches for Shaw. When he unwrapped the first one he discovered that the thoughtful cook had enhanced the dreary vegetarian repast with potted meat. GBS threw them away and hungered all the way to Wales. He was in Ireland with Charlotte when Kathleen went to the pre-opening private view of the

International Art Show in London, where her already completed bronze statuette of Shaw, standing, with arms folded across his chest, appeared to her "alone on the central table of the principal room, looking very small." After looking it over, Shaw would call it "a masterpiece."

To GBS, Kathleen could do no wrong—unless it was her having married Scott. (Shaw forgave her even that because the union produced Peter.) To her second husband, who was not amused, Shaw confided sharply late in life that Kathleen should have only been "secondarily famous as the wife of the world renowned wonderful Scott." Her authentic achievement was in art. "Now Scott was not wonderful: there was nothing wonderful nor uncommon about him; and he was so unsuited to the job he insisted on undertaking that he ended as the most incompetent failure in the history of exploration. Kathleen, on the other hand, was a wonderful woman, first rate at her job, adventurously ready to go to the ends of the earth at half an hour's notice with no luggage but a comb with three teeth left in it, and always successful. Scott's best right to his celebrity is that he induced her to marry him."

Although in part Shaw was indulging in his love of paradox, Kathleen would have remained far less friendly had she known of Shaw's private disloyalty to Scott, and how Cherry, with Shavian assistance, was treating her hero in the memoir he had begun early in 1917 as *Never Again: Scott, Some Penguins, and the Pole*. Cherry had been invited by the Captain Scott Antarctic Fund to write the official history of the doomed second Scott expedition. The Shaws lunched with Cherry-Garrard nearly every Sunday they were in the country, and on one crucial Sabbath he revealed the offer. But he was no explorer, he said dismissively: he had only been the young naturalist of the expedition, who as a boy had "a taste for snails and solitude." GBS and Charlotte urged him to undertake it although he had never written for publication. He felt daunted by the prospect, but Shaw offered editing help, and Charlotte even promised to correct his proofs.

Kathleen was delighted. In the circumstances, she felt, loyally, how could the result be anything but a hagiographic masterwork? But Shaw saw the project as more than a saint's life. First he set down for Cherry a half-page of punctuation rules, Shavian style, that emphasized the colon and semicolon. Then Shaw criticized the text, Cherry noted, "as it was written, word by word and chapter by chapter." As self-appointed editor, he asked questions to establish clarity, as in "What is pack?" Some of the questions, as this one, became rhetorical devices, as it introduced an explanation of pack ice. Beyond the pathetic end for Scott, Shaw also saw a drama in the race to the Pole—two rival protagonists on the Antarctic stage.

Cherry, Shaw recalled at the start, "still retained his boyish notions of Scott and his expedition. . . . One day, in his library, I asked him if there was any extant account of Amundsen's venture." Roald Amundsen, the Norwegian adventurer who had reached the Pole a month before Scott (as Scott discovered to his consternation), on December 14, 1911, had quickly published a book about the enterprise, *The South Pole*, in 1912. Cherry took down the book, which Shaw guessed from its mint appearance had not been opened. "I read it and found he was an explorer of genius, who had got to the Pole and back without losing a single man, having found a new route . . . by two inspired guesses and taking two big chances, and knowing exactly how to treat his men. Everything he did was original and right: Scott did what was done last time; and everything he did was wrong." Thus Cherry wrote, undoubtedly with Shaw's hand guiding him, of Amundsen's "sort of sagacity that constitutes the specific genius of the explorer," and that his expedition "was more highly endowed in personal qualities than ours."

During the three years when Cherry was writing, and the Shaws assisting—he was a wealthy country gentleman and had no working deadlines—he began to realize that harrowing deaths during "Scott's folly," however heroic, had their ambiguous dimension. Overextending his resources, "Scott had nothing to gain and a good deal to lose by taking an extra man to the Pole." Cherry had access to several of the journals of the men, and, unnervingly, had discovered the mottled, frozen corpses of his dead companions in their tent in 1912 as rescue arrived too late. Whatever their physical and moral resilience, they had failed in their quest for the Pole, and return. The elements had won. The buck stops with the expedition's leader, and his handling of the logistic details, and Cherry was tormented by having to bear witness to that, and to his pervasive gloom about not having returned in time to Scott's frozen and snowswept tent. Cherry quoted Scott from the journal he left behind, "We took risks, we knew we took them; things have come out against us, and therefore we have no cause for complaint." Although Cherry added, "No better epitaph has been written," with an uneasy conscience he withdrew from his commitment to the Fund, and opted to publish independently.

GBS had been drafting and rewriting passages for Cherry; and both

Shaws, as Cherry wrote, made marginal comments and textual emendations. (The plethora of full colons is also likely to have been Shaw's hand, as well as the discussion, recalling *Man and Superman*, of exploration as "the physical expression of the Intellectual Passion.") Shaw even arranged with his own printer, R. & R. Clark in Edinburgh, and his longtime publisher, Constable, for publication, and the proofs of the book, under its original title, were delivered on April 9, 1920. But Cherry was morbidly displeased with the seeming facetiousness of his "Penguins" allusion, although a central portion of the narrative dealt with his trekking to Cape Crozier in the seventy-below temperatures over five terrible winter weeks in 1911 with two companions to collect the substantial eggs of emperor penguins from their rookery for desperately needed food. It was, he concluded, "the worst journey in the world." It would have taken a saw to open his frozen outer clothes. "There's your title," said Shaw.

As the book inched closer to publication, GBS deflected Cherry's request that his considerable assistance be acknowledged. "It would be fatal," he advised on April 26, 1922, "to make any suggestion of collaboration on my part. The book would be reviewed on the assumption that I had written all the striking parts of it, and that they were 'not serious.' As my experience on the ice dates from the great frost of 1878 (or thereabouts) when I skated [in London] on the Serpentine, my intrusion into the Antarctic Circle would be extraordinarily ridiculous. Besides, the suggestion would be misleading. Beyond proofreading work, and paraphrasing your conversation here and there," he downplayed, "I have done nothing that is not covered by your device of quoting the practical man. You should not be at all uneasy as to the integrity of your authorship."

Cherry would confess to Lady Scott about the Shaws, "They taught me to write," and among the well-chosen epigraphs to chapters of the book he included one from *Man and Superman*, in which Don Juan in the interlude in Hell declares that men can be driven by ideas—"I tell you, . . . if you can show a man a piece of what he now calls God's work to do, and what he will later call by many new names, you can make him entirely reckless of the consequences to himself personally."

That concept as it applied to Scott should have appealed to Kathleen, but since Shaw realized, too, how she would react to other implications in the book, he had, accordingly, another and unconfessed reason to keep his distance. For when he (and Charlotte) began helping T. E. Lawrence, later that year, to turn his heat-drenched masterpiece about

Arabia in 1917–18, *Seven Pillars of Wisdom*, into a publishable book, he permitted a wry but open acknowledgment. It was remarkable that in the same decade GBS should have an editorial hand in perhaps the two greatest memoirs of adventure in English in the twentieth century, both at the climatic extremes—one set in ice, the other in sand.

Adventurers always intrigued Kathleen, and she would become friendly, too, with T. E. Lawrence, and sculpt him as well. When back in England, having reduced himself from lieutenant colonel to private, and concealed himself luridly in his own limelight by changing his name to *Shaw*, he would pop in and out of friends' homes (like the Shaws) within motorcycling range. Once, on a Sunday in July 1926, Kathleen was in her bath when her maid tapped and announced that Mr. Shaw was there. "Mr. Bernard Shaw, all right," she said. When her maid said no, Kathleen shouted through the door to ask the visitor what his business was. The maid went off, then returned with word that the stranger wouldn't tell his business. "Probably a beggar," Kathleen dismissed.

"I don't think so," said the maid. "He was in Air Force uniform."

"Colonel Lawrence! Dash after him!"

Off flew the maid to retrieve "Shaw." Brought back, he explained that he couldn't imagine what to say his business was, for "obviously" he had none. He was only an unskilled mechanic in the ranks, and was only dropping by.

A few days later she had lunch with the other Shaw, and mentioned the unexpected visit and surprise name. She hadn't known that Lawrence had become *Shaw*. The talk turned to *Seven Pillars of Wisdom*, and GBS's rather quiet role in it. Other than confessing that he recommended that a chapter be cut, Shaw said evasively, he had little share in it. But Kathleen confided to her diary that Lawrence had told her that "there was scarce a paragraph that G.B.S. had not amended." She had no idea what Shaw's part had been in Cherry's book either, which among other things had included writing at least some of the lines that praised Amundsen at Scott's expense. (GBS's later role was a jacket blurb for the Chatto & Windus reprint that hinted only slightly at that. Compared with Scott's "extraordinary and appalling" expedition," Shaw wrote, "Amundsen's victorious rush to the South Pole seems as cheerful as a trip to Margate. Even Dante's exploration of the icebound seventh circle of hell shews that men cannot imagine the worst that they can suffer." In a way that perspective toned down for Kathleen the criticism in the book itself.)

Kathleen's first postwar years included hectic travel that the war had precluded, in part to escape her past, in part to escape an new and intent admirer. In 1919 she recorded a March weekend at Lamer Park with the Shaws, their Irish playwright friend Lady Gregory, and Norwegian Arctic explorer and war relief activist Fridtjof Nansen. A hero at the new League of Nations, Nansen, in his late fifties, was, to Kathleen, "simple, frank, humble, childish, and altogether adorable"—and he was almost instantly in love with her. He would follow her round the world had she let him. But she wanted to remarry, and noted in her diary from Cherbourg, after travels across both Americas, "Lord will I ever find a man I altogether like—who do I want? No one will do. Maybe I am utterly and completely spoilt."

Another aspirant, however, had emerged from her surfeit of adventurers and heroes. In November 1922 she had Shaw and H. G. Wells to lunch, when they learned about her betrothal by accident. Kathleen had Shaw promise to read his new and yet-unproduced *Saint Joan* to her, and she asked him "if he was never coming to an end." He confessed, "I thought I must have dried up after producing *Methuselah*, but to my astonishment I found the sap rising again." Their discussion turned to her show of recent work at the Grosvenor Gallery, to which Wells had taken Shaw, and he was "awfully impressed," Kathleen noted, by her nudes, especially one she had titled, obscurely, *I Want*. Since she sculpted from life, he wondered about who posed for the statue. "Bill did it," she said.

Shaw looked puzzled. "Bill" was Edward Hilton Young, the Liberal MP and lawyer she would marry. But the statuette had two arms. In 1918 Hilton Young, then a naval officer, had lost his right arm in Belgium during the siege of Zeebrugge, and Kathleen had restored it in her bronze. She had felt immensely sorry for Hilton, and as her feelings for him intensified, Shaw tried to console her as he had done, wryly and unsuccessfully, with Robert Loraine. "I said," he recalled, his propensity for paradox again unsuccessful, "that as a man with two arms is not unhappy because he has not three, neither is he unhappy if, having one, he hasn't two, and she flew out at me so furiously that I discreetly shut up."

Kathleen was well past forty-four when she and Hilton were married in the crypt of the House of Commons by an Anglican bishop; he was younger by nearly a year. It was an opportune time for Shaw (March 23, 1923) to caution her as gently as he could about Cherry's just-published deflation of Scott, which Shaw had abetted but described to her as "a classic story of travel." Kathleen had the two-volume boxed set sent by Cherry inscribed "with very grateful thanks" and had already begun to pen "Rots!" in the margins. If she were able to bear "to treat the expedition judicially . . . by a man who was only 23 when it occurred," Shaw wrote, too late, she would put aside "every impression that has been made on you by selected scraps" in the press. That he was "more or less a witness" to Cherry's writing the book was all he admitted to. But he also suggested that she not visit Ayot as Cherry might be there; and he confessed that he had recommended to Cherry that "international courtesy and sportsmanship made it advisable to be scrupulously just and polite to Amundsen. I suspect this was the hardest pill he had to swallow; for the moment he went into the question he had to admit Amundsen was no scallywag, but a very good explorer." Then Cherry "was forced to contrast Amundsen's triumph with Con's tragedy."

Shaw wrote two long, delicate letters to Kathleen about Scott and the *Worst Journey*, attempting to make the distinction between hagiography, a word he left unsaid, and history. "Keep this," he began one letter defensively, "for a quiet hour: it is about Cherry and old times and sorrows." The facts would come out by some means or other, and as in "Cherry's narrative" Scott would be proved "reckless in travelling without sufficient margins in provisions and fuel; and he had accepted the official scientific formula for rationing, which was of course all wrong, and produced a starvation which was disguised until it was too late." The book, he explained, gently but unpersuasively, in his second letter, was not "an act of personal disloyalty to Con."

Loyally, Hilton Young was even more outraged than Kathleen, seeing on Cherry's part "a grievance against his leader, whom he believed to have neglected his, C.G.'s, merits, on the expedition." Although he saw Shaw's (and Cherry-Garrard's) undiplomatic assessment of Scott as irresponsible, it has stood up.

Shaw "seems unconsciously determined to make me angry and resentful against Cherry," Kathleen wrote, in misunderstanding, in her diary, "a thing I do not want to be at all. I have never admired Cherry but I am fond of him and don't want to have to cease to be . . . [but] his rendering of Con's character is so ludicrous it should not even make one cross, only Shaw seems determined I should be cross!" Scott had become a national icon for stoic endurance in terrible adversity, a quality glorified by a world war. Cherry (and Shaw) had tarnished the tragic moment. Yet she waited until early 1927 before she went to the publishers of *Worst Journey* to urge that "some effort be made to prevent a passage in Cherry-Garrard's book"—the use of his full, hyphenated surname suggested her hostility—"from gaining credence." The words about Scott she wanted expunged ("this silly opposite of the truth") were "weak and peevish." They might have been Shaw's.

Kathleen's friendship with Shaw survived *The Worst Journey in the World* because she never knew the extent of Shaw's hand in it. And Shaw never knew that, although she accepted his assessment. As keeper of the flame, she could never let him know it. When she discovered that Scott had falsified his own journals of the polar catastrophe, for posthumous exculpation, claiming a nine-day blizzard when none had occurred, Kathleen enlisted James Barrie to help her further falsify Scott's sledging diaries for publication to make Con's last journey seem more impossible than it had been.

Cherry-Garrard would see little of her afterwards, but he was gradually withdrawing into chronic, debilitating depression. "My own bolt is shot," he wrote near the close of his book; "I do not suppose I shall ever go south again before I go west." He had not been able to save Scott's marooned team. The memoir had attempted to explain why, but it could not purge him of his demons. One of the few people he was willing to see over the full course of his forty-six post-polar years was Shaw.

In August 1923, at forty-five, after four days of difficult labor, Kathleen gave birth to her second son, Wayland. The late, risky pregnancy and newborn child had not kept her from working. On Armistice Day, a cold, sunny morning, her war memorial, a larger-than-life brooding soldier, was unveiled at Huntingdon. Shaw remained in her life, now given over substantially to her new husband's career in the Commons. "I was awfully pleased to see him," she wrote of Shaw on March 11, 1924. "He sat holding forth on life, politics, and the drama, with our babe comfortably tucked up on his arm. There's summut [Scots for *something*] in a white-haired old man with a little baby that stirs all my heart."

In 1926, Hilton Young switched allegiance to the Conservatives, and politics became more intrusive in Kathleen's life. It was hard to be a sculptor, she wrote, when "there are . . . political parties in the world." People were beginning to forget exactly who her first husband was, other than that he was somehow connected with polar exploration. At a political dinner party in the Commons, an elderly guest greeted her with, "I knew your dear husband [Ernest] Shackleton." (At Charles Shannon's house a servant once asked him, as he ushered GBS out, "Excuse me, sir, is that the gentleman who wrote Shakespeare?") Despite her remarriage she could not escape Scott's shade, even when it was misidentified.

With his change of party Hilton was now seeking a seat from the Sevenoaks division, and early in 1928 Kathleen made speeches for him while he was on political business in East Africa. She served her "lord god" by hosting dinner parties, made time for overseeing her sons, the elder now nineteen, and worked on a statue commission of a former secretary of state for India, Edwin Montagu, for Calcutta. At one party, she recalled, Mrs. Stanley Baldwin, wife of the Tory prime minister, "looked down her nose at Bernard Shaw, and didn't get hold of him at all." Shaw often came to lunch, "which is fun," and on one occasion when she had the stellar Portuguese cellist Guilhermina Suggia also as guest, the onetime music critic (as "G.B.S.") "chid Suggia teasingly for having such a cumbrous instrument as a cello. Why not a nice little fiddle?" It reminded Shaw of the elderly removals laborer who, while weighed down by a grandfather's clock he was carrying, was stopped to be asked, "Excuse me, but at your age, wouldn't you find a wristwatch more convenient?"

Shaw was again at Buckingham Palace Road in April 1929 to lunch with American banker Otto Kahn and several English politicians. Kathleen and Hilton "had a bet" as to whether Shaw or Austen Chamberlain would "talk the other down." To their surprise, Kahn "beat them both, and Shaw came in a poor third." On one occasion the millionaire playwright boasted to a party of economists and financiers that he was a communist, a paradox that Kathleen found "unconvincing." At another, in 1932—he was often a raisin in her social cake—he brought her his newest book, the *Candide*-like *Adventures of the Black Girl in Search of God,* and "got on like a house on fire" with fashionable conductor Malcolm Sargent. Afterward she walked across Green Park with Shaw "at an immense rate." She was amazed at his stamina. "He is a grand old man.... May I be like him when I am seventy-five." Kathleen would have been peeved had she known that in Cherry-Garrard's gift copy of *The Black Girl,* GBS would write,

> For Cherry and Angela
> Greatest of my friends.

Only once in her own later years did Kathleen run into Cherry. Although she had put him out of her life, she had been telling people—ignoring the neighborly connection—that it was she who had introduced him to GBS. Cherry and Angela (he had married belatedly in 1938) were having tea at a London hotel, a rare occasion for a chronic depressive, when Kathleen entered with her husband and elder son. "Now, Cherry," she admonished on spotting him, "don't pretend you don't know me!" Cherry stood up politely, looked at the sturdy young man and said, "This must be Wayland."

"It's Peter," she corrected. But it demonstrated that despite her antagonism, Cherry had kept up with her.

Also in 1938, when Shaw was eighty-two, Kathleen had him sit for a head-and-shoulders sculpture. She was sixty, and in dark slacks and Nehru-like blouse she looked youthful to him. Watching her results, Shaw, who materialized under her fingers with his head in his hands, framing his face, deplored it facetiously as "a Shakespearean tomb." It did look remarkably like the iconic portrait of the Bard. For it (and her) Shaw wrote a rhyming commentary, on green paper, beginning, "Weep not for old George Bernard: he is dead"—a copy of which he sent to Lord Alfred Douglas, once Wilde's young friend and a minor poet. Kathleen, he wrote, rejected his "epitaph" (jokingly intended as inscription for a pedestal) as "nonsense verse"—which might have been too kind. He had once written of his bust in marble by Auguste Rodin that he—GBS—would be known mainly as "subject of bust by Rodin." Now he closed by versifying that "Kathleen plied" at his head

> Until one day the Lord said "No, my lass:
> Copy no more. Your spirit shall be your guide.
> Carve him *sub specie aeternitas*
> So, when his works shall all forgotten be
> He yet shall share your immortality.

At the Royal Academy exhibition in the spring of 1940, despite the Luftwaffe incendiary bombs beginning to reach London, she exhibited in bronze what she called "a half-figure, almost," pleased with the outcome. Under wartime restrictions, people got around far less, and Shaw saw little of Kathleen then and nothing of Peter, who now commanded a destroyer. Shaw lived largely in the country, as Charlotte was very ill, and the bombings made matters worse for her. Kathleen, too, lived more at Leinster Corner, the country place she and Hilton had acquired.

Returning painfully to London to be close to her doctors, Charlotte died on September 13, 1943, at eighty-six. At the end of October, after her private funeral and cremation, Shaw remained to help sort out her effects at Whitehall Court, and on October 30 Kathleen wrote, still maintaining her diary, that Shaw, eighty-seven, came to tea, traveling alone by tube. "He was more amazing than ever, and better company. He told us all about Charlotte's illness and death." Charlotte, GBS told Kathleen and Hilton—he was now Lord Kennet of the Dene, and she was Lady Kennet—had illusions that the service flat in which the elderly Shaws had lived since the mid-1920s was full of people who didn't belong there. "You must get up the housekeeper and the manager," Charlotte had appealed. "We pay for the flat and it is very expensive: we have a right to have it to ourselves." Shaw explained the phenomenon imaginatively to Charlotte as her clairvoyance—"all these people existed but they were in Australia or Oxford or anywhere," and because of the distance, the manager would not be able to see them.

Three years later, after Shaw had a fall, Kathleen went to visit, finding him sitting up in a dressing gown and "looking really very frail. . . . Oh dear he is the oddest maddest mixture. He told me yet again how many women wanted to marry him [since Charlotte's death], knowing that they would only have to look after him for a year or two and then have his fortune." It was October 14, 1946. "He is ninety, but his mind and gestures are as active as ever and his memory for what we had said and done thirty years ago quite prodigious, and putting me to shame." Feeling his mortality, at his suggestion they talked of possible Shavian memorials, including her bust. "I tried to go lots of times, lest he should get tired, but he wouldn't let me. He was a little sentimental, finally. Waning is a sad, sad thing."

Kathleen said nothing about herself, but she was waning more seriously, stricken by painful angina. Soon after Christmas she was bedridden. A few months into 1947 she went into St. Mary's Hospital, Paddington, realizing that it was the end. When she died on July 24, 1947, a year short of seventy, it was two days before Shaw would reach ninety-one. He wrote to Peter, now an eminent ornithologist, "The news from Leinster Corner reached me on my birthday, and for a moment struck it all of a heap. But I cannot feel otherwise than gladly about her, nor imagine her old. She was a very special friend."

At the time, Shaw was contemplating publication of his admittedly lightweight *Rhyming Picture Guide to Ayot Saint Lawrence*. He could not imagine a year without producing something between hard covers. Its origin, years before, had been picture-postcard doggerel verses for Ellen Terry. The last contribution to it was a photograph he had taken of Kathleen at Ayot. Accompanying it were his unmemorable yet deeply felt lines,

Widow of Scott, whose statue [I] cherished
She wrought when at the Pole he perished;
A later union of two hearts
Was with a man of many parts.
She wedded him, and then was seen
As Lady Kennet of the Dene.
Lest she should have her looks undrawn
I photographed her on my lawn;
And me she modelled at her Dene house
As I was sitting in its greenhouse.

It was the last book on which Shaw worked, published in December 1950, six weeks after his own death.

Bibliographic Essay

Kathleen recalled the paradoxical "homosexual" remark in her diary entry for September 19, 1929. All her diary entries following, unless otherwise cited, are from her *Self-Portrait of an Artist*, ed. Lord Kennet (London: John Murray, 1949). Her obituarist would be James Lees-Milne, *Fourteen Friends* (London: John Murray, 1996).

Aleister Cowley recalled Kathleen in John Symonds and Kenneth Grant, ed., *The Confessions of Aleister Crowley* (London: Jonathan Cape, 1969). For Rodin and Kathleen, see Frederic V. Grunfeld, *Rodin: A Biography* (New York: Holt, 1987). For Kathleen and Steichen, see Penelope Niven, *Steichen* (New York: Clarkson Potter, 1997); and Louisa Young, *A Great Task of Happiness: The Life of Kathleen Scott* (London: Macmillan, 1995), which also quotes Kathleen's hospital request to see Shaw. The "lonely widow" is from Shaw's letter to Lord Kennet of the Dene, August 16, 1947, in *Collected Letters*, vol. 4. All Shaw letters are from vols. 2, 3, and 4.

Captain Oates is quoted from Apsley Cherry-Garrard, *The Worst Journey in the World* (London: Chatto & Windus, 1965). Further quotations are from this edition. (The book was originally published by Constable in London in 1922.) The three-way relationship with Kathleen, Cherry, and Shaw, and how it was affected by *The Worst Journey in the World*, is drawn from Kathleen's diaries, Shaw's letters, and Sara Wheeler's *Cherry: A Life of Apsley Cherry-Garrard* (London: Jonathan Cape, 2001).

Shaw's story about the wartime Flanders episode is more fully described in Stanley Weintraub, *Journey to Heartbreak* (New York: Weybright, 1971), which also describes Shaw's wartime relations with Robert Loraine. That Lady Scott had procured Shaw's invitation to be a war correspondent in 1917 is clear from Shaw's letter to Delme-Radcliffe, April 23, 1917, in *Collected Letters*, vol. 3.

For T. E. Lawrence's encounters with Kathleen, see *Journey to Heartbreak* and Lady Scott's diary. Charles Shannon's anecdote about Shakespeare and Shaw is from Young, *A Great Task of Happiness*. Shaw's inscription to Cherry and his wife is in George Seaver's foreword to the Chatto and Windus reprint of *Worst Journey*. His verses on Kathleen's "Shakespearean" bust of him are in a letter to her, November 12, 1938, reproduced, with an illustration of the bust, in Mary Hyde, ed., *Bernard Shaw and Alfred Douglas: A Correspondence* (New Haven & New York: Ticknor and Fields, 1982). *Bernard Shaw's Rhyming Guide to Ayot St. Lawrence* (Luton, Herts: Leagrave, 1951), with its lines to Kathleen, although dated 1951, was released posthumously on December 14, 1950, six weeks after Shaw's death.

· 10 ·

Eugene O'Neill

THE SHAVIAN DIMENSION

Sitting in the offices of the Theatre Guild while being interviewed by a *New York Times* reporter, Eugene O'Neill looked up, with some anxiety, at a drawing on the wall. "I wish they'd take that down," he said. "The old man seems to be laughing at me." The year was 1931, and the image was a portrait of Shaw.

O'Neill was only five years away from winning the Nobel Prize for Literature. Shaw had been there, for O'Neill, at the beginning, and in the comedy about his adolescence that he was already contemplating, *Ah, Wilderness!* (1933). The callow boy of seventeen at the heart of the play, Richard Miller, O'Neill's nostalgic mirror of himself in the early 1900s, is surreptitiously reading the morally seditious Shaw. Soon, O'Neill's wife, Carlotta, would be writing to her husband's editor, Saxe Commins, "Gene has asked me to ask you if you can send him the dates of the publications of Shaw's *earlier* plays—*before around 1907.*" O'Neill intended to have them on young Richard's bedroom shelves and wanted to make sure that he was committing no anachronisms.

At the close of the 1930s, when he was working on a more deeply autobiographical play, about his father, Irish-American actor James O'Neill, and Eugene's mother, who paid the price for her husband's fame, Shaw's books would also be in the small bookcase in the Tyrone summer home in *Long Day's Journey into Night* (1939–40). Here the Eugene figure, Edmund Tyrone, would be older. The play is set in 1912.

It was not only the invented Richard Miller but also his prototype, O'Neill himself, who encountered Shaw's books as a schoolboy. Eugene must have first heard about Shaw at home even earlier. A friend of the elder O'Neill, Jimmie Durkin, wrote to GBS in 1909 that "while I am a stranger to you, your writings have endeared you to me, as an old acquaintance," for James O'Neill "has discussed you and your work with me for hours, with much enjoyment to the both of us." Two years before Durkin's reminiscence, in 1907, young Eugene had seen the great Russian actress Alla Nazimova in *Hedda Gabler*, the Ibsen play that focused his ambitions on the stage. To the editor of a Norwegian-American newspaper he recalled going back "again and again for ten successive nights. . . . It gave me my first conception of a modern theater where truth might live."

Eager to learn more about Ibsen, O'Neill sought out Benjamin R. Tucker's "Unique Bookshop" in lower Manhattan. The shop was the ideal venue in which to learn about Shaw as well as Ibsen, for Tucker, as editor of *Liberty*, an anarchist journal, had published, in 1895, Shaw's "open letter" rejoinder, written at Tucker's request, to Max Nordau's philistine polemic *Enartung*, translated as *Degeneration*. Shaw asked no fee for "A Degenerate's View of Nordau," a sardonic, thirteen-thousand-word demolition of Nordau's claim that contemporary artists (and their art) were either sick or lunatic. Tucker happily published a double number of *Liberty* to fit in all of Shaw's observations about the social utility of the arts, then sent copies to every paper in America for which he had an address. With some additions and revisions, it would become, in 1908, *The Sanity of Art*. Shaw would let Tucker publish the 104-page New York edition, which it is unlikely that O'Neill would miss in the Unique Bookshop.

Tucker got O'Neill's Shavian orientation going with *The Quintessence of Ibsenism* (1891). By the time he bought the book, O'Neill not only knew about Shaw from his father's conversation: the first American production of *Mrs Warren's Profession* (1893) had been shut down by the police for alleged indecency in 1905. Newspaper readers across America learned that the entire cast had spent opening night in a New York jail, inadvertently establishing Shaw's national reputation as controversialist. "Wildly excited," Eugene read through *Quintessence*, marking in red ink everything that impressed him or that he disagreed with. The book would be underscored on every page. As he carried the small book about in his pocket during his last year of school in Stamford, Connecticut, his disdain increased for his father's sort of theater, in which, Eugene later said, "virtue always triumphed and vice always got its just deserts. . . . A man was either a hero or a villain, and a woman was either virtuous or vile." In his last year at boarding school O'Neill armed himself with quotations from Shaw to fit every argument and convinced himself that the falsity in much of the popular art he knew only reflected the corruption and hypocrisy in contemporary society.

Eugene went, too, to Shaw's published plays, also available at Tucker's bookshop, and read all he could find, reinforcing his feeling that glib, happy endings, romantic rather than ironic, had no realistic relation to life. He absorbed the early Shaw so completely, an O'Neill biographer contends, too sweepingly, that "years later, when he created the character of Captain Brant in *Mourning Becomes Electra*, he would make him almost an exact duplicate of Shaw's Captain Brassbound [in the 1899 play *Captain Brassbound's Conversion*] without even being conscious of the plagiarism."

The play that Eugene first identified himself with was *Candida* (1894), in particular the eighteen-year-old aspiring poet tormented by unrequited love, Eugene Marchbanks. The coincidence of names intensified his passion for the play. In a romantic exchange with one young woman, O'Neill implored her, "I make the poet's plea in *Candida*." She went to the play for an explanation and found another aspiring writer named Eugene. Like O'Neill, Shaw's poet was shy and awkward, with a "haunted, tormented expression." She read the "auction" scene late in the play in which Candida Morell asks her puzzled husband and the young poet, more ironically than each realizes, what they are willing to bid for her love. Morell, who would be lost without her, proudly claims that he has the wherewithal to defend her and her quality of life. The poet, who desperately worships her, offers all he has: "My weakness. My desolation. My heart's need."

"That's a good bid, Eugene," says Candida, but she realizes that his world is not her own and that her husband, a smug and popular preacher, rather than Marchbanks, would fall apart without her. She sends the poet off. Anticipating rejection, Marchbanks announces melodramatically, "Out, then, into the night with me!" O'Neill's autobiographical Richard, not quite seventeen, quotes that line when his mother rebukes him for reading "indecent" books, among them *Candida*. At the bedroom door he adds, contemptuously, the enigmatic final comment in Shaw's stage directions for the play about the Morells, husband and wife: "*They do not know the secret in the poet's heart.*" O'Neill seems to have appropriated Shaw's sentimental irony.

In the bland, middle-class household in *Ah, Wilderness!* the "shy, dreamy, defiant" Richard conceals on his shelves, masking them unsuccessfully by other books, Carlyle's *The French Revolution* and Wilde's *The Ballad of Reading Gaol*, the plays of Ibsen, the poems of Swinburne (soon discovered), the once-sensational *Rubaiyat*, and two books, his mother charges, "by that Bernard Shaw."

"The greatest playwright alive today!" retorts Richard.

One of the books, Essie Miller goes on with sarcasm, "was so vile they wouldn't leave it play in New York!" The other, she informs her husband, "had a long title I couldn't made head or tail of, only it wasn't a play."

"*The Quintessence of Ibsenism*," Richard explains proudly.

As the third scene of act 4 opens, Nat Miller is leafing through the pile of books confiscated by Essie from their son's bedroom. Miller "*chuckles at something he reads*," then observes, "That Shaw's a comical cuss—even if his ideas are so crazy they oughtn't allow them to be printed. And Swinburne's got a fine swing to his poetry—if only he'd choose some other subjects beside loose women."

"I can see," Mrs. Miller says ("*teasingly*," O'Neill notes), "where you're becoming corrupted by these books, too—pretending to read them out of duty to Richard, when your nose has been glued to the page!"

Although the Millers want Richard to study, in family tradition, at Yale, his future is undefined when the curtain falls. The real Eugene, searching for what he described as "real life," would drop out of Princeton and sign up as a merchant seaman, then experience a physical breakdown that required a lengthy stay in a tuberculosis sanatorium. His enforced leisure to read convinced O'Neill that he wanted to be a playwright in the spirit of Ibsen and Shaw. On recovery in 1913, when he was already twenty-four, he studied playwriting at Harvard for a year and saw his early attempts performed by an amateur group—the Provincetown Players. Its stage became the proving ground where O'Neill learned how his plays actually worked in performance. Most were short and personal, as is typical of apprentice writers, and his growing pains are evident in them, as well as his reading and his experiences as a seaman—on deck, below deck, and in sleazy ports.

O'Neill seemed riveted by Ibsen and Shaw and their contemporaries. In an early play, *Fog*, his Poet—with a capital *P*—is a Marchbanks figure. Another, *A Wife for a Life*, reaches for Shavian domestic comedy. In *Now I Ask You*, more widely derivative, the recently married Lucy Ashleigh, his heroine, sounds like a Chekhov character, quotes Strindberg, acts like Hedda Gabler, and is fascinated by a young artist who tries to seduce her with echoes of *Candida*. Gabriel and Lucy closely parallel—almost to pastiche—the third act of Shaw's play as well as Ibsen's *Master Builder*, with Gabriel drawing his chair close to hers and offering to "come into your life and take you away, to the mountaintops, to the castles in the air, to the haunt of brave dreams where life is free, and joyous, and noble. . . . Can't you read the secret in my heart? Don't you hear the song my soul has been singing ever since I first looked into your eyes?" Her husband walks in, as did Candida's, and is immediately demoralized by what he erroneously thinks has already happened.

Just as derivative is *Servitude*, another 1914 effort beginning (in effect) when Nora Helmer slams the door in *A Doll's House*, and which continues as a sort of *Candida*, with the interloper this time a Nora rather than a Marchbanks. A play with Shaw-like dialogue about the role of women in contemporary marriage, it focuses upon a preachy playwright of advanced ideas, David Roylston, suggesting Rev. James Mavor Morell in *Candida*, whom women swoon over at his sermons, and a young married woman, Ethel Frazer, who has left her husband to live by Roylston's radical philosophy of self-realization.

Seeking out the playwright to reassure herself that she is living by his code, Ethel becomes infatuated with Roylston. But getting closer, she discovers that he is just another selfish husband exploiting a devoted wife who has submerged her own aspirations in coddling him into prominence. And it ends as does *Candida* with the departure of the intrusive third party and the reconciliation of husband and wife. "Mentally I am your creation," Mrs. Frazer tells Roylston, confronting him with the living result of his moralizing for the theater. "I demand that you restore my peace of mind by justifying me to myself." Attempting to do so, he confesses that a comfortable marriage in which he gives little back sustains his literary output. "My work comes first. As long as my home life gives free scope for my creative faculty, I will demand nothing further from it. . . . I accept my domestic bliss at its surface value and save my analytical eye for the creations of my brain." So-called love, he contends, "is the world upside down."

When Mrs. Roylston is forced to face the reality of her role as unpaid servant, Mrs. Frazer commiserates with her, "How unhappy you must have been!" But Ethel is startled by the paradox of Alice Roylston's impulsive and unexpected response. "Unhappy! . . . How little you know. I have been happy in serving him, happy in the knowledge that I have had my little part in helping him to success, happy to be able to shield and protect him." In a reversal of *Candida*, O'Neill's theme-and-variations on the play even has Mrs. Roylston confide that she is willing to leave her husband to Mrs. Frazer if that will enhance his professional success. Her offer awakens Roylston to his unsavory real self. Like Morell with Candida (who has offered to remain, rather than run off), he kneels beside his wife and begs forgiveness. But, she claims, restating the paradox of her answer to Ethel Frazer, "This *was* my happiness." And her husband, in O'Neill's stage directions, "*bends down and kisses her reverently.*" The young playwright, unsure whether to be satiric or sentimental, has it both ways.

In *The Quintessence of Ibsenism*, juxtaposing distancing with empathy, Shaw had referred to the ideal audience at a modern production as "guilty creatures at a play." In *Servitude*, neither sex was spared from that recognition of guilt, although O'Neill had not yet found his own voice. It would take the unsparing gloom of his 1920s tragedies to accomplish that. In the years before them he would see, in New York, not only Shavian "treats," as he put it, like *Pygmalion*, but also the repertory of the visiting Irish Players of Dublin, which included the plays of J. M. Synge, whose bleakness O'Neill would mirror. In the early 1920s he saw *Heartbreak House* and *Saint Joan*, presented by a new producing organization, the Theatre Guild, which would soon stage O'Neill's plays.

That conjunction made it all the more likely that Shaw would learn about O'Neill, and when biographer Archibald Henderson needed a money-spinning project and published a pseudo-dialogue in 1925, *Table-Talk of G.B.S.*, Shaw included his earliest references to O'Neill. "I have seen a couple of his plays," Shaw confirmed, "and read some others. They depend to some extent on false acting. For example, when Jean Cadell played *Diff'rent* in London, and played it so well that she made the woman absolutely real, the result was too painful to be bearable. . . . O'Neill's dramatic gift and sense of the stage are unquestionable, but as far as I know his work he is still only a Fantee[1] Shakespeare, peopling his tales with Calibans. I wonder what he would make of a civilized comedy like Moliere's *Misanthrope*."

Shaw had not known that while O'Neill was reaching for Shakespearean tragedy, he was also trying to write a Shavian comedy, attempting

---

1 The Fantee, or Fanti (first English usage 1819), are a tribe inhabiting the southern Gold Coast—now Ghana. Shaw seems to have been suggesting—perhaps with O'Neill's *The Emperor Jones* in mind—unpolished or unsophisticated writing, however powerful, in comparison to Shakespeare.

an anachronistic historical satire in the style of *Caesar and Cleopatra*. Critics have thematically associated *Marco Millions*, begun in 1923, with the publication of Sinclair Lewis's novel of the American Midwest, *Babbitt*, an evisceration of the go-getting businessman of the 1920s, yet Shaw had already included his own glib salesman as the Roman rug merchant Apollodorus. *Caesar and Cleopatra*, written in 1898–99, seems, like O'Neill's play, never intended to be actable in its entirety. Both are long by commercial stage standards, even O'Neill's truncated second version, while Shaw's own, later, script, shortened somewhat in 1912, begins with a prologue spoken before the curtain by an Egyptian god who recognizes the existence of a contemporary audience and warns spectators not to applaud him, O'Neill shifts his anachronistic equivalent to the epilogue, in which Marco Polo is found rising from his seat with the theater audience. O'Neill knew his first text, much trimmed in 1927, would be overly long, but he confessed to Kenneth Macgowan, "I'm letting the sky be the limit and putting every fancy in."

Glimpsing yet not really perceiving the close connections, O'Neill biographer Louis Sheaffer wrote, "While the central idea has possibilities, O'Neill was not the man to develop them. In the hands, say, of Shaw, the story could have been thoughtful, witty comedy along the lines of *Caesar and Cleopatra*; but O'Neill, though he had a sardonic sense of humor, and an Irishman's flair for comic exaggeration, was too slow on his feet for the kind of verbal Ping-Pong his story required."

Whatever historical fuzziness and contradictions exist in Marco Polo's history, O'Neill was entitled to the pegs on which to hang his play. It is more than seven hundred years since Polo returned from his twenty-four years' absence from Venice, seventeen of them allegedly spent in China. Three years after his return from wherever he had been in Asia, he found himself locked up in a Genoese jail for nearly a year, for his part in a Venetian war with Genoa, where he recounted—or invented—his experiences to a fellow prisoner, Rusticello (in O'Neill's play, Rusticiano). The alleged thirteenth-century original is lost, but Polo's claimed adventures were translated into many European languages, even Irish. Doubts about the authenticity of his travels arise from his reliance on earlier travelers' accounts for details and his omission of such obvious sights as the Great Wall, foot-binding of females, cormorant fishing in the Chinese interior, and the ubiquitous tea-drinking. He may have never crossed into China from Mongolia, bargaining, rather, with traders for porcelain and other objects he brought back, and for books.

Perhaps the basic flaw—after all, *Marco Millions* is a dark comedy rather than a satirical chronicle-history—was O'Neill's concept of Marco Polo as banal and superficial, entirely a thoughtless go-getter after quick wealth. The thoughtful characters, the Khan and his beautiful (and very young) granddaughter, Princess Kukachin, who loves Marco because she sees only his attractive surface, and misunderstands him, are given relatively minor roles. Although Kukachin is in effect the Cleopatra to Marco Polo's Caesar, her character is not given enough depth by O'Neill, and the bittersweet romance lacks balance. At the close, Marco returns to Italy laden with wealth, ready to marry his long-waiting, now middle-aged, virgin betrothed, while Kukachin, having lost the will to live, dwindles into premature death.

The passivity of the princess—hardly a Cleopatra—seems intended by O'Neill as ironic contrast to Marco's irrepressible ebullience, although audiences aware of his actual history know that prison lies in his future. The paradox at the close of Shaw's playful history is that Caesar, also abandoning a pretty—if imperious—young thing to return to Italy (Rome rather than Venice), is knowingly homeward bound to assassination plots and a grim end to glory, leaving an ambitious rather than a lovesick maiden to rule with a younger lover he is sending to her in his place—Marc Antony.

For a reader fresh from the script of *Caesar and Cleopatra*, the Shavian resonances in O'Neill's satire are striking, especially in the uncut earlier text. There are echoes of Shaw's straitlaced, proud Britannus in Marco's cellmate Rusticiano, who rejects Marco's rather cynical advice about authorship with "I shall write as becomes a gentleman." (O'Neill may be parodying Britannus's obsession with gentlemanly behavior.) Despite naive deviations into what he thinks passes for wit, O'Neill's Marco has a severe, unsentimental objectivity reminiscent of the older, sardonic Caesar. "Facts, statistics, useful data in general," he explains, "a book that'll do good, that's what I want to write." When Rusticiano insists, huffily, about his intentions for his own book, "I am writing it for Art, not for money," he reveals his Apollodorus side, Shaw having exploited his rug merchant to satirize the "art for art's sake" aspirants of the 1890s.

Pleased by the results of his juxtaposition of the present with the past, Shaw appended tongue-in-cheek historical notes to the published play to elaborate upon some of his anachronisms, suggesting that Shakespeare had done the same with striking clocks and such in his *Julius*

Caesar. O'Neill was content to let the clash of medieval with modern reverberate in the reader or listener without further gloss. His ironic lines, largely given to, or addressed to, Marco, are on business ethics, religious hypocrisy, Western obtuseness, and national jingoism. "Never forget," Marco's uncle, Maffeo Polo, tells him patriotically about Venice, "that by the blessing of God you were born in the finest little old spot on God's green footstool!" As if that had not echoed sufficient Irishness, O'Neill has Marco himself tell a story he claims to have heard "from an idol-polisher in Tibet": "It seems an Irishman got drunk in Tangut and wandered into a temple where he mistook one of the female statues for a real woman and. . . ." He then performs a comic pantomime more fit for a pub, which embarrasses his father and uncle. "Dolt!" scolds Nicolo Polo.

Shaw's happiest anachronism in *Caesar and Cleopatra* is a steam-operated crane that lifts supplies to the top of the lighthouse in Alexandria—"a machine with boiling water in it which I do not understand," Britannus confesses. "It is not of British design." O'Neill's challenge for the set designer is a conveyor belt leading from a moored junk to the Khan's wharf at Zaiton. It is given at first sight the ironic appearance of powered machinery:

> In the right, is a warehouse, from a door in which an endless chain of half-naked slaves, their necks, waists, and right ankles linked up by chains, form an endless chain which revolves mechanically as it were, on sprocket wheels in the interiors of the shed and the junk. As each individual link passes out of the shed, it carries a bale on its head, moves with mechanical precision across the wharf, disappears into the junk, reappears a moment later having dumped its load and moves back into the shed. The whole process in a man power replica of the endless chain engines with bucket scoops that dredge, load coal, sand, etc. By the side of the shed, a foreman sits with a drum and gong with which he marks a perfect time for the slaves, a four beat rhythm, three beats of the drum, the fourth a bang on the gong as one slave at each end loads and unloads. The effect is very like the noise of a machine.

Marco Millions strikingly echoes, too, other Shaw plays. When the philosophical Kublai Khan and Marco discuss the possibility of the soul's immortality, the prosaic Venetian responds, mirroring the recognition of death by Adam and Eve in the corpse of a deer, and how life is renewed, in *Back to Methuselah*, just staged by O'Neill's own producers, the Theatre Guild. If humans had no soul, Marco contends, "nothing" would follow when one died: "you's be dead—just like an animal." And at the close, when Marco finally returns to Venice, his now dowdy but faithful betrothed, Donata, gushes, while hurrying to embrace him—as does Raina in *Arms and the Man* when Major Sergius Saranoff returns from his war—"My hero!" (Soon after O'Neill began going to the theater, "My Hero!" became a popular song, from the unauthorized musicalization of Shaw's play as *The Chocolate Soldier*. By 1910 it was a long-running hit in New York.) And echoing the beginning of the fourth act of *Caesar and Cleopatra* itself, the tempestuous (although fragile) Princess Kukachin, like the young Cleopatra, makes demands of her servants with the warning, supposedly typical of mistress—slave relationships, "—or I shall order you beaten!"

Marco's surface acceptance of his Western religion is scoffed at by the Khan much as he rejects Eastern alternatives of "drown[ing] in dream until you become a dream." He mocks his Court theologian, Chu Yin, with a sardonic dismissal that mirrors Shaw's Don Juan in *Man and Superman* as he repudiates the Devil's cheap sentimentality. (The entire exchange has the ring of the play's "Don Juan in Hell" dream scene.) "I have found no new faith in your Way," Kublai Khan scoffs, "and I have lost the old faith in mine. I no longer believe in my significance nor in man's. That we should imagine a meaning for ourselves beyond the obvious one of gorging our greedy pride . . . is for me only a final proof of idiot vanity. No, man does not yet deserve a soul. He is still the least human species of ape and because he is the only house-broken one we call him civilized—but we shouldn't be cheated by our own make-believe."

A science adviser to the Khan describes Marco, in a term that suggests Andrew Undershaft's religious self-definition in *Major Barbara*, as a "mystic idealist." (Undershaft claims to be "a confirmed mystic.") Yet when a competing adviser scorns Marco as a materialist, the scientist gibes that Marco "knows nothing of Matter, not even his own body, of which he is piously ashamed, and he worships a grey-whiskered Ghost with a bad temper whose address is a golden street somewhere in the sky." The lines are even more scathing about orthodox faith than Shaw's, and the references to pious prudishness about the body seems to reflect the dialogue in Hell as well as its intellectual successor, *Back to Methuselah*. Even earlier, Shaw's Caesar teases Britannus about painting his body blue (with woad), about which the mock Briton explains in his own defense that "though our enemies may strip us of our clothes and our lives, they cannot strip us of our respectability."

A direct echo of *Major Barbara* appears in act 5, when Marco demonstrates his invention of artillery to the Khan, revealing a cannon from which a lead ball is shot to knock a breach in a wall of blocks. In *Major Barbara*, Undershaft the millionaire armorer demonstrates his new cannon, mangling a group of life-size models of soldiers. Cynically, he observes that efficient weapons "make war on war" by creating such awesome destruction that their very existence—and potential—will usher in an era of peace. "War," O'Neill's Marco explains with the facile persuasiveness of a traveling salesman, "is a waste of labor and material which eats into the dividends of life. . . . Then why war, I asked myself? Why not a lasting peace with profit? But isn't war a natural resource of our human natures, poisoned at birth by the justice of God with original sin? How are you going to end it? . . . There's only one workable way and that's to lick everybody else in the world. A tough proposition, you object? Not any more! This little invention you see before you makes conquering easy." And he employs the powder that the Chinese heretofore had used only for harmless fireworks displays to power his cannon.

"You see?" he points out enthusiastically when his father, Nicolo, retrieves the deadly cannonball. "Now just picture to yourself this little ball magnified. . . . The destruction of property and loss of life would be tremendous! No one could resist you. You'd conquer the world into one great peace-loving, hard-working brotherhood of man!"

The nihilist in O'Neill sees no such future, but Shaw more hopefully creates a debate about the possibility in the dream interlude in *Man and Superman*. "Has the colossal mechanism no purpose?" asks Don Juan. "None, my friend," retorts the Devil. "You think, because you have a purpose, Nature must have one. You might as well expect it to have fingers and toes because you have them." O'Neill's Kublai Khan concedes no purpose and points to the fading of the youthful beauty of Kukachin, and her inevitable unhappiness, even misery, with or without Marco Polo, as evidence that life is "insane." He asks Chu Yin, "Why is all this? What purpose can it serve? My hideous suspicion is that the very essence of life may be merely an infinite, crazy energy which creates and destroys without [any] other purpose than to pass infinite time."

Possibly struck by how Shaw dramatically managed Caesar's leave-taking from Egypt, with Cleopatra arriving dressed entirely (and awesomely) in black in contrast to the colorful crowd at the close, O'Neill stages the departure of Princess Kukachin almost as a direct echo. In his stage directions, "*A cry of adoration goes up from the crowd as with one movement they prostrate themselves as the Princess comes down from the cabin dressed in a robe of silver and stands at the rail looking down.*" In what O'Neill describes as "*a long ululating whisper*" they cry out, "Farewell—farewell—farewell." Even the usually casual Marco Polo is moved. Caesar, earlier, had to suppress his own emotions at the close of Shaw's play.

At the end of *Marco Millions*, O'Neill seems to return to *The Quintessence of Ibsenism* and Shaw's excoriation of Duty as one of the worst sins visited upon humanity. All of Marco's dubious accomplishments, he boasts, have come from his fidelity to Duty. "*Squirming*"—O'Neill writes—"*onto a high moral plane*," Marco declares to the Venetians who welcome him, wealth-laden, on his return, "I was true to a trust that was placed in me. I had a job to do and I did it, that's all there was to it. I acted as a man of honesty and integrity ought to act, for, thank God, my moral sense of duty has always proved stronger than any temptation."

"Yes," Rusticiano says, "*a bit slyly ironic*" after listening to Marco's account of himself, "you are a good man." The scene fades to a final one in which the Khan receives the body of his adored Kukachin, shipped home from Persia. The lights come up for the epilogue, an ironic presentational twist upon Shaw's prologue to *Caesar and Cleopatra*:

> The play is over. The lights come up brilliantly in the theatre. In an aisle seat in the first row a man gets up, conceals a yawn in his palm, stretches his legs as if they had become cramped by too long an evening, takes his hat from under the seat and starts to file slowly out with the others in the audience. But, although there is nothing out of the ordinary in his actions, his appearance excites general comment and surprise for he is dressed as a Venetian merchant of the later 13th century. In fact, it is none other than MARCO POLO himself looking a bit sleepy, a trifle puzzled and not a little irritated as his thoughts, in spite of himself, cling for a passing moment to the play just ended. He appears quite unaware of being unusual and walks in the crowd without self-consciousness, very much as one of them. Arrived at the lobby, his face begins to clear of all disturbing memories of what had transpired on the stage. The noise, the lights of the street, all recall him at once to himself. Impatiently

he waits for his car, casting a glance here and there at faces in the groups around him, his eyes impersonally speculative, his bearing stolid with the dignity of one who is sure of his place in the world, His car, a luxurious Pierce-Arrow limousine, draws up at the curb. He gets in briskly, the door is slammed, the car edges away into the traffic and POLO, with a satisfied sigh at the comfort of it all, comes back to life.

How much, if any, of the action in the epilogue was meant for production, and how much, for the reader, is left to the imagination—including that of the director? How much of the play itself evidences O'Neill's Shavian homework, and how much emanates from memory of books and performances, is also anyone's guess. Nevertheless, the echoes are striking.

By the mid-1920s, O'Neill had found his own voice, a somber and realistic one that earned him an enthusiastic reception in the United States. And Shaw was reading, and even viewing, O'Neill's early productions as they found stages in London. Shaw wrote that by 1923 he had seen O'Neill performed "once or twice." If he recognized any Shavian reverberations, he kept that to himself, yet there were, but for the more mordant plays, hints of Shaw, and when O'Neill's urge toward satire returned, more echoes would emerge, for he continued to keep up with Shaw through the Theatre Guild. (It may have had nothing to do with Shaw, but even one of O'Neill's homes, a house on Sea Island, Georgia, would have a study that recalled the interior setting of *Heartbreak House*, a sea captain's quarters on an old sailing ship.)

O'Neill had hoped for an elaborate production of *Marco Millions*, but even in the prosperous mid-1920s the staging of its many scenes seemed too costly. One producer, Gilbert Miller, claimed that he could not find what O'Neill described as a "romantic, handsome hero"—a casting that the playwright deplored because it would have undermined the satirical focus in order to sell tickets. O'Neill returned to another play that would distress producers, the overly long *Strange Interlude*. He saw precedents for long plays in Shaw. *Man and Superman* was now being performed complete to the Hell scene. Its first full production in London had been in 1925, as O'Neill was beginning his new play, and Shaw's five-play cycle, *Back to Methuselah*, had been daringly done in both London and New York over two evenings. *Strange Interlude*, "which occupied an afternoon and an evening with an interval for dinner," Shaw joked to London publisher Baliol Holloway, "was such a success that the Theatre Guild begged me to write my next play in eight acts."

Travis Bogard argued that it was "not essential to posit a direct connection between Shaw's massive statement of the myth of creative evolution [in *Methuselah*] and O'Neill's long choric drama *Lazarus Laughed*, which he wrote in 1925. The two plays are attempts to frame new religious doctrine, suitable to their nations and their epochs. Both plays emerge from evolutionary conceptions. Like Shaw, O'Neill had responded creatively to conceptions that Darwin and Lamarck had loosed into modern thought. . . . Neither playwright, faced with the consequences of evolutionary theory, was willing to exist in a world without God, and both sought to describe the nature of divinity in plays that were essentially religious. The difference in the myths each formulated lies in the direction of the search."

One striking parallel seemingly beyond coincidence is what might be termed the invention of death as a good. In the striking Garden of Eden opening play of Shaw's cycle, *In the Beginning*, Adam and Eve come upon a fawn dead in an accident. It has "a queer smell" as it decays, and the first humans recoil from it. But the Serpent describes death as a necessity to renewal, and in *Lazarus Laughed*, O'Neill argues that the cosmic processes require it. "As dust," Lazarus preaches, "you are eternal change, and everlasting growth." To both, evolutionary progress is as dependent upon death as upon length of life.

Strange Interlude was based not only on a story that O'Neill had heard in Provincetown in 1923 but also, Louis Sheaffer claims, on *Man and Superman*, another work that stretched traditional commercial length. O'Neill's Nina Leeds is by Sheaffer's reckoning an Everywoman just as is Shaw's Ann Whitefield—an embodiment of feminine vitality enhanced by an unscrupulousness necessary to work her genetic will. "If women were as fastidious as men, morally or physically," Shaw wrote sardonically in his preface to the play, "there would be an end to the race." Ann's purpose, claims John Tanner, the man she intends to marry, to his supposed rival, Octavius Robinson, "is neither her happiness nor yours, but Nature's. Vitality in a woman is a blind fury of creation. She sacrifices herself to it: do you think she will hesitate to sacrifice you?" As Bogard puts it, "Both dramatists feel that woman stands near the philosophical centre of life, and that men circle around the force she radiates." O'Neill's superman, to Bogard, is "the risen Lazarus." Much as in the Lilith close in *Methuselah*, "The loss of consciousness, the end of thought, the disappearance into the whirlpool of matter, are for O'Neill the supreme good."

Although Shaw's *Man and Superman*, despite the kind of dialogue between lovers described from Restoration drama as a "duel of sex" and the subplot of a not-quite-concealed pregnancy, is ironic in tone in comparison with O'Neill's preoccupation with coupling and its results, other echoes from Shaw's plays emerge in *Strange Interlude*. Nina's first lover, who dies in World War I, is named Gordon *Shaw*. An early aviator, he parallels John Tanner, who, in the dawn of powered flight, is an early automobilist. (In the first American production Tanner was played by Robert Loraine, known as a pioneer aviator.) A later aspirant for Nina's affections is Charles Marsden. However much he is based on another O'Neill friend (the suggested prototypes for Gordon and Charles, both artists, had little interest in women), Marsden seems also to be Shaw's Octavius, a genteel poet and Tanner's professed rival for Ann. However, she does not take him seriously. "Men like that," she confides to Tanner, who resists her almost to the end, "always live in comfortable bachelor quarters with broken hearts."

Octavius sighs, rather than lusts, after Ann. O'Neill's equivalent to Tanner, Edmund Darrell, is Nina's second lover, succeeding the man she first marries, Sam Evans, after Gordon Shaw's wartime death. Darrell, in O'Neill's complicated sexual roundabout, regards himself, as does Tanner, as "too knowing about the nature and wiles of Woman to succumb"—not because, like Shaw's smug hero, he has read all the relevant philosophers and scientists on sex, but because—as a physician—he considers himself "immune to love" through his "understanding of its real sexual nature." Both men, Louis Sheaffer observes, are "overpowered," nevertheless, by what Shaw and his protagonist label the "Life Force"—the "universal creative energy" for which human beings are only the agents. Darrell is swept by it into Nina's arms as Tanner is drawn inexorably to Ann. The Life Force "enchants" him, John Tanner confesses, resorting to his philosophical label for what appears to be passion: "I have the whole world in my arms when I clasp you." But to both Ann and Nina it makes little difference what higher motive is involved.

Rehearsals for the marathon Theatre Guild productions of both the nine-act *Strange Interlude* and the lengthy (but now shortened) *Marco Millions* went on almost concurrently late in 1927. Alfred Lunt, then playing the rogue artist in Shaw's *The Doctor's Dilemma* to his wife's Jennifer (who would be Louis Dubedat's widow by the end of the play), was to be Marco Polo, and O'Neill went to see Shaw's play in order to size up Lunt.

Unfortunately for *Marco Millions*, Lunt, who disliked the burlesque role, was cast in it anyway and performed without enthusiasm. The sardonic contrasts between Western materialism and Eastern idealism seemed, to him, unsubtle, the artistry artificial. O'Neill was operating, for Lunt, in an uncongenial dimension. The play was only a tepid success.

O'Neill turned next to the tragic mode, in which he felt more comfortable, and which met audience expectations for him. Again his play would be overly long, taking up both a matinee and an evening. As *Mourning Becomes Electra*, it suggested classic Greek tragedy. Setting his equivalent to the Agamemnon story during the American Civil War, his link to Homeric Troy, O'Neill created a melodrama fueled by the oedipal passions of son for mother and daughter for father, then brother for sister. The adulteries within the Mannon family include that of Captain Adam Brant, who is the Aegisthus to Christine Mannon's Clytemnestra. Even here, however, O'Neill seemed unable to escape Shaw. Captain Brant, Doris Alexander observes, becomes a completely different personality in O'Neill's second draft of the play than he had been in the first. A complete new character, she asserts, "walked into his play and blended so fully with his fated family that O'Neill never saw himself that his Captain Brant was really . . . Shaw's Captain Brassbound stepped intact out of *Captain Brassbound's Conversion.*" O'Neill had read Shaw's tragicomic play about justice and revenge in the volume *Three Plays for Puritans* (1901), the volume in which he had also read *Caesar and Cleopatra*, and had seen *Brassbound* performed while he was studying playwriting at Harvard. Shaw's sea captain is embittered by his passion for revenge against his uncle, Howard Hallam, an English judge whom he charges "with the death of my mother and the theft of my inheritance." In O'Neill's play, according to Doris Alexander, Captain Brant similarly accuses his cousin, Ezra Mannon, "and does so out of the same feeling of guilt he had in Shaw's play because he had not been 'very fond' of his mother or 'very good' to her." Brassbound's mother had, Mannon asserts, "a very violent temper," and Brant concedes that his mother had been "very strict" with him, even beating him, while she petted and spoiled his cousin Ezra.

"In both plays," Alexander contends, "Captain Brassbound/Brant hides his own guilt by accusing his uncle-cousin of letting his mother die 'of sickness and starvation,' for he himself had fled from her. He is very touchy about her honor in both plays. In Shaw he springs at his uncle, crying, 'He did not spare my mother'—'That woman,' he calls her—'because of her sex. I will not spare him because of his age.'" In O'Neill's play, Brant rises up at Lavinia's scorn of her mother, crying, "Belay, damn you!—or I'll forget you're a woman—no Mannon can insult her while I—"[2] There the dialogue breaks off.

Alexander speculates that O'Neill made Brant a clipper captain because Brassbound skippered a sailing vessel, and that O'Neill also gave him the same romantic appearance, "more like a gambler or a poet," she writes, "than a ship captain." Although O'Neill may have drawn aspects of his Captain Brant from a historical figure, "otherwise he kept his Brassbound's origin, and even took from Shaw's character the irony of [his] judging a judge. Before Brassbound took over Brant, Ezra Mannon had been [in the earlier draft] only [the] town's leading citizen, Mayor before [the] war. He became a former judge as well when Brassbound came into O'Neill's play."

Although the parallels seem persuasive, Alexander sees the link weaken when in *Mourning Becomes Electra* the Captain quickly falls "passionately in love, which he never would have done for Shaw." Yet Brassbound does indeed fall in love, his self-discipline eroding when he encounters the charming but somewhat older Lady Cicely (a hint in the direction of O'Neill's mother-son incest?), and he proposes to her. Tempted as she is, the indomitable lady traveler refuses him, and Cicely Waynflete breathes, at the close, "What an escape!" Even there, O'Neill sailed close to his likely source.

As his play was being prepared for performance, he tried to convince Maurice Wertheim of the Theatre Guild that *Mourning* was "a trilogy and not three separate plays" and that it required what he characterized as "the driving impact of a trilogy concentrated in one week—a bigger [*Strange*] *Interlude* in that sense!" However "seemingly impossible," he contended, the producers "may well lose out by [not] doing what is [now] a commonplace stunt, done before with Shaw's *Methuselah*."

O'Neill by then had divorced and remarried, going on a honeymoon to London early in 1928, traveling incognito to avoid notoriety and staying at the Berkeley in Mayfair. There is no evidence that he tried to see Shaw, who had not written a play since *Saint Joan* in 1923, and whose

---

2 Lavinia Mannon is the daughter, or Electra, figure. Her brother, Orin, is the Orestes figure.

next play, *The Apple Cart*, would not be begun until later in 1928. Shaw would be on the mind, however, of O'Neill's editor when *Mourning* was being prepared for print. Since the published text of *Strange Interlude* had, remarkably for a play, sold over a hundred thousand copies, Saxe Commins, still O'Neill's editor, hoped for a similar success after the Broadway opening. To help promote the book version, he planned to precede it with a brochure of short pieces about O'Neill and his work by theatrical and literary luminaries. He solicited such notables as Thomas Mann, Bernard Shaw, Sinclair Lewis, and Sean O'Casey. Mann offered regrets, while conceding that he saw "epic" qualities in O'Neill's plays. Lewis wrote that O'Neill had "revolutionized" what had been a "rather stupid and tawdry drama." O'Casey wrote gushily that O'Neill had redeemed the stage "from the shame of a house of ill-repute and a den of thieves." Shaw's secretary, Blanche Patch, wrote for him to Commins, characteristically, that "nothing is more revoltingly unreadable than logrolling[3] and that he implores you to abandon the project. . . . Otherwise O'Neill will probably sue you for damages."

That did not keep Shaw from the play. Someone told him, he wrote to Stella Campbell on May 2, 1932, "that you were wonderful and beautiful as O'Neill's Electra, which, as it happened, I had just read." The next day he learned that his informant "had made a slight error." Mrs. Campbell was playing the original Clytemnestra of Aeschylus, "not O'Neill's." On returning to the Riviera from New York and finding Shaw's letter, she shot back, "I found O'Neill's *Mourning Becomes Electra* horrible. [Alla] Nazimova had one fine emotional moment, worth something to see, but not [worth] all I suffered that afternoon and evening." But the play won for O'Neill his third Pulitzer Prize.

For all his admiration of O'Neill, especially his handling of sexual psychology, Shaw was still ambivalent about sex onstage. Although he had King Magnus and his mistress, Orinthia, wrestle—but clothed—onstage in the futuristic fantasy *The Apple Cart*, a vein of Victorian Irish prudishness left him uneasy about O'Neill's more direct sexuality. In the year of *Mourning* he wrote to Frank Harris, who was writing a biography of Shaw to pay debts and wanted to include Shaw's own sexual history, to warn him about money-grubbing pornographic memoirs, "This book is your chance of recovering your tall hat; and you want to throw it away

---

3 *Logrolling*, an American political term now in disuse, referred to the exchange of votes, or favors.

for the sake of being in the fashion of O'Neill, Joyce and George Moore." Yet Shaw would also write to English impresario Charles Cochran, "If only someone would build you a huge Woolworth theatre (all seats sixpence) to start with O'Casey and O'Neill, and no plays by men who had ever seen a five-pound note before they were thirty or had been inside a school after they were thirteen, you would be buried in Westminster Abbey." Shaw did not have O'Neill's school days exactly right, but he was clearly on his side.

That popular appeal became even more obvious after the rapturous reception of *Mourning* (notwithstanding Mrs. Campbell). Despite expensive tickets for the two-part performance, and the drawback of the Depression, it ran for 130 performances. Wits described it as "Mourning Becomes O'Neill" and "Evening Becomes Impenetrable," but critics and audiences perceived a grandeur in the somber play. The year after, when Shaw and W. B. Yeats were planning an Irish Academy of Letters that would include some associate members of Irish ancestry who were not Irish by birth, Shaw recommended American-born O'Neill and Welsh-born T. E. Lawrence. James Joyce, an authentic Dubliner, rejected his appointment, but O'Neill wrote to his elder son, "I regard this as an honor, whereas other Academies don't mean much to me. Anything with Yeats, Shaw, A.E., O'Casey, Flaherty, Robinson is good enough for me."

Four years later, in November 1936, O'Neill, at forty-eight, received the Nobel Prize for Literature. Shaw told a reporter that it was "an excellent decision. I always thought that this year's prize should go either to Upton Sinclair or O'Neill, so America would have received it in either case. Of course, I am very pleased." (Sinclair proved too political for the Nobel committee in his lifetime, but would not be so now.) What especially pleased O'Neill, he told fellow playwright Russell Crouse, was that the Irish ambassador in Washington congratulated him for "adding, along with Shaw and Yeats, to the credit of old Ireland." What, he asked, "could be more perfect?"

"Oddly," Travis Bogard, O'Neill's most thorough critic, thought, O'Neill resembled Shaw more than he did other playwrights of their century often associated with him. Bogard pointed not only to the "triangle play," the "melodramatic thriller," the drawing-room comedy, the chronicle history, and the plays "disquisitory in content and mythic in intention." Even Shaw's late "expressionistic" play *The Simpleton of the Unexpected Isles* (1934) he saw as much "experimental in its way as O'Neill's theatrical experiments."

Thwarted in the completion of his last plays by illness—O'Neill was handicapped by the tremors of Parkinson's disease and its attendant psychological devastation—he worked with intermittent intensity but finished little he began after 1940. One of his attempts, for which he wrote a scenario and some scenes, was "The Last Conquest," which has echoes of Shaw's "Don Juan in Hell" interlude from *Man and Superman*. It has as its principal characters Caesar, Satan, and an Everyman figure who may be Christ and who is, in one draft, a statue carved by Satan. The Hell scene, of course, has a talking statue as one of its four characters. A philosophical dialogue basically between Man and the Devil, the scenes are dominated by a proud, boastful, although warm, Satan, who, like Shaw's, has grown bored and possesses a satiric bravado rather than a fire-and-brimstone evil, while the Man (or Christ figure), for whom he has little but contempt, seems engaged in an eternal charade of resistance to Satanic temptation and longs for solitude from a humanity that disappoints him. He craves crucifixion, while Satan begs to take his place or at least to suspend the events that will lead inevitably to it.

As late as 1948, O'Neill was still struggling with his mordant parallel to "Don Juan in Hell." His darker version reflected the bleak O'Neill personality now even more burdened by physical deterioration. He died in November 1953, three years after Shaw. Obituaries saw no connection between the tragic outlook of O'Neill and the sardonic perspectives of Shaw, but O'Neill's playwriting journey had begun with Shaw, and the fading echoes of that initiation were still there at the end.

Bibliographic Essay

Shaw's plays are quoted from the *Complete Plays with Their Prefaces*. O'Neill's plays (but for the early "lost" texts) are quoted from *The Plays of Eugene O'Neill* (New York: Oxford University Press, 1988). Other than where noted, others are from Eugene O'Neill, *Ten Lost Plays* (New York: Random House, 1964).

O'Neill's anxiety over the Shaw portrait is from S. J. Wolf, "O'Neill Plots a Course for the Drama," *New York Times,* October 4, 1931. Carlotta Monterey wrote to Saxe Commins in September 1932, quoted in Dorothy Commins, ed., *"Love and Admiration and Respect": The O'Neill-Commins Correspondence* (Durham: Duke University Press, 1986). Commins responded on September 20, 1932, with a Shaw bibliography.

Jimmy Durkin's letter to James O'Neill, Spokane, Washington, February 20, 1905, is British Library Add. MS 50516, fols. 228–29, first published in Stanley Weintraub, "Eugene O'Neill: The Shavian Dimension," *SHAW* 18 (1998). Eugene O'Neill's letter to Norwegian editor Hans Olav, May 13, 1938, is in Travis Bogard and Jackson Bryer, eds., *Selected Letters of Eugene O'Neill* (New Haven: Yale University Press, 1988) (hereafter *Letters*).

Louis Sheaffer quotes O'Neill on *Quintessence* ("red ink" and "virtuous or vile") in his *O'Neill: Son and Playwright* (New York: Little, Brown, 1968). Other references to Sheaffer are from Schaeffer, including Blanche Patch's writing to Commins for Shaw. Don Alexander's study is *The Tempering of Eugene O'Neill* (New York: Harcourt, Brace, 1962); later, when she again refers to *Mourning Becomes Electra*, it is from her *Eugene O'Neill's Creative Struggle* (University Park: Penn State Press, 1992).

Now I Ask You and *Servitude* are quoted from *Ten Lost Plays* and were first viewed as Shavian by Travis Bogard in his *Contour in Time: The Plays of Eugene O'Neill* (New York: Oxford University Press, 1988). Shaw's quotes on O'Neill's early plays from Archibald Henderson, ed., *Table-Talk of G.B.S.* (New York: Harper, 1925), are actually supposed conversations written by Shaw, who permitted Henderson, then hard up, to collect the royalties as editor.

The performance text of *Marco Millions* is in *Plays*; the earlier and longer text is in Travis Bogard, ed., *The Unknown O'Neill: Unpublished or Unfamiliar Writings of Eugene O'Neill* (New Haven: Yale University Press, 1988). Doris Alexander, letter to Stanley Weintraub, Venice, June 22, 1996, observes that Bogard has apparently misread the manuscript title, which at first was *Marco Million*, after the satirical name for young Polo, "Il Milione." ("In Italian one gives a name to the article. Later, O'Neill decided the idea would be conveyed better if he called it *Marco Millions*.") Other misreadings, she notes, include "My hideous intuition is" for "My hideous suspicion is." I have corrected such misreadings in the text as quoted.

O'Neill's letter to Angles Boulton O'Neill, November 27, 1927, is in the O'Neill *Letters*. His letter to Maurice Wertheim, June 15, 1931, to Eugene O'Neill Jr., November 11, 1932, and to Russell Crouse, November 25, 1936, are also in *Letters*. Shaw's letter to Basil Holloway, June 12, 1930, is in Dan H. Laurence, ed., *Theatrics* (Toronto: University of Toronto Press, 1995); his letters to Mrs. Stella Patrick Campbell, May 2 and May 3, 1932, are in

Alan Dent, ed., *Bernard Shaw and Mrs. Patrick Campbell: Their Correspondence* (New York: Knopf, 1952). His letter to Frank Harris, April 21, 1931, is in Stanley Weintraub, ed., *The Playwright and the Pirate* (University Park: Penn State Press, 1982); his letter to Charles Cochran is quoted by Eileen O'Casey in her *Sean* (New York: Coward-McCann, 1972). His comment on O'Neill's Nobel Prize appeared in the *New York Times*, November 13, 1936.

O'Neill's incomplete play *The Last Conquest* was published in Virginia Hoyt, ed., *Eugene O'Neill: The Unfinished Plays* (New York: Ungar, 1988).

· 11 ·

Noël Coward and the Avuncular Shaw

A child actor since he was eleven, Noël Peirce Coward spent nine months in the British army in 1918, after which roles like Slightly in *Peter Pan* and the schoolboy Charley in *Charley's Aunt* were no longer credible. As a juvenile he had often played opposite Esmé Wynne, already known for the children's musical *Where the Rainbow Ends*, which included Coward, Hermione Gingold, and Jack Hawkins. Prematurely political, Esmé fueled Coward's rebellious nature. "We were rooted and grounded in Bernard Shaw who said the majority were always wrong," and like GBS they were wartime pacifists; yet as Coward reached draft age, he was called up, proved medically fragile, and was invalided out before the Armistice. Seeking parts he could play himself once he became twenty on December 16, 1919, he wrote a comedy, *I'll Leave It to You*, which, despite good notices, closed in five weeks. It was his fourth attempt, the earlier three written and wisely discarded by the time he was seventeen.

Trying his hand at fiction at eighteen, before his army call-up, he had written a novel, *Cats and Dogs*, after Shaw's comedy *You Never Can Tell*, with a pert pair based on GBS's teenage twins Phillip and Dolly. According to Coward's biographer Cole Lesley, Coward's "bright young things prattled away with unparalleled vivacity for nearly eighty thousand words until the story mercifully and untidily came to an end." It seemed unpublishable, but he recalled it after he saw a matinee of Shaw's comedy at the Garrick, and in 1921, chancing that he could play the impetuous brother if he were aged somewhat, Coward turned the novel he had "filched unscrupulously" from Shaw (as he described it at a literary luncheon forty-three years later) into a play, *The Young Idea*. Coward's stage brother and sister, rather than twins, as in Shaw, were now twenty-one and eighteen.

To display his own characters where their inhibitions might be loosened, Shaw set his comedy at a beachfront resort hotel; Coward moved the action to a lodge in hunt country. *You Never Can Tell* had focused its irony on the encounters with staid Victorian manners of the play's precocious twins, who had grown up in sunny Madeira under their feminist mother's tutelage. Coward had first learned of the world beyond London at fifteen, when he was invited by the socialite Mrs. Astley Cooper, an eccentric "old duck" enchanted by his acting, to her country house at Hambleton Hall, and then to her Italian villa at Alassio. The Madeira of *You Never Can Tell* became Lombardy and added Continental sophistication to young Coward's ripening social verve. Shaw's play, the exotic backgrounds for his impertinent siblings, and the mothering Mrs. Cooper in Alassio contributed most of the ingredients to *The Young Idea*, which Coward updated from the 1890s with postwar pleasure-seekers and their openly easy morals.

Confessing his guilt about the obvious plagiarism but hoping to see the comedy staged, Coward offered his script to John Vedrenne, who had produced Shaw's plays in the great Court Theatre seasons (1904-7) and beyond. Although Coward feared Shaw's wrath, Vedrenne sent the script to GBS, asking if he had any objections. Shaw returned the pages promptly with constructive interlinear comments to the author, including suggestions for rewriting the last act. Still, when Vedrenne told Shaw that he was unpersuaded about production and was returning Coward's pages, GBS on June 27, 1921, wrote encouragingly to the young playwright, whom he did not realize had intended to play the key role himself,

> I gather from Mr Vedrenne that he turned the play down because he had some misgivings about trying to repeat the old success of the twins in You Never Can Tell, and was not quite sure that you had pulled off the final scene which I suggested. But when once a manager has entertained a play at all, his reasons for discarding it are pretty sure to be business and circumstantial ones. When you put impudent people on the stage they are very amusing when the actor or actress has sufficient charm to make the audience forgive the impudence: in my youth Charles Mathews lived on impudent parts; and every comedy had a stage cynic in it. [Charles] Hawtrey

has kept up the tradition to some extent; but impudence has long been out of fashion; your twins will take some casting to make them pardonable. I daresay Vedrenne did not know where to lay his hands on the right pair.

I have no doubt that you will succeed if you persevere, and take care never to fall into a breach of essential good manners, and above all, never see or read my plays. Unless you get clean away from me you will begin as a back number, and be hopelessly out of it when you are forty.

Faithfully,
G. Bernard Shaw

Coward was awed, for (as he wrote in his autobiography) "there was more than brilliance in the trouble that great man had taken in going minutely over the work of a comparatively unknown young writer." Coward's "comparatively" was a much later stretch: he *was* unknown. Yet he did not take Shaw's advice completely. He saw several GBS plays, read many more, and—a generation later—even starred in one. After several rounds of submissions he managed to find a producer, Robert Courtneidge, who toured *The Young Idea* for six weeks, beginning in Bristol on September 25, 1922, then opened it in London at the Savoy Theatre on February 1, 1923, where it ran for sixty performances.

For twenty pounds a week Coward played Sholto Brent, his updated version of Shaw's teenage Phillip Clandon. As in Shaw's comedy, the high-spirited young people, Gerda and Sholto, have lived their lives abroad, tutored by their divorcée mother, Jennifer, a successful writer of romantic novels. (Shaw's emancipated Mrs. Clandon writes tracts on modern manners.) Remarried uneasily to the quickly "tiresome" and flagrantly unfaithful Cicely, George Brent has invited his children for the first time to his lodge in hunt country, perhaps hoping that their proximity would inhibit his wife's dalliances. Since they do not know Brent, having been separated from him for sixteen years, Gerda must ask, introducing herself in overly childlike fashion, "Please, are you our daddy?" (In Shaw, the grumpy Fergus Crampton is long separated from the lady who now publishes as Mrs. Lanfrey Clandon. To complicate the action, the seemingly irresponsible twins have an attractive elder sister, Gloria, in Shaw's stage directions "the incarnation of haughty highmindedness.")

Coward's George Brent has even taken a rare day off from hunting (which he privately finds tedious) to await Sholto and Gerda, and Brent's reference to his former wife, Jennifer, prompts the bitchy Cicely to bluster, "To have her children here is bad enough, but for you to hold her up to me as an example! . . . Don't expect me to be nice to your children when they arrive. I consider it an insult to me for you to have asked them at all." The presence of Sholto and Gerda complicates the odious Cicely's open affair with Rodney Masters, her most recent lover, and the children are quickly aware of the affair. Unnoticed, Sholto impudently posts on the mantelpiece, for Cicely and George's insufferable houseguests to see, two photographs of the still-attractive, sun-bronzed Jennifer writing in her garden in Alassio.

Cicely soon has another distraction. Unable, with the children about, to join Rodney for their usual tryst, she discovers from him that his brother, a planter in Jamaica, has suddenly died, and that he will have to leave shortly and assume the estate's management. For Roddy it is an inconvenience. For the twins it is an opportunity. To increase Cicely's discomfort, they pretend that they are happy in the country, residing with their father, and absurdly, despite showing him happy pictures of Jennifer at home, claim, to the others, abandonment in Alassio—that their mother, allegedly an alcoholic, has run off with a bearded Italian claiming to be a count. Whether their aim is to keep their unpleasant stepmother from running off with the attractive but alcoholic Rodney or to induce her to do so, they realize that their father remains with Cicely only out of avoiding open scandal, and to maintain his country gentleman lifestyle.

When alone with their father, Sholto and Gerda intrigue to magnify his obvious discontent with their stepmother, and with his empty life. "The climate is so lovely in Alassio—all balmy with orange trees. Mother looks perfectly adorable in an orange-grove." (Jennifer's nonexistent indiscretions are only tall tales for the vapid guests.)

"Does she, indeed?" George exclaims, taken in—and Sholto hands him a photograph to admire while Gerda, looking over her father's shoulder, explains. "That's Mother—and that's us in the distance, and those are the oranges."

Voluble and outgoing, the children accelerate the domestic unease, and George cautions them, "Well, if you'll forgive me for mentioning it—don't assert yourselves quite so much—be more retiring. . . . I'm afraid you won't have much in common with the others, so you mustn't mind feeling a bit out of it." Sholto promises, but he and Gerda are not retiring types. Julia Cragworthy, a houseguest, observes to Claud Eccles, "It must be a crisis to any second wife to have the first wife's offspring suddenly foisted upon her." Eustace Dabbit, learning from Cicely that she dreads having Sholto and Gerda about, agrees. "One instinctively mistrusts the idea of young people bred on the Continent. I don't wish to depress you, Cicely, but they're certain to be precocious." Although in years they are beyond precocity, Julia confirms, "They know all the things they ought not to know."

In terms more like Shaw's younger twins than a precociously worldly twenty-one—Coward has difficulty in aging his siblings—Sholto soon gushes to his stepmother, who is contemplating a convenient headache, to distance herself from them, "We're frightfully excited, you know. It's the first time we've been in England, anyhow since we were tiny. So don't be cross if we're stupid about things." Interrupting, Gerda explains, in language more suited to fifteen than eighteen, "It's all, naturally, new and thrilling to us here. You can't imagine how funny it is, everything being grey instead of brightly coloured, and everyone talking English, and not waving their arms much, and—"

As the second act opens a week later, George Brent's guests are still hanging on, although Roddy is to leave the next day for Jamaica to exercise his obvious incompetence. All are weary of trying to be pleasantly unpleasant. Brushing aside some embarrassing gossip, George explains, wearily, "We all have reputations and traditions in the county, Gerda. Some of us try to live up to them, and others hope to live them down." Sholto is equally direct, impulsively telling his stepmother, "You *do* hate us being here, don't you?"

Not quite honest about her feelings, Cicely answers, "I'm afraid I haven't given the matter enough thought. You amuse George, and after all—" and she shrugs the idea off.

Claiming to understand, Sholto commiserates, "After all, it is not easy at a moment's notice to become an adoring adopted mother."

"I have never had the slightest intention," Cicely says sharply, "of being your adopted mother." (She seems an equivalent to Shaw's ill-tempered father figure, Fergus Crampton.)

Neither have Sholto and Gerda intended as much. After a further outburst from Cicely about "lack of breeding," and her huffily leaving the sitting room, Gerda concedes to Sholto that they were "asking for it" by egging Cicely on. "Still, we had to give her a chance to be nice. Wouldn't it have been awful if she'd got all impulsive, and wept a little and said she wanted us all to be girls together? Thank heaven, she really is an unpleasant woman. Now we'd better start in and get busy."

The devices of Shaw's twins are only one of several plots playing out simultaneously, none akin to Coward's insistent reliance upon sexual infidelity in his dozens of plays. To her own surprise, the elder Clandon sister, Gloria, is quickly involved in a lovers' duel with an infatuated (and impecunious) young dentist, Valentine, who explains their mutual infatuation (Gloria having failed her mother's feminist tutorials) as "chemistry." The long-separated parents, who go under the names of Crampton (clearly a Shavian charactonym) and Clandon, are accidentally brought together in a seaside hotel in Devon. Recognition leads to renewed animosity as the unreconciled parents become adversaries for the oversight of the children. Shaw's twins, as in the action about "second chances" adapted by Coward, scheme for the reunion of their parents, which comes about during a costume ball at which even the frigid Crampton warms to life.

Coward borrows from the scene to have Sholto and Gerda return from a local "Hunt Ball" in time to spy upon Cicely and Roddy's arrangements to run off—an elopement frustrated by George, who had been tipped off by a houseguest. Wanting to avoid the public indignity certain to ensue, Brent tells his "young devils" Gerda and Sholto that his "honour and good name" in the county are worth protecting. "You think I'm still in love with your mother—well, I'm not. I don't love anyone. I'm content and peaceful here," he claims; "my life is perfectly happy." He had invited them not out of "any sentimental desire" to see them, but as Sholto is his heir, "it is right that he get some idea of his future position in life." Brent contends that he need never see them again, and has no intention of unsettling his obviously unsettled life. "I'm entrenched here, and I mean to stay." He is willing to endure the open hypocrisy of his marriage, reminding the thwarted Cicely that adulterous life in a cramped colonial society would be extremely unpleasant and that she is not really in love with Roddy—only bored by her stodgy husband.

Cicely wavers—until the siblings announce dramatically, as if happy at her return, "We're going to live here always!" For their stepmother it is the last straw. After a final bitchy outburst she flees with Roddy. As they slam the door behind them, Sholto exclaims, "Great Scott! They've forgotten their bags"—and he and Gerda each seize a suitcase and chase after the couple.

While Shaw does not shift locales for the reconciliation of the separated parents, which is arranged with éclat in *You Never Can Tell* by the imperturbable hotel headwaiter, the genial "William," and his resourceful lawyer son, Walter, who coincidentally—as happens in farces—has arrived as Mrs. Clandon's attorney, Coward shifts the action to Italy, where in Alassio, Jennifer Brent is visited by a wealthy American suitor long in futile attendance on her, who wants to propose marriage. (Hiram Walkin may owe something to Coward's further reading in Shaw—the Irish-American millionaire Hector Malone, in *Man and Superman,* who turns up in Spain to rescue his son from an apparently mercenary marriage, only to find he has wed secretly.) As Hiram Walkin awaits Jennifer in an anteroom, Sholto and Gerda arrive home with a "surprise" for their mother and are dismayed by what they learn of Walkin's intentions. And he is dismayed by discovering that his prospective stepchildren are frighteningly sophisticated young people. Obviously, another fraud is foreshadowed.

While Gerda is explaining to Walkin preposterously that they live with Jennifer because their remote father is insane, and that their mother's sanity is also doubtful, the quite sane George Brent enters, identified by Sholto as "Mr. Peasemarsh." Aware now of being taken in, Walkin is unamused. "If you didn't want me to marry your mother," he says, "why couldn't you say so?" As everyone shouts at each other, including, in Italian, Jennifer's maid, Maria, Jennifer enters. Offended at what seems a long-planned repulse, Walkin stalks off, declaring that he is returning to Chicago. The young people quietly slip away to permit their parents to reunite.

Although Coward's script which Shaw interlined with suggested changes has been lost, one can guess that whether or not Shaw recognized traces in Hiram Walkin of Hector Malone, the character was unnecessary to Coward and added little but another stage salary. Walkin's excision would have helped to eliminate, also, the humorless absurdities about parental insanity. Neither Shaw nor Coward explained, and unless the lost script turns up, we shall not have any answers. Shaw did refer to "the final scene" and to "essential good manners." Coward only remembered, at one place in the script, Shaw's warning, "No you don't, young author!" GBS's letter to Coward had also been mislaid (or filched), but resurfaced in a dealer's sale catalog in 1954.

London reviewers failed to recognize the play's origins in *You Never Can Tell.* James Agate in the *Saturday Review* wrote, obtusely, "Broadly speaking, all but two of Mr Coward's characters are real; the comedy consists in the way in which these are led to act by two deliberately unreal people of the genus *enfant terrible*, horrific as humanity would be if it were put together with synthetic malice in the laboratory." But *The Young Idea*, he conceded, had some clever Wildean qualities in it, recalling *The Importance of Being Earnest*. Had Agate realized that Shaw had deliberately played upon Wilde's farce in *You Never Can Tell*, repeatedly having the romantic dentist, transparently christened Valentine, while wooing Gloria, insist that he is always in earnest—and in having the Shavian twins double the preposterousness of Wilde's inventive young Algernon, the source of Coward's less gentle wit would have been more apparent.

As Coward began succeeding in the theater in his own brittle style, leading lady Gladys Cooper accused him of "overweening conceit" when he compared himself to Shaw and to Somerset Maugham. That, she said, was like comparing herself to Sarah Bernhardt or Eleonora Duse; but Coward, flushed with box-office success, shot back that "the difference was not quite as fantastic as that."

For a time Coward remained fairly faithful to Shaw's injunction not to see his plays, lapsing at least once, in 1926, to see *Pygmalion* in a New York production, noting to his mother that Lynn Fontanne as Eliza Doolittle was "perfectly wonderful, much better than Mrs. Pat ever was." Had he seen Mrs. Campbell in the role long before? Perhaps—although he may have guessed from reputation. Much of his playgoing then is unrecorded. Very likely he also saw one of the 1920s revivals of *Overruled*, a one-act burlesque of what Shaw called, in his critic days in the 1890s, a "tissue of artificialities" by Sydney Grundy employing "a quadrille of lovers instead of a pair." In a preface to *Overruled*, Shaw proposed his play as a "model to all future writers of farcical comedy"; Coward may have read it. In Coward's *Private Lives* (1930), Michael Holroyd writes, "this option was to be taken up by Noël Coward," in whose comedy "the mixed-up couples once again meet in an hotel with each other's [new] partners." Coward would even borrow *Quadrille* for the title of another comedy about his perennial theme, in 1952. Later he saw revivals of *Saint Joan* (where the actress was "lacking in guts and rather like Peter Pan"), *Caesar and Cleopatra, Getting Married,* and even, again, *You Never Can Tell*. ("Oh, what a brilliant comedy!" Coward wrote.)

Their differences in dialogue would become apparent later when *Pygmalion* was being musicalized by Frederic Loewe and Alan Jay Lerner as *My Fair Lady*, using many of Shaw's scenes and much, too, of his language, even borrowing from his preface. Several years earlier, Coward had turned down the opportunity when invited by the Theatre Guild to adapt *Pygmalion* as a vehicle for the too-old Mary Martin, but "Mrs. Pat" had been even older (at forty-eight!) in creating the Eliza Doolittle role.

Rex Harrison, Lerner's unmusical Henry Higgins, attempting to sing in recitative, had been unhappy learning "Why Can't the English?" It sounded, he explained, "like an inferior Noël Coward." It occurred to Lerner that the Cowardly clue was the rhyme scheme. He had written

> Why can't the English teach their children how to speak?[1]
> In Norway there are legions
> Of literate Norwegians . . .

Lerner rewrote the lines as

> Why can't the English teach their children how to speak?
> This verbal class distinction by now should be antique

Shaw had made it clear in his preface and in the play that abuse of the language cut the lower classes off "from all high employment." Lerner's revisions—and there were more—made the lines more dramatically Shavian and less "lyricky" (in Lerner's term, as "Cowardly" could be misunderstood)—and Rex Harrison became more comfortable in his character.

As Shaw aged, he saw fewer and fewer plays and attended fewer and fewer concerts, but in 1931—when he was seventy-five—he was impelled to see Coward's emotional recapitulation of England since Victoria, the nostalgic panorama *Cavalcade*. Coward's powerful antidote to postwar malaise and economic hard times, Shaw wrote, "will survive in history. With *Cavalcade* alone he did more for Britain than all the generals at Waterloo." Nevertheless, not all of Coward's plays in the 1930s were box-office or critical successes. After the "flop" (his own term for it) of *Point Valaine* in 1935, Coward wrote to novelist G. B. (Gladys Bronwyn) Stern, who had commiserated with him, "After all, Ibsen and Shaw got bad notices, didn't they, once?"

Shaw himself reappeared in Coward's life formidably only once, years after *The Young Idea*. In October 1941, Coward had been quietly working out of his own financial resources for British intelligence via the Ministry

---

[1] In Shaw's preface to the play it was "The English have no respect for the language and will not teach their children to speak it."

of Information. During the early years of the war he was traveling ostensibly on personal theatrical business, however dubious that seemed under rigid travel restrictions. Since one bureaucratic hand did not know what the other hand was doing, he received a summons for two counts of evasion, while in the United States, of wartime currency regulations. He had left care of his finances to his friend and former companion Jack Wilson, counted on him to get his affairs "tidied up," and considered the summons "celebrity baiting."

Earlier, the dramatist and composer Ivor Novello ("Keep the Home Fires Burning") had been charged with using petrol in excess of personal rations and was sent briefly to prison. Coward had to employ counsel, and the eminent lawyer Dingwall ("Dingo") Bateson advised simply pleading guilty of taking £11,000 out of the country to cope with overseas expenses, and paying the fine. A month earlier, film star George Arliss (*Disraeli*) had pleaded guilty to a similar infraction, and Shaw, now eighty-five, wrote to him (September 27) that guilt was not merely a matter of the facts: "If you were firing at a target for practice as a Home Guard, and your bullet missed the target and killed me, and you said, 'I cannot deny it: I killed him: I plead guilty' the judge would have to sentence you to death. You would of course plead Not Guilty and be acquitted on the ground that the killing was an unintended accident." He recommended that Arliss seek a retrial. Prudently, Shaw also wrote to the chief solicitor of the Royal Treasury to ensure that his own foreign funds were being legally managed.

When similar news about Coward made the press, further damaging his already fragile reputation, often on the edge for lifestyle reasons, Shaw offered equivalent advice:

> The other day George Arliss, being in trouble about his American securities, pleaded Guilty under the impression that he was only admitting the facts and saving the Lord Mayor useless trouble. There was nothing to do but fine him £3,000.
>
> He should have admitted the facts and pleaded Not Guilty, being as innocent as a newborn lamb. Of course the facts have to be established before that question arises, but when they are admitted or proved they leave the question of innocence or guilt unsettled. There can be no guilt without intention. Arliss knew nothing about the Finance Clauses, and he did not even know that he owned American securities. He was Not Guilty, and should have said so and thereby put his defence in order.

Therefore let nothing induce you to plead Guilty. If your lawyers advise you to do so, tell them that I advise you not to. You may know this as well as I do; but after the Arliss case I think it safer to warn you.

On October 28, 1941, two days later, Coward replied, without being able to explain what he had been doing abroad undercover,

> Dear G.B.S.
> I can't tell you how touched and grateful I am for your wise and kindly advice which I will certainly follow.
> I need hardly tell you I am completely innocent over the whole business and have done the best I could since the war began to work for the country. I intend to fight this tooth and claw and feel most enormously encouraged by your great kindness in writing to me.
> I haven't seen you for many years and would so like to if you ever have the time.
> With again, so very, very many thanks.
> Yours,
> Noël Coward

Coward followed Shaw's advice rather than that of his counsel, who nevertheless appeared with him. Coward explained his war activities, "except the secret stuff." It was also already known that he working on a screenplay about the Royal Navy, about which press gossip scoffed as he was considered a lightweight writer of amorous farces and had no business dabbling in heroics. He left the courtroom in a "daze of relief," fined £200 and £20 costs at Bow Street for the technical error, far less than the £5,000 minimum fine established for the offense. His reputation repaired, and back at work on the film, he cabled Shaw: "DEAR GBS THE RESULT OF MY HAVING FOLLOWED YOUR ADVICE IS ONLY TOO APPARENT STOP I AM ETERNALLY GRATEFUL TO YOU NOT ONLY FOR YOUR WISDOM BUT FOR THE DEEP KINDNESS THAT PROMPTED YOUR MOST OPPORTUNE AND VERY REAL HELP."

Coward's troubles were not yet over, for the Lord Mayor now prosecuted him (as Arliss had been charged) for undeclared securities, and another hearing ensued, this time at the Mansion House mayoral offices. As securities were different than mere money, he was viewed less generously and fined an affordable £2,000. After the war, on September 9, 1947, with tight currency restrictions still in effect, he had dinner in New

York with William Stephenson, who had run the covert wartime British security and propaganda office under which Coward had operated, and William Donovan, President Roosevelt's chief wartime spymaster. Coward wrote his devoted secretary Lorn Loraine—she had been with him since 1924—that "Little Bill . . . very emphatically warned me not to go back to England without leaving myself a concrete reason for getting out again. Big Bill Donovan was also there and apparently has great pull. . . . It is really very curious for an eminent and frightfully pretty Englishman to have to solicit help from an American in order to prevent himself being imprisoned in his own country!" Yet Coward was now a national hero, having written, directed (with David Lean), and starred in the moving cinema epic about a doomed destroyer and its crew, *In Which We Serve* (1942).

While meanly deprecating the film, Gabriel Pascal tried to ensnare the aging Shaw about further rights to his plays. The émigré producer, after successes with *Pygmalion* and *Major Barbara*, and already offered *Caesar and Cleopatra*, was eager to tie up more titles for filming. "We have a terrific chance to get back the artistic leadership of the British cinema if we play our cards well," he cajoled Shaw the next year. "I am offended and hurt when second-rate writers like Noel Coward are hailed as the Saviours of the industry and are heard to boast that you do not count any more." Shaw did not rise to the bait.

Four years later, at a crotchety ninety-one, Shaw insisted to Pascal, who continued bad-mouthing GBS's successor generation of playwrights, and blandished him to dramatize St. Francis, "I will not touch St Francis. All I have to say about saints is in St Joan." And he would not "go on repeating myself like . . . Priestley and Coward." Even later, at nearly ninety-two, when Shaw's influential New York show-biz attorney tried to inveigle him into permitting Coward, also her client, to musicalize *Pygmalion*, she enlisted Gertrude Lawrence, whom Fanny Holtzmann also managed, to promote the scheme. GBS was crankily furious. "Stop cabling crazy nonsense," he wired back. "What you need is a month's holiday. Noel could not possibly interfere in my business. My decision as to Pygmalion is final." The play would not be set to music until Shaw's estate posthumously reversed his refusal, but Coward would be involved much later in another musicalized Shaw, in 1966, when he played Caesar in Richard Rodgers's television adaptation of *Androcles and the Lion*. By then Coward's memory was failing and he had trouble memorizing his lines. He claimed that he "didn't enjoy any of it. . . . However, I was apparently very good."

Having played a wartime naval captain, Coward would play a postwar king. Shaw's futuristic and long-running *The Apple Cart* (1929) was being revived in 1953 for the coronation year of Elizabeth II. At the Haymarket Theatre, Coward played King Magnus, opposite Margaret Leighton as the royal mistress Orinthia. Shaw, who had died at ninety-four in November 1950, would have been pleased at the bravura performances. "I am getting quite excited about it," Coward wrote to Violet Bonham-Carter while on winter holiday in Jamaica. Although as he began memorizing his lines he feared that Magnus's rhetorical first-act tour de force calibrated with memorably cadenced phrases was "a bit of a pill," he soon changed his mind. "There is a twelve-minute speech in the first act," he had complained, "that is quite frightening." More than a bit of a monarchist, Coward soon discovered that the old socialist's eloquent characterization of the king as a symbolic continuity of Britain above politics was a thrill to declaim. "Mr. Shaw is tricky to play," he told his diary on April 12, "because of his long sentences in which every word counts. The speeches cannot be hurried and yet if they are spoken too slowly they become ponderous—it is essential to find places to pause effectively and *think* effectively." In a letter he wrote, "I have rather enjoyed learning it. Magnus is a part that might have been written for me. I don't think he goes 'soppy' in the last scene. He actually wins hands down."

On May 12 Coward observed as the run continued, "The play was an immediate and triumphant success and has remained so in spite of some silly, patronizing notices.[2] I have done better than usual on the whole, but they"—the critics—"will never give me ungrudging praise, or very rarely. We have played to capacity since the opening night and I have cut down on smoking and concentrated on my voice."

Later the American songwriter Hugh Martin wrote to him, "I am enclosing a clipping from *The New Yorker* about you [in *The Apple Cart*] which you have undoubtedly already seen. I love their description of

---

[2] Very likely Coward was referring to the *Times*, May 8, 1953, which commented, condescendingly, that his casting as King Magnus "turns out smoothly, amusingly, yet somehow oddly. Mr. Coward, so used to writing brief colloquial sentences and uttering them with a staccato clatter, has seemingly made a great effort to master the longer Shavian rhythm. He carefully refrains from the temptation to treat the clauses of a long sentence as though they were short sentences. Evidently he immensely relishes the eloquent periods of Magnus, but the odd effect is that the longer speeches lack the vocal power on which these sudden variations on a theme depend."

you 'wearing a streamlined uniform and perfectly timing a lot of crisp Coward lines that happen to have been written by Shaw'!"

Bibliographic Essay

The Young Idea appears in Sheridan Morley, ed., *Noël Coward: Collected Plays*, vol. 8 (London: Methuen, 2000). All quotations from the play are from this edition, as are extracts from reviews of the first London production in 1922. Coward's correspondence is from Barry Day, ed., *The Letters of Noël Coward* (New York: Knopf, 2007). Hugh Martin's letter to Coward, July 15, 1953, about *The Apple Cart* and quoting *The New Yorker* is from the Day edition.

Esmé Wynne's recollection is from Philip Hoare, *Noël Coward: A Biography* (London: Sinclair-Stevenson, 1995), as is that of Gladys Cooper. Shaw's letters are from Day (the 1921 exchange and the unsourced Shaw comment on *Cavalcade*) and from Dan H. Laurence, ed., *Bernard Shaw: Collected Letters*, vol. 4 (London: Max Reinhardt, 1988). Michael Holroyd's suggestion of Shavian influence on Coward's amorous interludes, such as *Private Lives*, is from his *Bernard Shaw*, vol. 2 (New York: Random House, 1989).

Coward's diary extracts, with commentary, are from Graham Payn and Sheridan Morley, eds., *The Noël Coward Diaries* (Boston: Little, Brown, 1982). Coward's personal history, except where otherwise cited, is from Cole Lesley, *Remembered Laughter: The Life of Noël Coward* (New York: Knopf, 1976). Included is Coward's luncheon reminiscence of his abortive early novel *Cats and Dogs*, and another text of the 1921 Shaw letter to Coward.

Alan Jay Lerner's juxtaposition of his "Cowardly" lines in a lyric from *My Fair Lady* with lines that Rex Harrison found more authentically Shavian is from Lerner's *The Street Where I Live* (New York: Norton, 1978). Pascal's bad-mouthing Coward and his memorable wartime film appears in his letter to Shaw, ca. June 1943, in Bernard F. Dukore, ed., *Bernard Shaw and Gabriel Pascal* (Toronto: Univ. of Toronto Press, 1996). Coward's fear of Shaw's "twelve-minute speech" by King Magnus is from Hoare, as is Coward's comment about playing Caesar in the television *Androcles*. Shaw's refusal "to touch St. Francis" letter to Pascal is dated October 8, 1947. Shaw's cable to Fanny Holtzmann, April 5, 1948, is in *Collected Letters*, vol. 4.

· 12 ·

King Magnus and King Minus

A PLAY AND A PLAYLET

Early in December 1936, when Britain was shaken by the breakdown of press self-censorship about the affair of the king and the American divorcée Wallis Warfield Simpson, Winston Churchill saw in the crisis his way out of the political wilderness. He might become leader of a "King's Party" to back Edward VIII against the Conservative diehards led by the prime minister. Stanley Baldwin insisted that the king disavow Mrs. Simpson—or his throne. "England promptly went mad," Hesketh Pearson recalled. "Archbishops, bishops, peers, cabinet ministers, debated the matter behind closed doors. Could an English king contract a morganatic[1] marriage? Could British peeresses and royal highnesses walk behind an American commoner? Why could not this English king do as many previous English kings had done? The questions were endless. Nothing else was discussed.... Nearly everyone treated it as a matter of life and death. Nearly everyone suddenly became conscious of the Church of England, the British Constitution, Duty, Virtue, and the Ten Commandments. Even football was temporarily forgotten."

Resisting the Establishment threatened to compromise the political neutrality of the Sovereign, essential to constitutional monarchy. Yet the king could relinquish the throne to a legitimate successor, and might

---

1 A form of marriage in which a person of high rank marries a spouse of lower station with the prenuptial stipulation that neither the spouse nor any children of the marriage will have any claim to rank or property. Churchill had already proposed to the king that if he went through with a morganatic marriage, Mrs. Simpson could become the Duchess of Cornwall—a title adopted by a later Prince of Wales for his divorcée bride, Camilla Parker Bowles.

then, so recent fantasy suggested, campaign for elective power as leader of a parliamentary party. Taking his cue from Bernard Shaw's satire *The Apple Cart* (1929), John Grigg, the king's close friend, who would surrender his title as Second Baron Altringham to remain in the Commons, proposed to Edward that if he adopted, at the polls, the domestic politics of Lloyd George and the foreign policies of Churchill, he could become "a well-nigh irresistible force."

That never-employed electoral alternative had been the tipping point of the futuristic *The Apple Cart*, Shaw's hit comedy of 1929 set in remote 1960s England. The first London production ran for 258 performances, a long-running success for its time. In Shaw's political whimsy, King Magnus is warned by his "official mistress," the witty and voluptuous Orinthia, as they tussle playfully, that she wants her horizontal position formally recognized. Should he placate her? Can he do so? He has a lawful, homebody queen, and a public to reckon with. The king is also beset by the constitutional limits on his freedom of action laid out by Prime Minister Proteus. "If you flourish your thunderbolts," the king rejoins, "why may I not shoulder my little popgun?"

"What we say," Foreign Secretary Nicobar explains sweepingly, "is that the king has no right to remind his subjects of anything constitutional except by the advice of his Prime Minister, and in words which he has read and approved."

Not given to dithering, Magnus announces after a brief recess with Orinthia that he will resolve all disagreements with his Cabinet by abdicating in favor of his son, Robert, the Prince of Wales, although, the king concedes, "I have never been able to induce him to take any interest in parliamentary politics."

Relieved, Proteus agrees that abdication would be the "intellectually honest solution of our difficulty." And his colleague, Pliny, the Chancellor of the Exchequer, reflects, "One king is no worse than another, is he?"

"I suppose the King must do as he thinks right," concedes Boanerges, the president of the Board of Trade, happily, and the tame Cabinet impulsively choruses "For he's a jolly good fellow," assuming Magnus's public farewell. But King Magnus asserts, contrarily, "I have no intention of withdrawing from an active part in politics." Before stepping down, he plans to dissolve Parliament and call for a general election. "I shall be in a better position as a commoner than as a peer.... It is my intention to offer myself to the Royal Borough of Windsor as a candidate at the forthcoming General Election."

"He'll be at the top of the poll," Pliny predicts.

"There are several possibilities," Magnus goes on blandly. "I shall endeavor to form a party. My son King Robert will have to call on some Party leader who can depend upon the support of the House of Commons to form a Government. He may call on you," he tells Proteus. "He may even call on me."

Consternation follows. The king is highly popular with the people, and even with the press. The risk for the prime minister is too great. "There is not going to be any general election," Proteus declares. "We go on as before. The crisis is a washout." Magnus gets his way.

Suddenly, in December 1936, the future threatened to turn into the here and now. Magnus and Orinthia had not materialized, but an abdication loomed, and a king's mistress, long kept out of the newspapers, resurfaced. Rather than a Platonic philosopher-king in the Magnus mold, Edward VIII seemed an empty Savile Row suit, a King Minus.

On Friday, December 4, Churchill was guest at dinner at Fort Belvedere, Edward's castellated weekend retreat, known for its raffish ambience, on the edge of Windsor Great Park. Long its informal chatelaine, Mrs. Simpson was now prudently abroad in Cannes. Abdication seemed more of a solution than a fight to cling to the throne as advocated by the King's camp. Alfred Duff Cooper, MP for Oldham and First Lord of the Admiralty, agreed absurdly with fellow MP Henry ("Chips") Channon that the question of whether the king stayed or went was "a war to the knife between the past and the present." At the Palace on November 17, 1936, Cooper argued that ex-kings were miserable creatures, cited the example of the deposed king of Spain, and asked what Edward would do with himself. (Balbus in Shaw's *Apple Cart* had observed, "A retired king cant have plans and a future.) "Oh, I shan't be like Alfonso," said Edward. "He was kicked out. I shall go of my own accord.... You know me, Duff," his Royal Highness said airily, "I shall find plenty to do."

Out of Cabinet office, Churchill saw his political rehabilitation linked to the king's future. Before succeeding to the throne early in 1936 on the death of his father, George V, Edward had long been Prince of Wales by day, carrying on his ceremonial royal duties, and David, his playboy real self and his actual forename, by night. For more than twenty years as heir presumptive, his liaisons with married, often older, women had been the staple of society gossip in an era of press discretion and restraint. The fading Prince Charming appearance he cultivated into his early forties had disarmed hostility. He confided to intimates that he could not cope with the pressures of his two selves much longer and was "prepared to go," claiming that he was having "mental blackouts." Churchill urged him not to do anything precipitately. In time, matters would sort themselves out.

The king's entanglements with Wallis Simpson, who long had her claws into the king, and was now proceeding through her second divorce with the connivance of her husband, Ernest, had burgeoned into a government crisis. The decree *nisi*, uncontested, had been granted on October 27, 1936. Only the legal waiting period for the divorce to become valid remained. A loyal cabal of press barons had kept most of the scandal out of the newspapers, but for the "muck and slime" slipped in from the Continent and from America.

When the press blockade collapsed on December 2, broken by Claud Cockburn's radical *The Week*, the king's private secretary, Sir Alexander Hardinge, recommended that Mrs. Simpson leave the country at once, which she quickly did. Further, Hardinge advised, if the king persisted on marrying her when she became legally free, Stanley Baldwin's Cabinet was likely to resign. Bureaucratic chaos would be inevitable, for leaders of the Opposition had concurred that Wallis Simpson, a tawdry and ambitious American, could not be accepted as queen. Since Edward's travels to Commonwealth countries had made him immensely popular abroad, he pinned hopes on support from them, but no groundswell had emerged. Mrs. Simpson seemed the Wicked Witch from the West.

Harold Nicolson, then an MP, wrote in his diary on December 3, "The storm breaks." Newspapers were covering the story "in sorrow rather than anger." Returning from his north London constituency in Islington to the Commons, where the prime minister had assured members that no constitutional crisis had "yet" arisen, Nicolson reported, rather, "The streets flame with [press] posters, 'King and Mrs Simpson.'" Since the inarticulate majority wrote no pained letters to the editor, or to their representatives in Parliament whose names they rarely knew, his first soundings were insignificant, but he did not find people in his circle angry with the twice-married Mrs. Simpson—only with the king himself. "In eight months he has destroyed the great structure of popularity which he had raised." A Prince of Wales might have a mistress, but a king . . . ?

Late on Saturday, December 5, after a dinner that was largely liquid, Churchill wrote to Edward in a jaunty mood about the day on the political front. No one in the government, Churchill reported without indicating any evidence, would "hold a pistol" at the king's head. "Therefore no final decision or Bill till after Christmas—probably February or March." The Simpson divorce would take until April to be final, affording a further delay. Edward should not leave the country (to join Wallis), as Windsor Castle was his "battle station." He should see Max Aitken, Lord Beaverbrook, who owned the high-circulation *Daily Express* and the *Evening Standard* and would be "a *devoted* tiger" in his behalf. Then Churchill added, "And for real wit Bernard Shaw's article in to-night's *Evening Standard* should be read. He is joyous."

The GBS piece was almost certainly the reason for Churchill's euphoric late-evening letter—and Shaw very likely placed his skit in the *Evening Standard* because he knew that Beaverbrook was on the king's side. Like Channon, although *The Apple Cart's* King Magnus saw himself as representing *both* the past and the future, Shaw saw the question not as the choice of a matrimonial partner but the choice of a culture in change between the past and the future.

As *The King, the Constitution and the Lady*, Shaw's playlet was described as a "fictitious dialogue" set in a country identified as "The Kingdom of the Half-Mad." Shaw at eighty seemed at the top of his form, yet this one-act playlet, complete with Shavian preface, never would surface in collections of his plays or shorter pieces; it could also not be performed in England, as the Lord Chamberlain's censor of plays, by law, banned from the public stage any representation of the Deity, the Royal Family, recognizable living persons, and the recently dead. Shaw wrote, The new King, though just turned 40,[2] was unmarried; and now that he was a king he wanted to settle down and set a good example to his people by becoming a family man. He needed a gentle soothing sort of wife, because his nerves were very sensitive, and the conversation of his ministers was often very irritating. As it happened he knew a lady who had just these qualities. Her name, as well as I can remember it, was Mrs. Daisy Bell;[3] and as she was an American she had been married twice before and was therefore likely to make an excellent wife for a king who had never been married at all. All this seemed natural and proper; but in the country of the Half-Mad you can never count on anything going

---

2 Born in 1894, Edward VIII was forty-two.
3 "Daisy Bell" ("A Bicycle Built for Two"), by Harry Dacre, and with a plethora of alternative lyrics, became a London music-hall hit in 1892: "Whether she loves me or loves me not, / Sometimes it's hard to tell, / Yet I am longing to share the lot of / Beautiful Daisy Bell."

off quietly. The Government, for instance, would let whole districts fall into ruin and destruction without turning a hair, and then declare that the end of the world was at hand because some foreign dictator had said bluntly that there are milestones on the Dover Road. And so the King was not surprised when he was suddenly told one day at noon or thereabouts that the Archbishop and the Prime Minister had called and insisted on seeing him at once. The King, having spent the morning with Mrs. Bell, was in a good humor, so he had them up and offered them cocktails and cigars. But they not only refused this refreshment quite sternly but exhibited such signs of mental disturbance that the King had to ask them, with some concern, what was the matter.

"The rest," Shaw continues, "may be given in dialogue form":

> PRIME MINISTER: How can you ask, sir? The newspapers are full of it. There are photographs. We are not spared even the lady's little dog. What is your Majesty going to do about it?
>
> KING: Nothing out of the regular course. I shall be crowned in May; and in April I shall marry Daisy.
>
> PRIME MINISTER (*almost shrieking*): Impossible! Madness!
>
> ARCHBISHOP (*whose public voice is a triumph of clerical art*): Out of the question. You cannot marry this woman.
>
> KING: I had rather you called her Mrs. Bell; or Daisy, if you prefer it.
>
> ARCHBISHOP: If I were to officiate at your proposed marriage, I should have to speak of her as "this woman." What is good enough for her in the House of God is good enough for her here. But I shall refuse to officiate.
>
> PRIME MINISTER (*shouting*): And I shall resign.
>
> KING: How awful! Would it be too brutal to remind you that there are others? Sandy McLossie will form a King's Party for me in no time. The people are behind me. You may have to resign in any case long before the Coronation.
>
> ARCHBISHOP: Your taunt does not apply to me. The Church will not solemnize an unconstitutional marriage.
>
> KING: That will get me out of a grave difficulty. Religious matters are not so simple for me as they were for William the Conqueror, of whose death some of you don't seem to have yet heard. William had only a handful of adventurers to consider, all Christians, and Christians of one sort. I have to consider 495 millions—call

it 500—of my subjects. Only eleven per cent of them are Christians; and even that tiny minority is so divided into sects that I cannot say a word without hurting somebody's feelings. As it is, my Protestant Succession is an insult to the Pope and his Church. If I get married in a church, especially one with a steeple on it, I shall offend the Quakers. If I profess the Thirty-Nine Articles of the Church of England, I shall bind myself to hold most of my loving subjects as accursed, and oblige hundreds of millions of them to regard me as an enemy of their God. Now, though all the religious stuff in the Coronation business is out of date, I cannot alter it: that is your affair. But I can get legally married without offending the religious feelings of a single soul in my Empire. I shall be married civilly by the district registrar.[4] What have you to say to that?

ARCHBISHOP: It is unheard of and outrageous. But it would certainly get me out of a very difficult situation.

PRIME MINISTER: Archbishop, are you deserting me?

ARCHBISHOP: I cannot on the spur of the moment find the reply to his Majesty's very unexpected move. You had better take up the constitutional point while I consider it.

PRIME MINISTER: It is impossible for your Majesty to defy the Constitution. Parliament is all-powerful.

KING: It has that reputation as long as it does nothing. However, I am as devoted to the Constitution[5] as you are. Only understand that if you push me to a General Election to ascertain the wishes of my people on this question, I am quite ready to face that extremity. You will get a glorious licking. Your very mistaken ballyhoo in the press does not impose on me.

PRIME MINISTER: But there is no question of a General Election.

---

4 As would the Prince of Wales on April 9, 2005, in marrying Camilla Parker Bowles.
5 Asked about constitutional limits on the king through the advice of his ministers, Shaw told a reporter for the *New York American*, "Nonsense! Suppose they give him medical advice. Suppose they advise him to dye his hair, or change the color of his tie, or have his favorite dog shot. He will reply that their tastes and his differ, but that their fancies are not constitutional reasons and their advice therefore is not constitutional advice. Limits to the power and personal liberty of a constitutional monarch are not the personal prejudices of his ministers. He may not legislate except by the advice of his ministers. . . . If the ministers cannot advise the King in his choice of a necktie, still less can they force his hand in his choice of a bride, unless the lady be clearly ineligible of the alliance and politically mischievous."

Are you prepared to act by the advice of your ministers or are you not? That is the simple issue between us.

KING: Well, what is your advice? Whom do you advise me to marry? I have made my choice. Now make yours. You cannot talk about marriage in the air—in the abstract. Come down to tin tacks. Name your lady.

PRIME MINISTER: But the Cabinet has not considered that. You are not playing the game, sir.

KING: You mean that I am beating you at it. I mean to. I thought I should.

PRIME MINISTER: Not at all, sir. But I cannot choose a wife for you, can I?

KING: Then you cannot advise me on the subject. And if you cannot advise me, I cannot act by your advice.

PRIME MINISTER: This seems to me to be a quibble. I should never have expected it from your Majesty. You know very well what I mean. Somebody of Royal stock. Not American.

KING: At last we have something definite. The Prime Minister of England publicly classes Americans as untouchables. You insult the nation on whose friendship and kinship the existence of my Empire in the East finally depends. All my wisest political friends regard a marriage between a British king and an American lady as a masterstroke of policy.

PRIME MINISTER: I should not have said that. It was a slip of the tongue.

KING: Very well, we will wash that out. But you still want a bride of Royal stock. You are dreaming of a seventeenth-century dynastic marriage. I, the King of England and Emperor of Britain, am to go a-begging through Europe for some cousin, five or six times removed, of a dethroned down-and-out Bourbon or Hapsburg or Hohenzollern or Romanoff, about whom nobody in this country or anywhere else cares one single dump. I shall do nothing so unpopular and so silly. If you are still living in the seventeenth century, I am living in the twentieth. I am living in a world of republics, of mighty Powers governed by ex-house-painters, stonemasons, promoted ranker soldiers, sons of operators in boot factories. Am I to marry one of their daughters? Choose my father-in-law for yourself. There is the Shah of Persia. There is Effendi Whataturk. There is Signor Bombardone. There is Herr

Battler. There is the steel king of Russia.[6] That is the Royal stock of today. I wonder whether any of these great rulers allow a relative of his to marry an old-fashioned king! I doubt it. I tell you there is not a Royal House left in Europe today into which I could marry without weakening England's position; and if you don't know that you don't know anything.

PRIME MINISTER: You seem to me to be entirely mad.

KING: To a little London clique some two or three centuries behind the times I no doubt seem so. The modern world knows better. However, we need not argue about that. Name your lady.

PRIME MINISTER: I cannot think of anybody at the moment, though there must be lots available. Can you suggest anyone, Archbishop?

ARCHBISHOP: No; the unexpectedness of the demand leaves my mind a blank. I think we had better discuss the possibility of an abdication.

PRIME MINISTER: Yes, yes. Your Majesty must abdicate. That will settle the whole question and get us out of all our difficulties.

KING: My sense of public duty, to which your friends appeal so movingly, will hardly allow me to desert my post without the smallest excuse for such an act.

ARCHBISHOP: Your throne will be shaken to its foundations.

KING: That is not my look-out, as I happen to be sitting on it. But what will happen to the foundations of the Church if it tries to force me to contract a loveless marriage and to live in adultery with the woman I really love?

ARCHBISHOP: You need not do that.

KING: You know I will do that if I listen to your counsel. Dare you persist in it?

ARCHBISHOP: I really think, P.M., that we had better go. If I were superstitious, I should be tempted to believe that the devil was putting all these arguments into his Majesty's head. They are unanswerable; and yet they are so entirely off the track of English

---

6 Shaw had written his political satire *Geneva* between February 11, 1936, and April 29, 1936. Included in it were a Hitler caricature as "Battler" and a Mussolini travesty as "Bombardone." Many times revised to keep up with the newspapers, *Geneva* would premiere in Warsaw, in Polish, on July 25, 1938, and be produced in English at the Malvern Festival on August 1, 1938. The other rather transparent names represent Mustafa Kemal Atatürk, Francisco Franco, and Josef Stalin.

educated thought that they do not belong to your world and mine.

KING (*rising as his visitors rise*): Besides, my brother, who would succeed me, might strongly object. And he is married to a home-grown lady,[7] who is more popular than any foreign ex-princess could be. And he would never be the real thing as long as I was in the offing. You would have to cut my head off. You can't tomfool with the throne: you must either abolish it or respect it.

PRIME MINISTER: You have said enough, sir. Spare me any more.

KING: Stay for lunch, both of you. Daisy will be there. Or must I make it a command?

ARCHBISHOP: It is past my lunch hour; I am very hungry. If it is a command, I will not demur.

KING (*whispering to the stricken Prime Minister as they go downstairs*): I warn you, my dear Goldwyn,[8] that if you take up my challenge and name your lady, her photograph shall appear in all the papers the next day with Daisy's beside it. Daisy and her little dog.

The Prime Minister shook his head sadly, and so they went in to lunch together. The Prime Minister ate hardly anything; but the Archbishop left nothing on his plate.

Through the newspapers, Shaw was advising Edward VIII indirectly, and the British public directly, that the king could do as he pleased if he cultivated popular support. As Shaw's playlet was going to press, Prime Minister Stanley Baldwin had already conceded that the king could marry without "consent from any other authority," and had based his constitutional objections on the fact that "the lady he marries . . . necessarily becomes Queen. She herself therefore enjoys all the status, rights and privileges which . . . attach to that position." But Edward had no stomach for kingship, and wanted out, while the country was divided on the king's future.

Perhaps he would have been a mistake in any case had he remained on the throne, and Wallis, who was given, post-abdication, the title of Duchess of Windsor but was kept at a distance from Windsor itself, would almost certainly have been a disaster as queen.

---

7 Prince Albert, the king's brother next in line, and the future George VI, had married Lady Elizabeth Bowes-Lyon, of an aristocratic Scottish family. She became Duchess of York.

8 Transparently, the prime minister, Stanley Baldwin.

Shaw's intimate friend Beatrice Webb worried as much in an incisive diary entry written on the date of his *Evening Standard* playlet. In some ways her lines are an unacknowledged critique of it. She refused to accept the widespread "suspicion" on the Left that a conspiracy against the king by "a reactionary government" existed:

> What comes out of the whole business is that neither the Church nor the Court circle would have objected to a King's mistress—Edward VII had a succession of these, openly accepted by all concerned; what they do refuse to endure is a Queen who does not conform to Court usage, still more a King who dislikes conforming to Church rites and is on the side of the common people. If the King refuses to relinquish the proposed marriage, or to step down from the throne, the Cabinet will resign. The Opposition will refuse to take office, the scratch government he will get together (Winston Churchill, Lloyd George?) will have to dissolve [itself], and the electorate will be divided according to a distorted class bias.... If he withdraws the question of marriage and just "carries on," he might win through. No Conservative government would risk a general election on the Cabinet's right *to compel a King to promise not to marry*, if he had the common people on his side. No one knows what are Edward VIII's opinions, except that he loathes the Anglican Church, associates with a bad-mannered lot, and cares for the comfort of unemployed men. Whether he is Atheist or tends to[ward] the Roman Catholic Church, [or is] Communist or Fascist is unknown. He may not know himself. Some say he is intimate with the German Embassy and is a reactionary: [Lord] Rothermere and [Sir Oswald] Mosley support him. He is neurotically excitable, obstinate, hates show and has a warm heart for the underdog; but he is not an intellectual.... "*What do you really believe, Mrs Webb?*" in an earnest tone and with a nervous gesture, is the only sentence in his talk with me that I remember! What struck me as most certain is that he is an unhappy man who has not found as a royal personage a comfortable private life. Which is to his credit.

Ironically, Mrs. Webb's conversation with him, at a dinner at his London home, York House, in 1930, which she hardly now could recall, had resulted in her diary entry, "As I talked to him he seemed like the hero of one of Shaw's plays, the Dauphin of *St. Joan* or King Magnus of *The Apple Cart*."

Two generations later, the Duke of Windsor's great-nephew and

Britain's future king, the Prince of Wales, married an aristocratic lady he did not love, for the sake of the succession, and after her death in an auto crash, when they were already divorced, he married the divorced commoner to whom he had been attached for years, and now likely to become his queen. By the turn of the new century most of the bourgeois monarchies left in Europe had been resuscitated through marriages with commoners, and even the austere imperial house of Japan absorbed a commoner, now a princess, as bride of the future emperor and his empress-to-be. Darwinian pressures also have an impact on thrones.

Shaw was not ready to relinquish the king to legal quibbles, religious qualms, or class snobbery. Impelled by his long disappointment with Shakespeare's unsuccessful fairy-tale play *Cymbeline,* he was working on an alternative ending, beginning a draft on December 3, 1936, as he was posting his Edward playlet to the *Evening Standard.* Inevitably, there would be some intersections, particularly when Guiderius feels "plagued" by the followers of Cloten,

> This kingly business has no charm for me. . . .
> Compelled to worship priest-invented gods.
> Not free to wed the woman of my choice,
> Being stopped at every turn by some old fool
> Crying "You must not," or, still worse, "You must."
> . . . I abdicate, and pass the throne to Polydore.

When Arviragus objects that the decision is unwise, the king responds, "Do you, by heavens? Thank you for nothing, brother."

Shaw's intention in *Cymbeline Refinished* was to make the play more contemporary, for the Shakespeare Memorial Theatre, but the producers fell back on the original fifth act, and the Shavian recasting would have only a three-week run in London a year later, after its political references had faded.

By Tuesday afternoon, December 8, Members of Parliament who had been home for the weekend to assess among their constituents the king's chances of hanging in had learned that Mrs. Simpson, whose reputation was little more than adventurer among the elite, had no support whatever in the country. The day before, Robert Bernays, a rather liberal Tory MP, reported, when Churchill gave his "let the king choose his girl" speech, "Winston was absolutely howled down . . . and is in a very chastened mood. . . . In three minutes his hopes of return to power and influence are shattered." The then-influential Robert Boothby sent him a hasty note he later regretted, that "this afternoon you have delivered a blow to the King, both in the Commons and in the country, far harder than Baldwin ever conceived of. You have reduced the number of potential supporters [of the king] to the minimum possible—I should think now about seven in all."

On Thursday, December 10, Baldwin arose in the House to review his handling of "the King's matter," explaining through a confusion of dates and a mixup of his red-monographed papers in hand that Edward had brought himself to realize that there was no useful outcome for himself, if he wanted Mrs. Simpson in his life, other than by signing a deed of abdication. The king had few qualms, other than financial ones, about leaving duties he found more and more confining. As early as the 1914–18 war, when as Prince of Wales and already surfeited with ceremony he was a junior officer in the Guards, and officials wanted to keep him out of danger, he had remarked, "My father has four sons, so why should I be fettered?"

Unwilling to be Albert I, and suffer comparison to Victoria's consort, the Duke of York had determined on the imminent abdication to succeed his brother as George VI. "We are all staggered with shame and distress," Nicolson wrote. The "sentimental shock" had given way among the people to a feeling that Edward had proven by his priorities that he was unworthy. The Earl of Crawford judged of Wallis that "the upper classes mind her being an American more than they mind her being divorced. The lower classes do not mind her being an American but loathe the idea that she has [had] two husbands already." A nautical joke circulated, a now-disillusioned Chips Channon noted, that the king, who by his position had also been Admiral of the Fleet, had now settled on becoming "the third mate on an American tramp." Shaw's contrary pitch in the *Evening Standard* had failed.

Late that afternoon, with his three brothers, the dukes of York, Gloucester, and Kent, as witnesses, the king signed the instrument of abdication. Sir John Reith, director of the BBC, had made time available for the king's broadcast of his decision to the nation and empire that evening, and told Sir Claud Schuster, Clerk of the Crown, that he planned to introduce the withdrawing sovereign on the air as "Mr. Edward Windsor."

Sir Claud reported the proceeding. "That's quite wrong," said Prince Albert—who would be King George VI. He suggested identifying his brother as "His Royal Highness the Duke of Windsor, a title the new king now planned to give him as the first act of the succession. "He cannot be Mr. Edward Windsor as he was born the son of a Duke. That makes him [by courtesy title] Lord Edward Windsor anyhow. If he ever comes back to his country, he can stand & be elected to the House of Commons. Would you like that?"

"No," said Sir Claud, thinking, as many suddenly did once more, including Albert, of King Magnus's threat to abdicate, become a commoner, and stand for election, upsetting the political apple cart. (Shaw had also reminded readers of that in his playlet fable—that in the unnamed king's contention, no successor "would be the real thing as long as I was in the offing.")

"As Duke of Windsor, he can sit and vote in the House of Lords. Would you like that?" Sir Claud again said no, and Prince Albert went on, "Well, if he becomes a Royal Duke he cannot speak or vote in the House of Lords, & he is not deprived of his rank in the Navy, Army, or Royal Air Force." Albert realized the implications of having a possibly bitter and vindictive brother returning in a new guise as a rival for dominance. He had not only read Shaw's play of 1929, probably at the urging of concerned courtiers, but also the *Evening Standard* skit, which suddenly seemed no joke.

With the document transferring the Crown signed, the new king went to Fort Belvedere at seven, just before the broadcast, to have a final talk with his brother. "You are not going to find this a difficult job at all," the ex-king recalled telling his successor, whom he had always called Bertie. "You know all the ropes, and you have almost overcome the slight hesitation in your speech which used to make public speaking so hard for you."

"By the way, David," said the new king, trying to sound as if the question were off-hand, "have you given any thought as to what you are going to be called now?"

"Why no, as a matter of fact, I haven't."

"I shall create you a Duke," Bertie said. "How about the family name of Windsor?" The silence that followed was deemed assent.

After a farewell dinner with members of the family in the Royal Lodge nearby, the Duke of Windsor–designate made his broadcast from Windsor Castle. He had written it himself, on instructions in a comma-free admonition from Wallis on December 6: "Don't be silenced and leave under a cloud I beseech you and in abdication no matter in what form unless you can let the public know that the Cabinet has virtually kicked you out. . . ." The draft address was discarded after the king had shown it to Churchill, who wrote a more diplomatic alternative, keeping the line declaring the king's inability to go on "without the help and support of the woman I love."

Edward then left Windsor for self-exile, huddled in the back seat of his Daimler and covering his face from prying photographers. In the first weekly issue of *Time* for 1937, Mrs. Simpson would be on the cover without tongue in cheek as "Man of the Year."

At the time of the coronation of the ex-king's brother, in May 1937, Shaw joked in a long letter to the editor in *Time and Tide* that he thought it would be appropriate "to institute a Society for the Prevention of Cruelty to Royal Personages." And in an observation to the Labour organ *Forward* that December, Shaw stubbornly continued to see something in the former sovereign that few others perceived. "The notion of the ex-King of England vanishing from the news as a private person is not workable," he wrote, "unless Edward proves a genuine nonentity, which is hardly consistent with his abdication." Yet rather than a Platonic philosopher-king in the Magnus mold—Edward VIII had proved, romance apart, a King Minus. Diana Duff Cooper would tell Chips Channon about the difference between past and present, "That was an operetta, this is an institution."

The abdication spurred a revival of *The Apple Cart* at the Malvern Festival in the summer of 1937, following the Coronation. For the festival's souvenir book Shaw observed, dissatisfied at the outcome in reality, "how natural and reasonable and probable the play is, and how improbable, fantastic, and outrageous the actual event was. There was not a single circumstance of it which I should have dared to invent." If a Disraeli or a Macaulay could be raised from the dead to see *The Apple Cart* and asked, "Could this thing happen?" Shaw thought the response would be, "Oh, quite possibly. Queen Elizabeth threatened to abdicate and Queen Victoria used to hint at it once or so." But Shaw added, if you had told either one about the exit of Edward VIII, as Disraeli or Macaulay would have warned, "If you put a tale like that into a play you will spend the rest of your days in a lunatic asylum. So much for holding the mirror up to nature." Yet the royal affair, he felt, confirmed his misgivings about the ineffectiveness of democratically elected governments and offered "enough to tempt any playwright in the comedy of the utter helplessness of Earl Baldwin and the British Parliament while the affair was settled over their supposedly omnipotent heads by the Royal Family."

The aspirations of Winston Churchill to propel his own political rehabilitation through the rescue of a modern model of a monarch, as Edward briefly seemed, were a self-induced fantasy. Shaw's own vision of the ex-king through a rosy *Apple Cart* lens would also prove more fantasy than he imagined. Shaw's playlet king was far more shrewd and articulate than the exiting Edward VIII. As for Wallis Simpson, who had dominated the king since 1934, she had nothing of the beguiling charms of a Shavian Orinthia—and even among her few admirers, no one would confuse her with sweet Daisy Bell.

Several years later, Churchill still insisted he had been right, telling the American army chief of staff, General George C. Marshall, that the great mistake the king made was just not going ahead and marrying Mrs. Simpson. "The king could do no wrong if he had married her; then they could have scratched around and tried to settle this thing." Shaw had long before said much the same, telling Dorothy Kilgallen of the *New York Evening Journal* in May 1937 that Edward "didn't want to be King. If he wanted to be King, he would be King today and Mrs. Simpson would be Queen. Who could have stopped him? He had all the cards in his hand and threw them away." As for coming back, Shaw claimed that a private deal, including a financial settlement, had been made to keep Wally from England, "They could return tomorrow if they liked. . . . But I am sure they won't. They are better off where they are."

Had Churchill, and Shaw, succeeded in persuading Edward VIII to insist upon his throne, the outcome might have been far different than they imagined. The king was covertly pro-Nazi, and becoming more so under German wooing. When the new European war, already imminent, materialized late in 1939, Edward and Wallis were already under suspicion as coveting his brother's throne. Kings, Shaw had foreshadowed, in the words of his "refinished" Cymbeline, "do rarely love their heirs."

Charles Peake, a Foreign Office official, learned from Sir Walter Monckton, Edward's former attorney and in wartime the head of the Press and Censorship Bureau, of "a frightful interview" between the Duke of Windsor and Lord Beaverbrook in January 1940 in which both agreed that the war should be ended by a peace offer to Germany. (Beaverbrook had been influential in appeasement circles before the war.) "The Beaver suggested," Peake wrote acidly, "that the Duke should get out of uniform,[9] come home, & after enlisting powerful City support,

---

9 To find him a safe wartime role, his brother the king made the Duke of Windsor a liaison officer with the French army.

stump the country, in which case the Duke would have a tremendous success. W. M. contented himself with reminding the Duke that if he did that he would be liable [by residence] to UK income tax. This made the little man blench & he declared with great determination that the whole thing was off."

Still, the Nazis intended to exploit Edward. Shaw sensed this very early in the war. Writing wryly to Nancy Astor on November 8, 1939, after Poland had been subjugated and divided between Hitler and Stalin, he proposed, "If public opinion in Europe forces us to produce a war aim, what would you say to a constitutional monarchy in Poland, with the Duke of Windsor as monarch and Queen Wally as his consort? Unemployed kings are a bit dangerous." After the war, captured German documents exposed the Duke of Windsor's contacts with Foreign Minister Joachim von Ribbentrop through go-betweens in Lisbon. The Duke was to "hold himself in readiness for further developments" which promised to take him back to an occupied England.

George VI, his most thorough biographer, Sarah Bradford, has written, based on compromising papers found in Hesse in 1947, "must have reflected on the similarities between the scenario put forward by the Duke and the plot of *The Apple Cart*, a possibility which he had envisaged, perhaps only half-seriously, when discussing the question of his brother's title in December 1936. . . . In view of repeated evidence of his brother's willingness to stage a comeback, however ill-thought and woolly his plans to do so were, it is hard to say that he was entirely wrong." But the new king had become immensely popular during the war, while the Duke of Windsor, more and more seen as Wallis's lapdog, hovered on the margins in embittered and ostentatious, yet tawdry, exile. As the suitor in the music-hall ballad about "Daisy Bell" had prophesied, it would not be "a stylish marriage."

Shaw's *Apple Cart*, vastly more influential than anyone could have imagined in 1929, would still work onstage thereafter, and indeed does, when reset in an era much farther into the future. Its echoes of 1936 continue to resonate quietly. Yet the remarkable playlet recalling it receded into a rueful footnote to history.

Bibliographic Essay

Much abridged, my rediscovery of Shaw's satire appeared in the December 2006 issue of *History Today* (London) as "Playing the King." Shaw's playlet on the abdication is reproduced courtesy of the Society of Authors on behalf of the Bernard Shaw Estate, through Jeremy Crow, Head of Literary Estates.

For copies of Shaw's 1936–37 newspaper articles, interviews, and news releases I am indebted to Lorne Bruce, archivist of Special Collections at the University of Guelph, Ontario, Canada. Two typescripts of Shaw's playlet originally owned by Hearst's London correspondent William Hillman were sold by Litchfield Auctions, Litchfield, Connecticut, in May 2003.

Shaw's *The King, the Constitution and the Lady: Another Fictitious Dialogue* appeared in the *London Evening Standard* on December 5, 1936, as *Name Your Lady*. It also appeared on that date in the *New York American*. It was reprinted in the pamphlet *Cavalcade* soon after (London, 1936), and again in Hesketh Pearson's *G.B.S.: A Full Length Portrait* (New York and London: Harper, 1942). The text appears here by permission of the Society of Authors acting per the estate of Bernard Shaw. Pearson's comments on the abdication are from the same volume. Shaw's *Apple Cart* first appeared in English (a German translation, as *Der Kaiser von Amerika*, preceded it in 1929) as *The Apple Cart: A Political Extravaganza* (London: Constable, 1930). Shaw's *Cymbeline Refinished*, facetiously subtitled *A Collaborator's Note*, was first published by Constable in London as a rehearsal copy in October 1937.

The stage censorship law of 1737, revised in an act of 1843, is described, along with its repercussions until its fading and demise in the later 1960s, in John Johnson, *The Lord Chamberlain's Blue Pencil* (London: Hodder and Stoughton, 1990).

Winston Churchill's letter to the king referring to Shaw's playlet appears in Roy Jenkins, *Churchill: A Biography* (New York: Farrar, Straus, 2001). Robert Bernays and Robert Boothby are also quoted from Jenkins. Baldwin's role is described in *The Baldwin Age*, ed. John Raymond (London: Eyre & Spottiswoode, 1960). Edward's objections, as Prince of Wales, to being "fettered" are quoted by Churchill in his essay on George V in *Great Contemporaries* (London: Butterworth, 1937).

Harold Nicolson's diary is *Diaries and Letters, 1930–1939*, ed. Nigel Nicolson (London: Collins, 1966). Nancy Astor's diary entries are from Norman and Jeanne Mackenzie, eds., *The Diary of Beatrice Webb*, vol. 4 (Cambridge: Harvard University Press, 1985). Shaw's letter to her of November 8, 1939, is from *Bernard Shaw and Lady Astor*, ed. J. P. Wearing (Toronto: University of Toronto Press, 2005). References to the Duff

Coopers and Henry Cannon are from Philip Ziegler, *Diana Cooper* (New York: Knopf, 1982), although the "Admiral of the Fleet" quip attributed to Channon is from Ralph Martin, *The Woman He Loved* (New York: Simon and Schuster, 1973).

The exchanges between the ex-king and the new king are from Sarah Bradford, *King George VI* (London: Weidenfeld and Nicolson, 1989). Shaw's *Time and Tide* quip about cruelty to royal personages appeared on May 22, 1937, as "The Coronation." Shaw's "On the Festival Habit" appeared in the *Malvern Festival Book* for 1937 and was reprinted in E. J. West, ed., *Shaw on Theatre* (New York: Hill and Wang, 1958). Churchill's conversation with General Marshall is recalled by the general in Forrest C. Pogue, ed., *George C. Marshall: Interviews and Reminiscences* (Lexington, Va.: George C. Marshall Research Foundation, 1991).

· 13 ·

Who's Afraid of Bernard Shaw?

VIRGINIA WOOLF AND GBS

On the day before Bernard Shaw's ninety-third birthday in 1949, a sale of his library in London attracted press attention. Up for auction at Sotheby's were shelves of books he had emptied from the flat he was vacating at Whitehall Court. He now lived entirely at Shaw's Corner, the former rectory at Ayot St. Lawrence in Hertfordshire. To push up the prices Shaw had put, in the spidery holograph of his last years, autobiographical flyleaf inscriptions in some of the most rare volumes, including T. E. Lawrence's privately printed *Seven Pillars of Wisdom* and editions of Bunyan, Dante, and Shakespeare. The meager prices—Londoners had been struggling in straitened circumstances since the war—were disappointing. Lawrence's memoir of Arabia, which might have brought many thousands between the wars, fetched only £460. An original edition of the striking Aubrey Beardsley–illustrated *Morte Darthur*, not quite as valuable, brought only £58. Without Shaw's flyleaf assistance, a presentation copy of *A Room of One's Own* (1929) from Virginia Woolf brought a meager £6.10.

Had Shaw written an inscription in the Woolf book, in which he would have recognized echoes from his own *The Quintessence of Ibsenism* (1891), and much more, what might he have disclosed? In her lifetime he told her, and she reciprocated. Yet even devotees of Virginia Woolf see little association with GBS other than that in March 1907 she and her brother Adrian Stephen took over, from Shaw, the lease of 29 Fitzroy Square, where he had lived with his mother until his marriage to Charlotte Payne Townshend in 1898.

Virginia's sister, Vanessa, was now Mrs. Clive Bell. The unmarried

Stephen siblings needed their own address, preferably within walking distance of Bloomsbury. Although the tall row house with iron railings was run down and seemed not as respectable as Gordon Square, Virginia's builder had checked for her with local police, who reassured her, as Duncan Grant, a friend—and neighbor with two rooms nearby at number 22—recalled, that a relic of earlier grandeur "was a beadle to march round the square . . . in a top-hat and a tail-coat piped with red and brass buttons." It would cost £150 to refurbish the interior to her liking, a rather large investment for a house with a lease to expire in October 1911, when the Stephens relocated to 38 Brunswick Square.

At Fitzroy Square, with most of its houses now broken up into flats, studios, and offices, Virginia and Adrian, relatively well fixed, were rare tenants, occupying the entire structure, complete with live-in cook and maid, front-door bell, and a dog, Hans.

While Virginia remained satisfied with the house and the neighborhood, she had always seemed impatient with the works of the previous occupant. Living with his ghost changed nothing. "Bernard Shaw kept us on the rack for 3 hours last night," she complained to a friend about Shaw's new, and talky, country-house comedy, *Misalliance*, then at the Duke of York's Theatre; "His mind," she deplored, "is that of a disgustingly precocious child of 2—a sad and improper spectacle to my thinking." Her outraged tone made her sound less like a Bloomsbury rebel than her father's daughter. Shaw had long identified Sir Leslie Stephen with what he called the sect of "Secular Morality—the party of Matthew Arnold, George Eliot and Mrs Humphry Ward, of the Ethical Societies of America, of South Place [Chapel], Leslie Stephen and so on."

Virginia must have known, then, a Shavian play more to her frame of mind, *Mrs Warren's Profession* (1893), banned from the stage by the Lord Chamberlain's censor but notorious thereby and easily available in print, for her early novel *The Voyage Out* (1915) employs as symbol of the double standard its ultimate victim, the prostitute. Unlike sentimental late-Victorian melodrama, *Mrs Warren* evokes the complicity of a male-dominated society, an injustice recognized by Virginia's Evelyn Murgatroyd, who, like Vivie Warren, who also loses her idealism, learns her mother's history and the price she has paid for being unmarried, while the only price paid by a prostitute's clientele is a few pounds.

There was no reason for Virginia to encounter Shaw in person before she married Leonard Woolf. Since one of her conditions for their marriage in 1912 was that he could not return to Colonial Service administration—he had spent nearly seven years in Ceylon, then considered part of India—he sought work in London that might exploit his experience. Becoming involved in journalism and in Labour Party politics, he was soon involved with Sidney and Beatrice Webb, and Bernard Shaw. The Webbs, Virginia wrote in 1915, in the early months of the Great War, had "clawed" her Leonard "for a huge job." Woolf had begun doing preliminary studies of what Beatrice described as "supernational law" for the Fabian Society's Research Department. Through funds supplied by Quaker cocoa manufacturer Joseph Rowntree, Leonard had been offered £100 to produce a monograph on the practicalities of international government. It would become the seed of the postwar League of Nations.

Since Shaw rather than Webb was the chairman of the Research Department, the work put Woolf next to some giants of the generation before his own—activists who "lifted the burden of Victorianism" and were "on the same side of the barricades" as he felt he and Virginia were. In her strongest language, Virginia at first would disagree.

In 1916 the Webbs rented Windham Croft, a country house near Turners Hill in Sussex, for their long weekends in late spring and summer, and invited the Woolfs for mid-June. They discovered that they were to be joined by Leonard's ostensible employer—Bernard Shaw. Virginia had never met him, but had noted in her diary about a "divine concert" of Haydn, Mozart, and Bach at Queen's Hall in February 1915 that to her surprise, "Opposite me was Bernard Shaw, grown a whitehaired benevolent old man." (He was fifty-eight to her thirty-four.) She could now validate that curious perception. At Queen's Hall she had been too timid to talk to him. Her elderly "Aunt Anny"—Anne Thackeray Ritchie—had compared contemporary writers unfavorably to her own generation, including GBS. "Some of them have a touch of that [earlier] quality; Bernard Shaw has; but only a touch."

The social weekend on the edge of summer marked the completion of Leonard Woolf's book. For the American edition to appear in mid-August, Shaw had written a preface noting that the author had researched and written *International Government*, proposing "a supernational authority that will prevent [further] war," on public-spirited financial terms "which would certainly have been rejected with emphasis by a dock labourer." But Woolf had rejected something else—Shaw's preface as chairman of the commissioning group—so far as the English edition was concerned, "on the ground that, as a young man and writer, I wanted my book to be judged on its own merits and defects; it should stand solely on its own legs, and not on those of as great man's preface." (Shaw conceded to a friend the next year that Woolf had been "quite right" to do so.)[1]

"We're just off to the Webbs," Virginia wrote with trepidation to James Strachey, "possibly to meet the Shaws, and if it weren't for the boasting, I should collapse altogether."

Afterward she reported to Nelly (Lady Robert) Cecil, who lived nearby but whom she had no opportunity then to visit, that when they were not indoors at Windham Croft they were "marching through woods with Mr and Mrs Sidney Webb, and Mr and Mrs Bernard Shaw, who all talked so incessantly upon so many different subjects that I never saw a single tree, and rather wished I could open your garden gate. Still, they were very kind."

The hours were not all consumed by walking and talking, Leonard remembered in his eighty-eighth year. "Shaw went into the garden every morning and wrote on a writing pad on his knee." He was jotting down ideas about how to continue the intractable play about the war which he had begun and then put aside. "I don't know what it's about," he had confessed to Stella Campbell, the Eliza Doolittle of his *Pygmalion*, on May 14. "I began it on the 4th [of] March: and I have hardly come to the beginning of the first scene yet." His Pitman shorthand first draft is now lost, but his title for it, repeated in his much-revised typescript, was the now almost meaningless "The Studio in the Clouds," apparently a place that was not yet Windham Croft.

To Vanessa, Virginia repeated a little of her Strachey letter. "We talked quite incessantly—we were taken for brisk walks, still talking hard. . . . Mrs Webb pounces on one, rather like a moulting eagle. . . . However I got on with her better than I expected." And we see Virginia dissecting everyone—including herself—in such Shavian terms that some of her perceptions seem to leap, as if shared, onto GBS's writing pad. Beatrice, she explained to Vanessa, "seems very open minded, for an elderly person"—she was fifty-eight—"and with no illusions or passions, or mysteries, so I daresay one would find her dull in the long run; she reminded me," Virginia added paradoxically, "of one of the undergraduates of our youth."

Mrs. Webb knew that Virginia had already attempted, at least once

---

[1] For the French and American editions, and in the second English edition, the Shavian preface did appear to help promote the book.

since her marriage in 1913, to commit suicide. Beatrice recalled her later as "beautiful . . . but with a queer, uncertain, almost hysterical manner." Curiously, in Beatrice's diary entry for the Windham Croft weekend, she never alluded to the Woolfs. Yet Virginia, in her letter to her sister, had a lot to say about the Webbs and the Shaws. Even the aged, garrulous, hoary-bearded Captain Shotover of the early pages of Shaw's new play, who falls asleep in company despite his efforts to concentrate his mind, seems anticipated in her letter. "Shaw went fast asleep, apparently, in the midst of all the talk and then woke up and rambled on into interminable stories about himself . . . and his uncle who tried to commit suicide by shutting his head into a carpet bag, and his father who played on the ophicleide and died insane"—Virginia probably meant to write *inebriated*—"as they all do, and so on and so on. Poor Mrs Shaw was completely out of it; and told me all about her conversion to Indian mysticism, and lent me little books, which unluckily, Mrs Webb got hold of, and she jeered at poor old Mrs Shaw, who sat in her corner, like a fat white Persian cat."

"I liked it better than I expected," Virginia wrote to Katherine Cox about the long weekend. "At any rate, one can say [there] what one likes, which is unusual with the middle aged; indeed I felt much more of a mature woman with a passionate past than Mrs Webb, who seemed to me astonishingly young and crude . . . and keen as a knife." Charlotte, she deplored, seemed "very stupid, and has rolled herself up . . . like a caterpillar in a cocoon." GBS was "rather more remote than the others"—clearly, when he was absorbing impressions he could imaginatively exploit—"but when stirred up he told stories, all about himself, without stopping." When he drafted letters to the newspapers, a favorite pastime, "he read them aloud."

Shaw did fire off letters from Windham Croft to at least three papers, but his ideas about his play, which he would title, finally, *Heartbreak House*, were also beginning to jell. Later he told a biographer that the play "began with an atmosphere" and did not contain "a word that was foreseen before it was written." The "over-heated drawing-room atmosphere," he would claim in his preface to the play, came from his having seen Chekhov's *The Cherry Orchard* just before the war. Other dimensions of *Heartbreak House* would come from Shakespeare (*King Lear* and *Othello*), Wagner (*Siegfried* and *Parsifal*), Lewis Carroll (the *Alice* stories), and Homer (*The Iliad*). Even before the war he was contemplating a Chekhovian play, to be charged with symbolism and prophecy about

England's moral paralysis as "cultured leisured Europe" drifted toward catastrophe. Events would validate his scheme.

Later, in *The Common Reader* (1925), Woolf in "The Russian Point of View" would contrast Shaw and Chekhov without realizing their affinities, writing that Chekhov was "also aware of the evils and injustices of the social state, . . . but the reformer's zeal is not his. . . . The mind interests him enormously, but he is a most subtle and delicate analyst of human relations. But again, too, the end [for him] is not there." She would not see herself in *Heartbreak House* either.

Shaw's play would be set in a country house "in the middle of the north edge of Sussex" with an interior suggesting an old sailing ship. A long-retired and seemingly half-mad sea captain haunts rather than possesses it. Old Shotover had his origins in the actress Lena Ashwell's eccentric and irascible seafaring father, Captain Charles Pocock, who worked out of a sailing ship in the Tyne, on which his family lived. Shaw also borrowed from the cranky mid-Victorian prophet Thomas Carlyle, who had even used, in *Past and Present*, a character named Undershot. Yet readers who turn to *Heartbreak House* will recognize in Virginia's recollection something of the gestating play. As remote—yet genial—as he appeared, Shaw was preoccupied with assimilating, inventively, his weekend companions.

The "astonishingly young and crude . . . and keen as a knife" early perception of Beatrice Webb may turn up, surprisingly, in the ingenue Ellie Dunn, whom heartbreak turns hard, while Virginia becomes transformed, as does Leonard, for Shaw's purposes. Neither would notice it. There is even more of GBS himself than he would have owned up to, but creativity has its secrets as well as its mysteries.

In the opening scene appears Shotover's fortyish and eternally feminine elder daughter, Hesione Hushabye, patterned—so Shaw confided to her original—after Mrs. Campbell. Hesione's husband, Hector, developed, Shaw confessed, from the politician and adventurer Robert Cunninghame Graham as well as from an even older friend, Fabian pioneer and journalist Hubert Bland, whose swashbuckling was limited to the boudoir. At the start was the plot device of a young and bewildered visitor to the Shotover house, Ellie Dunn, an Alice with traces of Helen of Troy, who would lose her innocence and become, in those words of Virginia which Shaw never knew, "crude . . . and keen as a knife." A comfortable civilization would be evoked, to be undermined by its own apathy. It would take on much of that weekend at Windham Croft.

Beatrice Webb had a habit, Leonard Woolf has written, "of classifying all her friends and acquaintances in a kind of psychological and occupational card-index. I was 'the ex-colonial civil-servant.'" If the attractive but haughty and high-strung Virginia Woolf were transmuted by Shaw, who was quick to pick up a person's mannerisms, into his play's imperious, snobbish, younger Shotover daughter, Lady Ariadne Utterword, he may have picked up Beatrice's shorthand. (Curiously, too, Virginia's first name was actually Adeline, and Ariadne is called "Addie"—to her annoyance—by Shotover's old housekeeper.)[2]

Ariadne's absent husband—he never appears onstage but is much talked about—is Sir Hastings Utterword, whose baptismal name suggests the Indian subcontinent. (Warren Hastings had been a stern governor-general of India in the decade of Victoria's birth.) In the play he is described as "governor of all the crown colonies in succession."

Leonard Woolf's far more modest but geographically relevant colonial background may well have been in Shaw's mind, as a curious echo of the weekend suggests. Lady Utterword, apparently repeating a boast by her husband, remarks that imperial rule required shedding "ridiculous sham democracy" in favor of "a good supply of bamboo"—presumably for caning malcontents—"to bring the British native to his senses." Leonard, who did not subscribe to such ways, instinctively employed a condescending noun he had heard used daily, and remembered that at a Fabian meeting Shaw "gave me the only serious dressing down I have ever had from him, my sin—a somewhat inadvertent sin—having been to use the word 'natives' of Indians."

Thanks to Windham Croft, the setting and characters were coming together, and one can even see elements of the scholarly political radical, Sidney Webb, emerge in the unassuming veteran radical Mazzini Dunn, whose daughter, Ellie, has some of the harder as well as some of the immature qualities which Virginia imagined in Beatrice Webb.

Why Virginia turned to an early Shaw novel after returning from

---

2 Michael Holroyd in volume 3 of his biography of GBS (1991) sees Charlotte Shaw, however "out of it" to contemporaries, as "well disguised" for the role of Ariadne; yet she resembles no aspect of the character. He also identifies the "splendid drumming" heard outdoors on the terrace in the last act as—improbably—"the guns of the Somme offensive" rather than the rumbling of the Zeppelin which would drop one of the first bombs of the war on the Shotover property. Echoes of a "goods train" on the railway line nearby are suggested by Hesione, as the war has not yet erupted, although its outbreak is feared. The Somme offensives were years away.

Windham Croft is unknown, but if she were looking for something by a newly interesting GBS to read she would have found in Leonard's library Shaw's satire on prizefighting as a socially unacceptable occupation and his depiction of a very liberated and bookish young woman. (Leonard owned copies, then, of two of Shaw's early novels in 1914 reprints, as well as several of his plays.) "Have you read *Cashel Byron's Profession*?" she queried Molly MacCarthy. "Much the best thing Shaw ever wrote, to my mind." Shaw's next novel, *An Unsocial Socialist* (1883), also on Leonard's shelves, seems to have had a more direct impact, evident strikingly and almost immediately in *The Voyage Out*. Henrietta, the young wife of Shaw's wealthy and eccentric socialist, Sidney Trefusis, dies of pneumonia under the ministrations of a physician so mediocre and loftily rude that, given the opportunity, Shaw observes, he might have decimated London. In Woolf's novel of 1915, young Rachel Vinrace, engaged to be married, dies of apparent typhoid under "the sulky masterful manner of Dr. Lesage," who dismisses the case as hopeless and, returning from the deathbed, lightly has a cup of coffee.

A further echo seems to appear in Virginia's *Night and Day* (1919), where William Rodney and Katharine Hilbery resemble GBS's aristocratic Gertrude Lindsay and the newly widowered Sidney Trefusis. "She, who had lived in the marriage market since she had left school, looked upon love-making as the most serious business of life. To him it was only a pleasant sort of trifling, enhanced by a dash of sadness in the reflection that it meant so little."

Late in October 1916, Virginia and Leonard went to a Fabian lecture given by Shaw at King's Hall, Covent Garden, at which Molly's husband, theater critic Desmond MacCarthy, was to introduce the society's star performer, whose topic had been announced as "how far the sacrifice of liberty to the energies created by war is really necessary." Since every seat had been sold, Shaw felt that he had to keep the audience "up to concert pitch" for ninety minutes. "The hall was quite full," a press report observed, "and judging by the congestion in the entrance . . . a considerable number of people had neglected to book their seats and had to be turned away in the rain." His title was advertised as "Life," and he lived up to its vagueness, talking about "biology, theology, and the super-man or super-Prospero, Zeppelins, Plato, poverty, the intelligent parent—and himself." Virginia wrote to Vanessa rather sympathetically that concert length was far too long: "the audience coughed him down, which was rather terrible." Listeners did not want what Shaw thought was their money's worth, only a sample of the famous GBS.

In 1923, after *Heartbreak House* was published and staged,[3] Virginia would write, playfully, *Freshwater*, a burlesque she never expected to expose beyond her Bloomsbury circle. The playlet, outdoing *Misalliance*, which she once deplored, in absurdity, is set in a country house on the Isle of Wight at a time when her aunt, the photographer Julia Margaret Cameron, and her husband, Charles Hay Cameron, who lived at Freshwater, are preparing to leave for India. There are echoes of *Heartbreak House*. Cameron, a colonial servant, would be a judge in India and would live his last years with his wife in Ceylon. (Leonard is penciled in to play him.)

The skit—as Virginia called it—is peopled with real-life Victorians. Shaw's Alfred Mangan in *Heartbreak House* is named, Mangan claims, for one of them, Tennyson. (The poet had a home at Freshwater.) There is also the painter George Frederick Watts and his childlike wife, Ellen Terry, whom he married in 1864 when she was sixteen. He was more than thirty years her elder—as old as her father, Ben Terry. (Young Ellie in Shaw's play had already claimed a "mystic marriage" with old Shotover.) The elderly Cameron is given to visionary speeches and to falling asleep in company much as is Shotover, and Ellen Terry—like Shaw's Ellie—arrives to find a somewhat mad household. "O how usual it all is," Ellen Terry says. "Nothing ever changes in this house. Someone is always asleep."

The skit closes with the Camerons leaving for India, "a land less corrupted by hypocrisy." And as they go, the aged queen is trundled in, seated in her wheelchair (many years too soon), having been driven across the island from Osborne. (Virginia writes *Balmoral*—perhaps for its patent absurdity. Osborne House *was* on the Isle of Wight, Balmoral far off in Scotland. There was, however, a sanatorium on the Isle of Wight called Balmoral House. Virginia may have been planting a wicked

---

3 When St. John Ervine, reviewing the London production, complained that Ellen O'Malley, who had already been on the stage as a leading lady for twenty years, was "seriously miscast" as Ellie Dunn, Shaw defended himself by retorting, "I did not cast Ellen for Ellie Dunn: I wrote the part for her; and it fits her like a glove" (October 23, 1921). Shaw had spoken of her as appropriate for Ellie since 1918, the year after he finished the play, but she could no longer carry off ingenue roles. In misplaced loyalty, Shaw did not care, intending his words to sustain stage illusions, as he did when Mrs. Campbell at forty-eight played the eighteen-year-old Eliza Doolittle in *Pygmalion*.

allusion for the knowledgeable.) A later version of the scrawled text was performed in Vanessa Bell's Fitzroy Street studio early in 1935—a burlesque, perhaps, on the play in which Virginia herself may have been burlesqued.

Shaw's next play after *Heartbreak House* was the gargantuan Bible-to-beyond cycle, *Back to Methuselah*, which Virginia's brother-in-law, Clive Bell, attacked in a review, leading to a prank by her bohemian friend Dora Carrington, who lived in a ménage à trois with Ralph Partridge and Lytton Strachey. Above a crude forgery of Shaw's signature, she had Partridge type out for her a letter utterly unlike, in form and style, anything that GBS had ever written:

Dear Clive Bell,

Thank you for the numerous compliments you have paid me in this week's New Republic. I am sorry that I can't return the compliment that I think you, or your prose, "Perfectly respectable."

In my young days a "taxicab" was a name given only to aged whores, ugly as Shaftesbury Avenue.

You do not, it would appear, lead a very enviable aesthetic life; to me it seems dull.

Yours,
Bernard Shaw

Bell was completely taken in by the letter, although the style was not remotely Shavian. Further, "taxicabs" (called so for their taximeters) did not exist in Shaw's "young days," and Shaw used printed notepaper that didn't require a typed address. Bell's indignant reply to Adelphi Terrace resulted in a postcard from Shaw disowning the diatribe. Carrington delightedly wrote a note to Strachey, who was away, that Bell's credulity proved he was "a greenhorn." And she wondered what "Poor Shaw" thought of Bell. "Clive Bell completely ga-ga," she imagined.

Since Strachey was her only friend with influence over the flighty Carrington, Virginia wrote to him with concern (February 23, 1922), "I think you *must* now tell Clive the truth. He is making himself the laughing stock of London.... I'm not sure he didn't say he was going to write to Shaw again.... He says that he has shown the letter to several good judges who all agree that Shaw has been driven mad by Clive." With no evidence whatever he had claimed as much to her. "These vegetarians, my dear Virginia, always go [off] at the top. He needs bullock's blood."

In her diary on March 30, while writing *Jacob's Room*, she wondered about "skipping to the end of the book, & thinking what I shall say about Shaw." But she did not skip to the end, and cautiously inserted Shaw, with Wells, into her third chapter, where young Jacob Flanders, a fictional Thoby Stephen (Virginia's brother Thoby died of typhoid fever on November 20, 1906) who goes up to Cambridge in 1906, is entertained at luncheon with three other undergraduates by Professor George Plumer and his wife, who have made it, from their beginnings in Manchester, up the rungs of class. Their severe politics, the better-born Jacob could see, appeared reflected in what they read. "Books were on the shelves by Wells and Shaw; on the table serious sixpenny weeklies written by pale men in muddy boots—the weekly creak and screech of brains rinsed in cold water and rung dry."

"I don't feel that I know the truth about anything till I've read them both!" said Mrs. Plumer brightly, fingering a table of contents "with her bare red hand."

The young men from comfortable backgrounds leave with "discomfort at the world shown them" in Shaw and Wells and the radical weeklies, and Jacob muses, "What were they after, scrubbing and demolishing, these elderly people? Had they never read Homer, Shakespeare, the Elizabethans?" He pauses in the street to light a cigarette, and Woolf notes ironically "the [restored] composure with which he hollowed his hand to screen a match. He was a young man of substance." Yet he feels threatened that such upstarts have become competitors for places once automatically his, that "there will be no form"—due or proper shape—"in the world." "The Plumers will try to prevent him from making it. Wells and Shaw and the serious sixpenny weeklies will sit on his head."

In the end she excoriated Arnold Bennett and John Masefield and recommended that their works be "burn[ed] to cinders." (In Virginia's *Night and Day*, in 1919, Mrs. Cosham accosts Mr. Popham with his alleged failure to read the earlier stylists. "You have your Belloc, your Chesterton, your Bernard Shaw—why should you read De Quincey?" But, he protests, "I do read De Quincey, more than Belloc and Chesterton, anyhow!" "Indeed!" she says, relieved, for he does read De Quincey *and* Bernard Shaw. And in *Mrs. Dalloway*, published in 1925, she imagined Septimus Smith "devouring Shakespeare, Darwin, [Mackinnon's] *History of Civilisation*, and Bernard Shaw.")

Although Leonard had seen Shaw often on literary and political business, it was usually without Virginia. At an exhibition of caricatures by Edmond Kapp in 1920 she criticized his ink-and-wash Shaw portrait as "diabolic" and inhuman. That was not her picture of him, she explained. "Gazing from the gallery of some dismal gas-lit hall, one has seen him, often enough, alert, slight, erect, as if combating in his solitary person the forces of inertia and stupidity massed in a sea upon the floor. On a nearer glance, he appeared much of a knight-errant, candid, indeed innocent of aspect; a Don Quixote born in the Northern mists—shrewd, that is to say, rather than romantic. Mr Kapp has the legendary version—the diabolic. Moustache and eyebrows are twisted into points. The fingers are contorted into stamping hooves." It was the result of knowing "little or nothing about the subject." She was no more sympathetic to caricatures of Shaw in words, having reviewed in *TLS*, anonymously as was then its practice, a book of parodies by J. C. Squire, *Tricks of the Trade*, judging his attempt at GBS his "least successful." Shaw's style, she explained, was "much too workmanlike to present any obvious weak points to the caricaturist; and to parody his manner you would have to be quicker and more agile of intellect than he is himself. Moreover, Shaw parodies himself far better than anyone else could do it."

Late in 1921 she and Leonard went to the Court Theatre in Sloane Square with Lytton Strachey and Ralph and Frances Partridge to see *Heartbreak House*. (At tea two weeks earlier, Partridge had predicted to Virginia, disconcertingly to her, that "no one [then writing] will be read 100 years hence save Shaw," and in the following May, while sitting with Leonard in Richmond Park at a Sunday band concert (so she wrote to Janet Case), the couple had "a terrific argument about Shaw. Leonard says we owe a great deal to Shaw. I say that he only influenced the outer fringe of morality. Leonard says that the shop girls wouldn't be listening to the Band with their young men if it weren't for Shaw. I say the human heart is touched only by the poets. Leonard says *rot*, I say damn. Then we go home. . . . But don't you agree with me that the Edwardians, from 1895 to 1914, made a pretty poor show. By the Edwardians, I mean Shaw, Wells, Galsworthy, the Webbs, Arnold Bennett. We Georgians have our work cut out for us, you see."

Virginia's insistence on a primary place for poets left little room for GBS. In another incendiary image about extirpating obsolescent writers (as in *Jacob's Room*) she would write, "Modern literature, which had grown a little sultry and scented with Oscar Wilde and Walter Pater, revived instantly from her nineteenth-century languor when Samuel Butler and Bernard Shaw began to burn their feathers and apply their salts to her nose. She awoke; she sat up; she sneezed. Naturally, the poets were frightened away.... Prose has taken all the dirty work on to her own shoulders."

Virginia hardly knew which side she was on, as ideology and emotion often conflicted where Shaw was concerned. When her circle argued over the merits of *Saint Joan,* a slight majority taking the "pro" side, she noted herself as a "hedge"—as she confessed to not having read it or seen it. Yet it was then difficult to evade: it was the play of the mid-1920s, for which Shaw would win a long-delayed Nobel Prize for Literature.

Also in the mid-1920s Leonard became literary editor of *The Nation,* a "sixpenny weekly." The position elevated him to peer status with the elite figures of his earlier years. By publishing *Mrs. Dalloway* in 1925, Virginia had moved up even more, now recognized as a major novelist, even by the Edwardians about whom she had little good to say. The novel incorporated her view of physicians, which had hardened since her experience in 1904 with a group of Harley Street specialists who had prescribed cures for her mental breakdown which she found little short of savage. In fact, one of her doctors, fittingly—and factually—Sir George Savage, would be pilloried in *Mrs. Dalloway,* which a Woolf scholar believes may owe something to Shaw's *The Doctor's Dilemma,* the Molieresque mockery of doctors that was a stage hit as Virginia was emerging from her first Harley Street regimen. "I do not know a single thoughtful and well-informed person," Shaw had written in his preface to the play, "who does not feel that the tragedy of illness at present is that it delivers you helplessly into the hands of a profession which you deeply mistrust."

Mrs. Dalloway incorporated Virginia's similarly mordant view of physicians, already evident. Joanne Trautmann Banks suggested that while Shaw drew a rogue's gallery of practitioners in his satire, Woolf poured out her scorn for four recognizable London medical men into the capacious personality of her fictional Sir William Bradshaw, who to Clarissa Dalloway is "a great doctor yet to her obscurely evil." Also to Mrs. Dalloway, "Death was defiance," as it is to Shaw's outrageous and doomed antihero, Louis Dubedat.

After *Mrs. Dalloway* the Woolfs were sought after by leading intellectuals, even invited to dinner with H. G. Wells at his London flat in posh Whitehall Court, where Shaw also had a town residence. When they arrived—it was November 4, 1926, according to Arnold Bennett's diary—only Wells and his wife were present, but soon the maid announced the Shaws, and a few minutes later the Bennetts. (Bennett, long estranged from his wife, Marguerite, lived with a young actress, Dorothy Cheston, who called herself Mrs. Bennett.) "We had hardly met Bennett before," Leonard recalled, "and I felt rather overwhelmed by the galaxy." Since he had reviewed "rather critically" Bennett's new novel, *Lord Raingo*, he was not at his ease. And both Leonard and Virginia could guess how ill Bennett spoke privately of her. Sitting between Shaw and H. G., she seemed insulated from his potential wrath. "Both gloomy, these two last," Bennett noted of the Woolfs. "But I liked both of them in spite of their naughty treatment of me in the press." That was not apparent to the Woolfs. "As soon as we sat down," Leonard wrote, "Bennett fixed me with his eye, leant across, and said, 'W-w-woolf d-d-does not l-l-like my novels.'"

Once Bennett repeated, then re-repeated the charge, to no response, Shaw confronted the awkwardness by dominating the table. "Arnold with his slow stutter had no chance of getting a word in and soon resigned himself to firing the minute gun at me.[4] H. G. did not give way without a struggle, but he was no match for Shaw and the Shavian pyrotechnical monologue." Woolf thought it was "extraordinarily charming," but not Bennett, who was especially aggrieved by Virginia's vicious 1924 polemic, "Mr. Bennett and Mrs. Brown," which faulted him, and also Wells, among Edwardians, for emphasizing circumstantial realism over character and psychology. GBS had come off much better, for in one version of her essay, "Character in Fiction," in making her point that "human character" as portrayed by writers "changed" about 1910, she saw the evidence in "the plays of Bernard Shaw [which] continued to record it," but not in his contemporaries Wells, Bennett, and Galsworthy.

"Shaw talked practically the whole time," Bennett complained, "which is the same thing as saying that he talked a damn sight too much. After dinner he and Dorothy and Virginia Woolf and H. G. formed a group and never moved. I formed another group with Charlotte Shaw and Jane Wells, and never moved either. I really wanted to have a scrap with Virginia Woolf; but got no chance."

Nevertheless, seeing world-class stature in Shaw—a recent Nobel laureate in literature—meant overvaluing the Edwardians at the expense of Virginia's own generation, and she would be exasperated, accordingly, by the Shavolatry of her teenage nephews. "I only wish," she explained to Vanessa, their mother, in May 1927, "they didn't both (Quentin and

---

4 A minute gun, fired at intervals of a minute, especially at funerals, poked private fun at Bennett's "slow stutter."

Julian, I mean) think Bernard Shaw greater than Shakespeare." Shaw was just as suspicious of the staying power of such new moderns as James Joyce, who challenged readers with what he called "blackguardly" language to show their liberation from traditional restraints. Woolf remained on Shaw's more restrained yet candid side.

When Shaw gave a thousand pounds for the start-up of *Political Quarterly*, he cautioned the editor-to-be, William A. Robson, tongue-in-cheek, that since "artistry" in language was essential, "all the political notes should be written by Virginia Woolf." Unlike her husband, Shaw knew, Virginia had little interest in politics, but wrote without "commonness." Virginia again encountered the first rank of Edwardians on October 10, 1927, at the funeral at Golders Green of Wells's wife, Jane. (She had died of cancer.) Afterwards the pale gray coffin was sent through a door for the cremation. Many of the congregants were in tears, among them the wife of John Maynard Keynes, Lydia Lopokova, who rushed, sobbing, to Leonard and Virginia. "Then Shaw came up," Leonard remembered, "and put his hand on Lydia's shoulder and made a kind of oration to her telling her not to cry, that death was not an event to shed tears upon." ("You mustn't cry. Jane is well—Jane is splendid.") It was meant kindly, Woolf thought, and was "beautiful and eloquent," yet although GBS knew Lydia, the tiny former ballerina, well, and liked her, Leonard felt that Shaw's consolation was "rather to 'someone in tears,' who indeed might have been any woman in tears." ("I am not sufficiently fond of myself," GBS later told Virginia and Maynard Keynes, "to wish for immortality.")

A year later, Shaw and Virginia were part of a small group of writers who offered to give testimony at the trial for obscenity of Radclyffe Hall for her openly lesbian novel *The Well of Loneliness*. They met, with Vita Sackville-West and Rose Macaulay, on November 1, 1928, at the home of the architect Clough Williams-Ellis, all determined to support the book's rather small literary values in order to affirm its symbolic significance in enlarging the boundaries of the printed word. The group, she told her diary, was, but for Shaw, "a dowdy lot." At the trial eight days later none were permitted to speak, as the magistrate presiding, Sir Charles Biron, ruled narrowly that only experts in obscenity could testify. He ordered that copies of the book be seized and destroyed. But the old Edwardian had proven to Virginia to be allied with the future.

At least one of her close friends, composer Ethel Smyth, considered her an expert on Shaw, and wrote to her in 1931 to trace a GBS quotation.

"Is it possibly this?" Virginia responded. And she set down the Bunyanesque lines from the preface to *Man and Superman* that seemed to showcase Shaw's personal philosophy: "This is the true joy in life, the being used for a purpose recognized as a mighty one; the being thoroughly worn out before you are thrown on the scrap heap; the being a force of Nature instead of a feverish selfish little clod of ailments and grievances complaining that the world will not devote itself to making you happy." Shaw's creed made for a crowded postcard.

The Woolfs caught up with Shaw again at lunch with Lydia and Maynard Keynes, in June 1932. Whether as reaction to the spate of lionization that had accompanied his seventy-fifth birthday the year before, or merely to make conversation, Shaw observed that he would have liked to have had a different career. "I should like to be a performer in music, & a mathematician." He claimed that he burned many of the letters he received from the great, which was not so, but that he could not burn those from Ellen Terry, which were "works of art." Since they had been published the previous September, the first long run of his letters to appear in print, it is clear how the subject came up. (Virginia had already tried to borrow the volume from Vita.) "I admit," she quoted Shaw as confiding, generously, "that when our correspondence was published I thought—I admit—I shall be the hero: not a bit of it: I have to admit that Ellen was the superior. She comes out far better."

Shaw even suggested that his famed speaking style was not really "spontaneous, colloquial," but studied. "I've taken long railway journeys & spent them saying the letters of the alphabet aloud to make my vowels strike out." He described his "mugging up" his history plays by drafting them first and doing the background research afterwards—certainly not the whole truth, as he had read deeply in Napoleonic biography before writing *The Man of Destiny*, read de Fonblanque's life of General Burgoyne before completing *The Devil's Disciple*, consulted with Gilbert Murray and read Mommsen's *History of Rome* before writing *Caesar and Cleopatra*, and read the transcript of the trial of Joan of Arc, and much else, before writing *Saint Joan*. Yet his claim of reversing the process made provocative conversation: "I imagine the sort of things people would have done & then say they did them & then I find out facts—one always can—that prove it." Virginia took it all down.

He revealed his joy at listening to music on the BBC, sitting with the score in his lap and conducting for himself—and being peeved when Sir Thomas Beecham did not follow him, as when a "solemn, slow, processional" segment of *The Magic Flute*—and he sang it—turned inexplicably into a "hornpipe." Shaw "leapt up his knees & clasped them" ("he is never still a moment") to make his point as Virginia "leapt in my seat." He flung himself "this way & that: he sprang up to go, as if he were twenty. . . . What life, what vitality! What immense nervous spring! That is perhaps his genius. Immense vivacity—& why I don't read him for pleasure." It looked like yet another performance, but he had enjoyed being with the Keyneses and the Woolfs: he was not merely enlivening a public meeting.

That quality of impulsive command performance always puzzled Leonard. "He was always extremely nice to Virginia and me," Leonard recalled. "If one met him anywhere, he would come up and greet one with what seemed to me warmth and pleasure and he would start straight away with a fountain of words scintillating with wit and humour. You might easily flatter yourself that you were the one person in Europe to whom at the moment the famous George Bernard Shaw wanted to talk." Yet to Virginia the paradox was that Shaw was, to her view, even at such moments, "almost the most impersonal person I have ever known." He was "looking through you or over you" while conducting his one-man show.

A chance meeting in London, in Hyde Park, suggested—yet with some clues pointing otherwise—what the Woolfs perceived. As Virginia and Leonard were walking toward the Serpentine on April 27, 1933, "Suddenly L. bore off; and there was Shaw, dwindled shanks, white beard; striding along. We talked by a railing for 15 minutes. He stood with his arms folded, very upright, leaning back: teeth gold tipped. Just come from the dentist and 'lured out' by the weather. That is his art, to make one think he likes one." Because of Shaw's open affability, it always seemed that he was performing, and it would take the suspicious Virginia all her life to discover that he really liked her. Leonard would remember the Hyde Park encounter as "a brilliant, unflagging monologue" about the round-the-world voyage from which Shaw had recently returned, having been greeted everywhere as the most famous man on earth.

Virginia noted snatches of his "great spurt" of talk, particularly about China and India. "You forget that an aeroplane is like a car—it bumps. We went over the great wall—saw a little dim object in the distance. Of course the tropics are the place. The Sinhalese people are the original human beings—we are smudged copies." He didn't mention that he was writing a new play, begun that February, *On the Rocks*, in which an elderly Sinhalese gentleman, Sir Jafna Pandranath, after denouncing the

British as barbarians, challenges his listeners, "Look at your faces and look at the faces of my people in Ceylon, the cradle of the human race. There you see Man as he came from the hand of God, who has left on every feature the unmistakeable stamp of the great original artist. There you see Woman"—Shaw could have also been thinking of Virginia— "with eyes in her head that mirror the universe." Although Sir Jaffna's concepts were beyond ordinary conversational exchange, Shaw was clearly trying out ideas on the Woolfs.

Shaw also spoke of exhorting students at the University of Hong Kong. "I told them that every man at 21 must be a revolutionary. After that of course the police imprisoned them by the dozens." He went on to confide that he could "only stand the voyage" itself by writing, and had kept himself busy. "I like to give the public full weight. Books should be sold by the pound. What a nice little dog," he observed, changing the subject and looking down at the four-legged reason why the Woolfs were out walking. "But aren't I keeping you & making you cold?" she recalled him saying. And he touched Virginia's arm.

"Two men stopped along the path to look," she noted. Thirty years later, Leonard wrote more dramatically, "When the fountain of words at last died down and we parted, I found that we were the centre of a wide circle of 15 or 20 people; they had recognised Shaw and had stopped to listen as though it were a public entertainment."

"Off he strode again on his dwindled legs," Virginia supplemented in her diary. "I said Shaw likes us. L. thinks he likes nobody. What will they think of Shaw in 50 years?"

That unexpected encounter may have resulted in an invitation to lunch with the Shaws at Whitehall Court on a hot day in mid-June. The occasion began badly. Shaw was distracted by thoughts of addressing, later in the afternoon, a conference at the Royal Academy in Piccadilly of the Friends of the National Libraries. His escort was to be the Keeper of Prints and Drawings, the very minor poet Lawrence Binyon, who, with his wife, was also at the luncheon. Virginia found the Binyons dreary, as was the meal, sent up from the building's service kitchen and attended by its staff. For once Shaw had little to say, as he could strike little off the Binyons. "Shaw's paddle actually out of the water," Virginia told her diary on June 16, the next day. "And I talked. And I said [to myself] This is d——d dull."

Shaw joked that he hoped "to say something unpleasant" at the conference—though he did not. He mentioned being offered the Order of

Merit by the prime minister and that he replied that he had already conferred it on himself. Leonard's right hand, which trembled more under tension than it normally did, "clattered."[5]

Shaw attempted further small talk, repeating a story about his trip to China. Then he dredged up some Dublin memories. "And I kept saying [to myself] no the drug won't work."

Finally it was over, and suddenly the formal stiffness vanished. As the Binyons waited, Shaw escorted the Woolfs to the windows overlooking the angle of the Thames, for a last glance at the glistening river. Then they went down the black-and-white passage into the corridor—"very jaunty, upright—sea green eyes [and] red face to the lift. A man of perfect poise—spring—agility—never to me [un]interesting[6]—no poet, but what an efficient, adept, trained arch & darter! His wires, his spring . . . entirely astonishing. And the hands flung out in gesture: he has the power to make the world his shape—to me not a beautiful shape, that's all. So home."

Yet soon Virginia was thinking otherwise, recording in her diary that Kingsley Martin of the *New Statesman and Nation* had been unhappy with the pessimism of Leonard's review of Shaw's *Collected Prefaces*. Leonard saw the 1914–18 war as curtailing the tremendous influence that Shaw had possessed over the generation which had come of age with the new century. "Nothing less than a world war," he wrote, "could have prevented [him] from winning the minds of succeeding generations to truth, decency, socialism, peace, and civilization. So they made a world war, and ever since the barbarians have been on top." Approvingly, Virginia quoted her husband's lines, but she was far less approving of the old sage when war broke out again in 1939 and Shaw published a piece in the *New Statesman* urging the impossible—a negotiated peace with Hitler. The proposal, she thought, was "scatter brained."

Clearly not "scatter brained" to Virginia had been Shaw's lengthy *The Intelligent Woman's Guide to Socialism, Capitalism, Sovietism and Fascism* (1928), published between *Saint Joan* and *The Apple Cart*. She had taken the two-volume Pelican reprint of May 1937 and re-covered the blue-green paperbacks she found repellent with cover art in her own distinctive fashion—a design on cream cardboard of red branches with two

---

5 In 1937, at Shaw's suggestion, Leonard consulted a Dr. Alexander and, Virginia wrote to a friend, "was becoming cured of his trembling hand. Isn't that a miracle?"

6 As written the word has the appearance of a Freudian slip; the context following suggests its opposite, thus the bracketed prefix.

leaves on either side among indefinite blue figures somewhat resembling a blurry butterfly. Each was labeled "Guide to Socialism," and differed from the other only in the volume numerals. Apparently she expected to refer to them often, and Pelicans were not only cheap but cheaply put together.[7] Having inhabited Shaw's former house, she was now inhabiting his books.

After her death Leonard conceded, "I think he did, in his own way, like Virginia and me." And he produced, as evidence, a correspondence in her last years in which, while writing a biography of a great friend of her early literary life, Roger Fry, she queried Shaw about him. Fry had been an increasingly influential art critic in the years when Shaw, busy as a playwright, no longer wrote much about the arts. In 1913 they had conducted a controversy in the letters columns of *The Nation*. Nearly eighty-four in 1940, Shaw responded with a reminiscence, adding, "I have a picture by Roger which I will give you if you care to have it: a landscape.... I wish we could see more of you and Leonard; but we two are now so frightfully old that we no longer dare to offer our company as a treat to friends who are still in the prime of life." (Virginia was fifty-eight.) He did not explain that Charlotte, suffering from a painful spinal ailment, could now hardly see anyone.

"There is a play of mine," Shaw closed, "called Heartbreak House which I always connect with you because I conceived it in that house somewhere in Sussex where I first met you and, of course, fell in love with you. I suppose every man did."

Shaw's letter was dated May 10, 1940—the day the Germans invaded the Low Countries and France, bringing again, soon, the sound of guns—and air raids—across the Channel, within hearing of the Woolfs at their cottage in Sussex. ("We shan't I suppose be killed," she wrote

---

7 Those Shavian titles then on the Woolfs' Monk's House shelves at Lewes surviving posthumous dispersal are now in the Holland Library (Modern British Literary Collections), Washington State University, Pullman, Washington. They include the novels *The Irrational Knot, Love Among the Artists* (in two editions), *Cashel Byron's Profession*, and *An Unsocial Socialist*, the plays *Arms and the Man, Candida*, and the four "Pleasant" plays, among which are the aforementioned two also in separate editions, and *Saint Joan* (in two editions). Also the *Collected Prefaces* of 1934, the early pamphlet "The Common Sense of Municipal Trading" (1904), clearly a pre-marriage Leonard Woolf acquisition, *The Intelligent Woman's Guide*, and the wartime *Everybody's Political What's What?* (1944), marked up by Leonard and purchased after Virginia's death. The nature of the surviving volumes (the "Pleasant" volume without its companion, for example) suggests that there were others, now missing.

without conviction to Ethel Smyth.) Five days later Virginia replied to Shaw that his letter "reduced me to two days silence from sheer pleasure." She lifted lines from it to insert in her proofs. "As for the falling in love, it was not, let me confess, one-sided. When I first met you at the Webbs I was set against all great men, having been liberally fed on them in my father's house. . . . But in a jiffy you made me re-consider all that and had me at your feet. Indeed you have acted a lover's part in my life for the past thirty years; and though I daresay it's not much to boast of, I should have been a worser woman without Bernard Shaw."

Since she understood the many demands that fame had brought upon him all the years between, she added, in the third person, vainly attempting to create some distance, "Leonard and Virginia have never liked to impose themselves on you. But . . . if ever Mr Shaw dropped his handkerchief—to recur to the love theme—we should ask nothing better than to come and see you." In a postscript she confided, "Heartbreak House, by the way, is my favourite of all your works." Did she recognize that she lives in it?

When next in London she found the Fry landscape waiting for her. To have it from Shaw, she thanked him on June 13, 1940, "adds to its beauty. One day I hope you will come and see it hanging in my room. And if ever you had time, and a half sheet of paper, and would write upon it that it was your picture and that you gave it [to] me, my debt of gratitude to you would mount, if possible, higher. But I'm not going to bother you any more." Her affection, "though suppressed, is always alive in the heart of yours gratefully, Virginia Woolf."

France had just fallen, followed by the Blitz, raining bombs on London and southern England, and a new emotional breakdown ensued for Virginia, during which, early in 1941, she stuffed the pockets of her raincoat with stones and resolutely waded into the Ouse.

Bibliographic Essay

The Sotheby's sale of Shaw's books with flyleaf inscriptions is described by Dan H. Laurence and Daniel Leary in *Flyleaves* (Austin: W. Thomas Taylor, 1977), 11–12. The relocation to Fitzroy Square by the Woolf siblings is described by Jean Moorcroft Wilson in *Virginia Woolf: Life and London; A Biography of Place* (New York: Norton, 1988), 59–60. Virginia's friend to whom she wrote about *Misalliance*, March 9, 1910, was Saxon Sydney-Turner, in Nigel Nicolson and Joanne Trautmann, eds.,

The Letters of Virginia Woolf, vol. 1 (New York: Harcourt Brace Jovanovich, 1975), 423. Shaw's "Secular Morality" comment to William Archer, January 24, 1900, is in Dan H. Laurence, ed., *Bernard Shaw: Collected Letters, 1898–1910* (New York: Dodd, Mead, 1972), 139. I have excised the *e* that Shaw mistakenly added to the name of Mrs. Humphry Ward.

Leonard Woolf describes his Fabian writing commission in *Beginning Again: An Autobiography of the Years 1911–1918* (London: Hogarth Press, 1964), 34, 124, 183–84. Virginia refers to the "divine concert" attended by Shaw on February 13, 1915, in Anne Olivier Bell, ed., *The Diary of Virginia Woolf*, vol. 1 (New York: Harcourt Brace Jovanovich, 1977), 33 (later volumes were edited by Andrew McNellie). Lady Richmond Ritchie, a daughter of W. M. Thackeray, is also referred to (March 5, 1919) in *Diary*, 1:247–48.

The Woolfs' and Shaws' weekend with the Webbs at Windham Croft is described by Stanley Weintraub in *Journey to Heartbreak* (New York: Weybright and Talley, 1971), 97–98, 163, 165; by Virginia to James Strachey, June 17, 1916, and Lady Dorothy Cecil, [June 1916], in *Letters*, 2:101; to Katherine Cox, June 25, 1916, and Vanessa Bell, June 28, 1916, in *Letters*, 2:102–4. The country house Windham Croft is reproduced in S. Weintraub, "Curtains Speech: A New Source for *Heartbreak House*," *English Literature in Transition*, 38 (1994). "The Studio in the Clouds" early version of *Heartbreak House* and its literary antecedents are described in Stanley Weintraub and Anne Wright, eds., *Heartbreak House: A Facsimile of the Revised Typescript* (New York: Garland, 1981), xiv–xv. Shaw's references to Chekhov and to the demise of "cultured, leisured Europe" are from his preface to *Heartbreak House*.

Virginia's comments on *Cashel Byron's Profession* are from her letter, August 26, 1916, to Molly MacCarthy in *Letters*, 2:129. The press report about Shaw's Fabian lecture is from *Journey to Heartbreak*. Virginia's *Freshwater* (written 1923) was posthumously published, ed. Lucio P. Ruotolo (New York: Harcourt Brace Jovanovich, 1976), and contains two variant texts. Andrea Adolph, in "Virginia Woolf's Revision of a Shavian Tradition," *SHAW* 21 (2001): 63–79, devotes pages comparing, quite unpersuasively, *Freshwater* to *Major Barbara* when its obvious antecedent is *Heartbreak House*.

The episode of the faked Shaw letter is documented in Virginia's *Letters*, vol. 3, February 23, 1922, to Lytton Strachey; and in David Garnett, ed., *Carrington: Letters and Extracts from Her Diaries* (New York: Holt,

Rinehart & Winston, 1971), 202–3. Virginia's diary reference to the episode, February 23, 1922, is from *Diary*, 2:173.

Quotations from Virginia's *Jacob's Room* (1922) are from the "definitive collected edition" (London: Hogarth Press, 1990). All quotations from her novels are from this edition. Her reference in her list of "must-read" authors includes *History of Civilisation* (1846), once a standard Victorian textbook, by William Alexander Mackinnon. Her art exhibition comments are from "Pictures and Portraits," *Atheneaum*, January 9, 1920, a review of Edmond X. Kapp, *Personalities: Twenty-four Drawings* (London: Martin Secker, 1919), the book of the exhibition at the Little Art Rooms, Duke Street, May–June 1919, repr. in Andrew McNellie, ed., *The Essays of Virginia Woolf*, vol. 2 (Harcourt Brace Jovanovich), 163–66. Virginia's *TLS* review, March 8, 1917, published anonymously, is also in this volume, 89–91.

The Partridge comment is in Virginia's *Diary*, vol. 2 (November 27, 1921), and the band episode in a letter to Janet Case (May 21, 1922) is in Joanne Trautmann Banks, ed., *Congenial Spirits: The Selected Letters of Virginia Woolf* (London: Hogarth Press, 1989), 143. Virginia's comment deploring nineteenth-century writers is from *Essays*, 2:223; and her "hedge" comment about *Saint Joan* to Roger Fry, July 28, 1924, is in *Letters*, 3:122. The Woolf scholar on the doctors in *Mrs. Dalloway* and their likely relation to Shaw is Joanne Trautmann Banks, "Mrs. Woolf in Harley Street," *Lancet*, April 11, 1998, 1124–26.

The awkward confrontation with Arnold Bennett in Whitehall Court is described by Bennett on November 4, 1926, in *The Journal of Arnold Bennett* (New York: Literary Guild, 1933), 910; and by Leonard Woolf in *Beginning Again*, 123–25. "Character in Fiction," which evolved from Virginia's "Mr. Bennett and Mrs. Brown," is reprinted in *Essays*, vol. 3 (1986), where the lines about Shaw are on 422.

Virginia's letter to Vanessa Bell referring to her sons Julian and Quentin, May 8, 1927, is in *Congenial Spirits*, 223. Leonard quotes Shaw on editing *Political Quarterly* in *Beginning Again*, 120–22. Virginia's diary reference, June 2, 1932, to Ethel Smyth on a Shaw quotation is in *Diary*, 4:106. Her conversations with Shaw, June 2, 1932, November 7, 1928, April 28, 1933, and June 16, 1933, are from *Diary*, 4:106, 3:207, 4:152–53, and 4:163–64. Leonard's comments on the meetings with Shaw, two of them paralleling Virginia's comments, are from *Beginning Again*, 122. Her reference, September 2, 1934, to Leonard's review of Shaw's *Collected Prefaces* is from *Diary*, 4:24.

Virginia's exasperated "scatter brained" remark about Shaw's impossible suggestion to negotiate peace with Hitler, October 22, 1939, is from *Diary*, 4:242. Shaw's polemic, "Uncommon Sense about the War," had been published in *New Statesman and Nation* on October 7, 1939, to much public criticism, and Virginia's diary continued, "Maynard [Keynes] has had a heart attack over it."

Virginia and GBS were originally quoted about *Heartbreak House* in *Journey to Heartbreak*, 165; Leonard is quoted from *Beginning Again*, 125; Virginia's letters to Shaw in complete texts, May 17, 1940, and June 13, 1940, are in *Congenial Spirits*, 428–29, and in *Letters*, 5:402–3. Whether Shaw responded on the requested "half sheet of paper" is unknown.

Virginia drowned herself in the River Ouse, near Lewes, Sussex, on March 23, 1941, leaving a farewell note for Leonard.

Index

Achurch, Janet, 108, 112
Addis, William Edward, 9–10
Agate, James, 167
Albert, Prince, 21
Alexander, Doris, 154–55, 159
Alma-Tadema, Laurence, 26
Amundsen, Roald, 128, 130
Anderson, Mary [de Navarro], 90
Antony, Mark, 17
Archer, William, 107–8
Arliss, George, 75, 170–71
Arnold, Matthew, 195
Asquith, H. H., xi, 124–25
Astor, Nancy, 96, 191
Atherton, Gertrude, 108, 115

Baldwin, Stanley, 68, 88, 134, 175, 184, 187
Banks, Joanne Trautmann, 206
Barrie, James, 110, 121
Barton, Kingston, 9
Bateson, Dingwall, 170
Beardsley, Aubrey, 194
Beaverbrook, Maxwell Aitken, 1st Baron, 190–91
Beecham, Thomas, 209–10
Bell, Clive, 194, 203
Bell, Julian, 207–8
Bell, Quentin, 207–8
Bell, Vanessa Stephen, 194–95, 197, 203, 207
Bennett, Arnold, 205, 206–7
Bennett, Dorothy Cheston, 206–7
Bernays, Robert, 186
Besant, Annie, 106

Bible, 1–16
Binyon, Lawrence, 211–12
Bird, Thomas, 102
Bismarck, Otto von, 69, 70
Bland, Hubert, 199
Blandford, Lord, 101–2
Blavatsky, Helena Petrova, 106
Blood, Bindon, 104, 116
Blood, Thomas, 103–4
Bogard, Travis, 152–53, 157
Boldini, Giovanni, 113–14
Bonaparte, Napoleon, xii, 106
Boot, Francis, 108
Boothby, Robert, 186–87
Bradford, Selina, 71
Bradlaugh, Charles, 9
Bright, John, 56, 67
Bunyan, John, 1
Burgoyne, John, xii, 39–50
Butler, Elizabeth Thompson, 102
Butler, Samuel, 205
Butler, William, 102

Cadell, Jean, 144
Caesar, Julius, 17–28
Cameron, Charles Hay, 202
Cameron, Julia Margaret, 202
Campbell, Colin, 99–103
Campbell, Gertrude Blood (Lady Colin), xiii, 99–117
Campbell, Stella (Mrs. Patrick Campbell), 156, 168, 197

Carleton, Guy, 47–48
Carlyle, Thomas, 19
Carrington, Dora, 203
Carroll, Lewis, 198
Cecil, Nelly, 197
Cetewayo, xii, 51–64
Chamberlain, Austen, 134
Chamberlain, Neville, 69
Channon, Henry ("Chips"), 177, 187, 189
Charles, Prince of Wales, 175, 186
Charrington, Charles, 108
Chekhov, Anton, 198–99
Cherry-Garrard, Angela, 134
Cherry-Garrard, Apsley, 121–35
Cherubini, Maria Luigi, 91
Chesterton, Gilbert K., 39
Churchill, Jennie, 113
Churchill, Winston, xi, 65–66, 175–79, 185, 186, 190
Cinquevalli, Paul, 114
Clayton, Henry, 92
Cleopatra, 17–28, 149
Clinton, Henry, 47
Cockburn, Claud, 178
Colles, H. C., 90
Commins, Saxe, 156
Conan Doyle, Arthur, 29, 110
Cooper, Alfred Duff, 177
Cooper, Diana Duff, 189
Corbett, James J., 59
Courtneidge, Robert, 163
Coward, Noël, xii–xiii, 151–74; *Cats and Dogs*, 151; *Cavalcade*, 169; *In Which We Serve*, 172; *Point Valaine*, 169; *Private Lives*, 168; *Quadrille*, 168; *The Young Idea*, 151–58
Crawford, David Lindsay, 27th Earl, 187
Crowley, Aleister, 119
Cunninghame Graham, Robert Bontine, 71, 116, 199

Dacre, Harry, 179
"Daisy Bell" ("A Bicycle Built for Two"), 179, 191
Delme-Radcliffe, Charles, 123, 138
Denman, George, 102
Dent, E. J., 85
Disraeli, Benjamin, 20, 65–78, 189; *Falconet*, 70–71; *Lothair*, 71; *Sybil, or The Two Nations*, 72–73
Donovan, William, 172
Douglas, Alfred, 135
D'Oyley, Christopher, 48

Duncan, Isadora, 118–19
Durkin, Jimmie, 140

Edward VII, 185
Edward VIII, xiii, 39, 76, 175–93
Elgar, Alice, 81, 90
Elgar, Carice, 89
Elgar, Edward, xii, 79–96; *The Apostles*, 84, 96; *A Dream of Gerontius*, 80; *Enigma Variations*, 80; *Falstaff*, 83; *The Kingdom*, 96; *Pomp and Circumstance*, 84; *Symphony No. 3* (unfinished), 93–96, 98; *Severn Suite*, 88–89
Eliot, George, 195
Elliott, Gertrude, 21
Ervine, John, 1–2, 202

Farr, Florence, 112
Forbes-Robertson, Johnston, xi, 17, 21–22, 26
Frere, Bartle, 53
Fry, Roger, 81, 213–14

Gates, Horatio, 44
George III, 39–41
George V, 120
George VI, 187–91
Germain, George (Sackville), 39–50
Gérôme, Jean-Léon, 27
Gingold, Hermione, 161
Gladstone, W. E., 56, 67, 68
Goethe, Johann Wolfgang von, 29, 30
Golding Bright, Reginald, 30
Grant, Duncan, 195
Graves, Clotilde, 111
Gregory, Augusta, 131
Grein, J. T., 110
Griffith, Troyte, 81
Grigg, John, 176
Grundy, Sydney, 168

Hall, Radclyffe, 208
Hardinge, Alexander, 178
Hardy, Thomas, 110
Harris, Frank, 99, 102–3, 156–57
Harrison, Rex, 169
Hawkins, Jack, 161
Heine, Heinrich, 31
Helburn, Theresa, 76
Henderson, Archibald, 144
Hitler, Adolf, 69

Hockman, Vera, 91
Holloway, Basil, 152
Holroyd, Michael, 168, 200
Homer, 198
Howe, William, 41–49
Hume, David, 11

Ibsen, Henrik, 143
Irving, Henry, 71

James, Henry, 108, 115
Jesus Christ, xii, 1–16, 39, 94
Joan of Arc, 94
Joyce, James, 157

Kahn, Otto, 134
Kapp, Edmond, 204–5
Kennet, Kathleen. *See* Scott, Kathleen Bruce
Keynes, John Maynard, 208, 209, 217
Knox, William, 49

Lawrence, T. E. ("T. E. Shaw"), xi, 91, 94, 129–30, 157, 194
Lean, David, 172
Lehzen, Louise, 21
Lerner, Alan Jay, 168–69
Lesley, Cole, 161
Lewis, George, 100, 102–3
Lewis, Sinclair, 145, 156
Lloyd George, David, 124–25, 185
Loewe, Frederic, 168
Lopokova (Keynes), Lydia, 208, 209
Loraine, Lorn, 172
Loraine, Robert, 125–26, 153
Low, David, 87
Lunt, Alfred, 153–54

Macaulay, Rose, 208
Macaulay, Thomas Babington, 189
MacCarthy, Desmond, 201
MacCarthy, Molly, 201
MacDonald, Ramsay, 68, 88
Macgowan, Kenneth, 76
Mahomet, xi–xii
Mann, Thomas, 156
Mapleson, James H., 79
Marshall, George C., 190
Martin, Hugh, 173–74
Martin, Kingsley, 212

Martin, Mary, 169
Masefield, John, 1
Maurel, Victor, 108
Mendoza, Daniel, 31
Merson, Luc-Olivier, 27
Meynell, Alice, 113
Millais, John, 3, 15
Miller, Gilbert, 151
Milton, John, 31
Mommsen, Theodor, 24
Monckton, Walter, 190
Montagu, Edwin, 134
Moore, George, 79, 111
Mosley, Oswald, 185
Murray, Gilbert, 24

Nansen, Fridjof, 131
Nathan, Matthew, 121
Nazimova, Alla, 156
Nicolson, Harold, 178
Nordau, Maz, 75, 78, 140
North, Frederick, 41–42
Novello, Ivor, 170

Oates, Laurence, 121
O'Casey, Sean, 156, 157
O'Malley, Ellen, 202
O'Neill, Eugene, xii, 139–60; *Ah, Wilderness!,* 139, 141–42; *A Wife for a Life,* 142–43; *Diff'rent,* 144; *The Emperor Jones,* 144; *Fog,* 142; *The Last Conquest* (unfinished), 156; *Long Day's Journey into Night,* 139; *Marco Millions,* 144–51, 153–54, 159; *Mourning Becomes Electra,* 141, 154–57; *Servitude,* 143–44; *Strange Interlude,* 151–54, 156
O'Neill, James, 139–40
Osborn, Melmoth, 53, 59

Palmer, Lilli, 21
Parker-Bowles, Camilla (Duchess of Cornwall), 175, 186
Parry, Hubert, 85, 88
Partridge, Bernard, 100
Partridge, Frances, 205
Partridge, Ralph, 203, 205
Pascal, Gabriel, 26, 172
Patch, Blanche, 156
Pater, Walter, 205
Payne, Anthony, 96

Payne-Townshend, Charlotte. *See* Shaw, Charlotte Payne-Townshend
Peake, Charles, 190–91
Pearson, Hesketh, 29, 65, 77, 175
Pickerill, W. J., 92
Pilate, Pontius, 12–15, 39, 95
Pollock, Walter, 110
Polo, Marco, 145–51
Poynter, Edward, 26
Priestley, J. B., 172

Rains, Claude, 26
Ramsden, John William, 71–72
Reed, William H., 90, 96, 97
Reinhardt, Max, 26
Reith, John, 92–95, 98, 187
Ribbentrop, Joachim von, 191
Ricketts, Charles, 124
Ritchie, Anne Thackeray, 196
Robson, William A., 208
Rodin, Auguste, 118
Roebuck, John Arthur, 71
Ronald, Landon, 93
Rothermere, Harold Harmsworth, 1st Viscount, 185
Rowntree, Joseph, 196
Russell, John, 1st Earl, 69

Sackville-West, Vita, 208
Sargent, Malcolm, 134
Savage, George, 205
Schiller, Friedrich: *Die Räuber*, xii, 29–38; *Jungfrau von Orleans, Die*, xi; *Wallenstein*, 30
Scheaffer, Louis, 145
Schuster, Claud, 187–88
Scott, Kathleen Bruce, xiii, 118–38
Scott, Peter, 120, 122–27, 135–36
Scott, Robert Falcon, xiii, 120–21, 127–37
Shakespeare, William, 2, 83; *Antony and Cleopatra*, 27; *Cymbeline* 186; *Julius Caesar*, 6, 17; *Henry V*, 19; *King Lear*, 198; *Othello*, 198
Shannon, Charles, 124
Shaw, Bernard: *The Admirable Bashville*, 59–63; *Adventures of the Black Girl in Search of God*, 90, 92, 134; *Androcles and the Lion*, 81, 86, 172; *An Unsocial Socialist*, 201, 213; *The Apple Cart*, xiii, 65–66, 75–77, 85, 91, 156, 173–77, 185, 189, 191; *Arms and the Man*, 30, 70–71, 81, 100, 146, 213; *Augustus Does His Bit*, 81; *Back to Methuselah*, xi, 30, 80, 125, 151–53, 203; *Caesar and Cleopatra*, 17–28, 68–69, 71, 145–51, 172, 209; *Candida*, 84, 141–44, 213; *Captain Brassbound's Conversion*, 27, 30, 71, 141, 154–55; *Cashel Byron's Profession*, 54–56, 65, 119, 201, 213; "The Common Sense of Municipal Trading," 213; *Cymbeline Refinished*, 186, 190; *The Devil's Disciple*, 30, 39, 43–44, 81, 209; *The Doctor's Dilemma*, 81, 112, 153–54, 206; *Don Juan in Hell*, xi, 9, 29–38, 75, 80, 117, 129, 149, 158, 209; "The Emperor and the Little Girl," 122–23, 138; *Everybody's Political What's What?*, 213; *Fabian Essays*, 107; *Fanny's First Play*, 81; *Getting Married*, 81; *Heartbreak House*, 84, 123, 144, 151, 197–203, 213–15; *Intelligent Woman's Guide to Socialism and Capitalism*, 86, 212–13; *The Irrational Knot*, 213; *John Bull's Other Island*, xi, 81; "Joy Riding at the Front," 123; *The King, the Constitution, and the Lady*, 179–84, 192; *Love Among the Artists*, 213; *Major Barbara*, 24, 73, 148–49, 170; *Man and Superman* (see also *Don Juan in Hell*), xii, 30–33, 38, 80, 114–15, 125, 129, 151, 153, 209; *The Man of Destiny*, 71, 106, 209; *The Millionairess*, xi, 72–73; *Misalliance*, 114, 120, 195; *Mrs Warren's Profession*, 112, 140, 195; *On the Rocks*, 39, 94–96, 210–11; *Passion Play, A*, 1–16; *The Philanderer*, 109–12, 117; *Pygmalion*, 84, 144, 168–69, 170, 172, 197, 202; *The Quintessence of Ibsenism*, 140, 142, 150, 194; *Rhyming Picture Guide to Ayot Saint Lawrence*, 136–37; *Saint Joan*, 86, 122–23, 144, 185, 206, 209; *The Sanity of Art*, 75, 140; *The Shewing-Up of Blanco Posnet*, 30; *Short Stories, Scraps and Shavings*, 39; *The Simpleton of the Unexpected Isles*, 81, 157; *Table-Talk of G.B.S.*, 144; *Too True to Be Good*, xi, 91, 94–95; *Village Wooing*, 95; *Widowers' Houses*, 109; *You Never Can Tell*, 71, 151–58
—and Lady Colin Campbell, 99–117
—and Noël Coward, 151–74
—and Edward VII, 175–93
—and Edward Elgar, 79–96
—and Eugene O'Neill, 139–60
—and Kathleen Bruce Scott, 118–38
—and Virginia Woolf, 194–207
Shaw, Charlotte Payne-Townshend, xi, 26, 96, 113, 123–27, 129, 135–36, 194, 213
Shaw, Eyre Massey, 102
Shaw-Disraeli connection, 65–78
Shepstone, Theophilus, 51–54, 63
Simpson, Ernest, 178

Simpson, Wallis Warfield, 175, 178–79, 184–87, 190
Sinclair, Upton, 157
Smyth, Ethel, 208–9
Sopwith, Thomas, 120
Squire, J. C., 205
Stanford, Charles Villiers, 85, 88
Stead, William T., 102
Steichen, Clara, 119
Steichen, Edward, 119
Stephen, Adrian, 194–95
Stephen, Leslie, 195
Stephenson, William, 172
Strachey, James, 197
Strachey, Lytton, 203, 205
Suggia, Guilhermina, 134
Sutherland, Duchess of, 115
Synge, J. M., 144

Terry, Ben, 202
Terry, Ellen, 71, 202
Trebitsch, Siegfried, 17, 27, 29
Tucker, Benjamin, 140

Vandervelde, Lalla, 81
Vedrenne, John, xii–xiii, 162
Victoria, Queen, 16–17, 26, 56–57, 63, 69, 70, 189, 202–3
Voltaire, François Marie Arouet de, xi–xii

Wagner, Richard, 198
Ward, Mary Augusta (Mrs. Humphry), 195

Warwick, Countess of, 115
Watson, Frederick, 126
Watts, George Frederick, 202
Webb, Beatrice, xi, 126, 184–85, 197–99
Webb, Sidney, 126, 197
Webster, John, 2,
Wells, H. G., 205, 207–8
Wells, Jane, 208
Wertheim, Maurice, 156
Whistler, James A. McNeill, 99–101
Wilde, Constance, 105
Wilde, Oscar, 103, 111, 168, 205
Wilhelm II, 122
Williams-Ellis, Clough, 208
Wirgman, Blake, 70, 77
Woolf, Leonard, 195–217; *International Government*, 196–97, 215
Woolf, Virginia, xii, xiii, 81, 97, 194–217; "Character in Fiction," 207; *The Common Reader*, 199; *Freshwater*, 202–3; *Jacob's Room*, 203–4; "Mr. Bennett and Mrs. Brown," 207; *Mrs. Dalloway*, 204, 206; *Night and Day*, 201, 204; *Room of One's Own*, 194; *The Voyage Out*, 210

Yates, Edmund, 103, 106–8
Yeats, W. B., 79, 157
Young, Edward Hilton (later Lord Kennet), 129–37
Young, Kathleen. *See* Scott, Kathleen Bruce
Young, Wayland, 133–34
Younghusband, Francis, 72

Stanley Weintraub, Evan Pugh Professor Emeritus of Arts and Humanities at Pennsylvania State University, is the author or editor of twenty books about or by Bernard Shaw, including *Private Shaw and Public Shaw, Journey to Heartbreak, Bernard Shaw: The Diaries, 1885–1897*, and Shaw's collected art criticism. He was editor of *SHAW: The Annual of Bernard Shaw Studies* and its predecessor journals from 1956 to 1990. He has written biographies of such notable Victorian figures as Victoria and Disraeli, and a life of Shaw for the *Oxford Dictionary of National Biography*.

The Florida Bernard Shaw Series

This series was made possible by a generous grant from the David and Rachel Howie Foundation.

EDITED BY R. F. DIETRICH

Pygmalion's Wordplay: The Postmodern Shaw, by Jean Reynolds (1999)
Shaw's Theater, by Bernard F. Dukore (2000)
Bernard Shaw and the French, by Michel W. Pharand (2001)
The Matter with Ireland, Second Edition, edited by Dan H. Laurence and David H. Greene (2001)
Bernard Shaw's Remarkable Religion: A Faith That Fits the Facts, by Stuart E. Baker (2002)
Bernard Shaw's The Black Girl in Search of God: *The Story Behind the Story*, by Leon Hugo (2003)
Shaw Shadows: Rereading the Texts of Bernard Shaw, by Peter Gahan (2004)
Bernard Shaw: A Life, by A. M. Gibbs (2005)
What Shaw Really Wrote about the War, edited by J. L. Wisenthal and Daniel O'Leary (2006)
Bernard Shaw and China: Cross-Cultural Encounters, by Kay Li (2007)
Shaw's Controversial Socialism, by James Alexander (2009)
Bernard Shaw as Artist-Fabian, by Charles A. Carpenter (2009)
Shaw, Synge, Connolly, and Socialist Provocation, by Nelson O'Ceallaigh Ritschel (2011; first paperback edition, 2012)
Who's Afraid of Bernard Shaw? Some Personalities in Shaw's Plays, by Stanley Weintraub (2011; first paperback edition, 2013)
Shaw, Plato, and Euripides: Classical Currents in Major Barbara, by Sidney P. Albert (2012)
Shaw and Feminisms: On Stage and Off, edited by D. A. Hadfield and Jean Reynolds (2012)
Shaw's Settings: Gardens and Libraries, by Tony Jason Stafford (2013)

www.ingramcontent.com/pod-product-compliance
Lightning Source LLC
Chambersburg PA
CBHW031433160426
43195CB00010BB/722